Japanese Marks And Seals...

James Lord Bowes

KUTANI.

Nine Valleys.

UPON KAGA POTTERY.

JAPANESE MARKS AND SEALS.

Part I.

POTTERY.

Part II.

ILLUMINATED MSS. AND PRINTED BOOKS.

Part III.

LACQUER, ENAMELS, METAL, WOOD, IVORY, &c.

BY

JAMES LORD BOWES,

JOINT AUTHOR OF KERAMIC ART OF JAPAN.

LONDON:

HENRY SOTHERAN & CO.,

36, PICCADILLY; 136, STRAND; 77 & 78, QUEEN STREET, CITY.

MANCHESTER: 49, CROSS STREET.

Printed by D. MARPLES & CO. LIMITED,
Lord Street, Liverpool.

DEDICATED

BY DIRECT PERMISSION

TO

HIS IMPERIAL MAJESTY

THE

MIKADO,

WITH EVERY FEELING OF RESPECT,

BY

HIS MAJESTY'S

OBEDIENT SERVANT,

THE AUTHOR.

PREFACE.

THE *marks and seals in this Volume have been gathered from many sources, amongst which may be named the collection of wares made by myself during the past fifteen years, for the purpose of forming the classification of pottery as set forth in "Keramic Art of Japan." I have also availed myself of the collection of Old Japan porcelain preserved at Dresden, the interesting and valuable series of examples of the same ware presented to the British Museum by Mr. Aug. W. Franks, and the specimens sent by the Japanese Government to the South Kensington Museum, as well as numerous other collections.*

The great variety of the characters, the several styles in which they are written, and the differences necessarily incidental to the rendering of them by the workmen upon productions executed during a period extending over more than three centuries, have made the translation of the inscriptions a work of extreme difficulty, which has only been surmounted by the assistance of my Japanese friends, Mr. Kawakami and Mr. Yamanobe. To the former my especial thanks are due for his careful revision of the whole of the translations, and I have the more thankfully accepted his system of transliteration of the Chinese characters into Japanese and English, as much difference of opinion exists upon this subject amongst European scholars who have studied it. Little progress has so far been made in the formation of a uniform system, and even in the proceedings of the Asiatic Society of Japan the name of the Eastern capital is rendered in the following ways:—Tôkiyô, Tōkiyō, Toukiyau, Tōkiō, Tôkiô, *and lastly,* Tokio, *the form used in this Work. Great latitude also exists in Japan in the rendering of proper names, which may often be read in two ways; for instance, the Chinese characters for the name of one of the chief potters in Hizen may be read as Fukugawa or Shinsen, the former being the Japanese style for the family name of the potter, and the latter the Chinese mode of expressing his professional name. I have therefore been exceedingly fortunate in having had the assistance of so able and accomplished a Chinese scholar as Mr. Kawakami in reducing the transliterations to uniformity. I must also express my thanks to him for having drawn for this Work the characters given in connection with the Zodiacal Cycle and Year Periods.*

The collection of marks and seals upon pottery is the most numerous and complete, for this branch of industry was pursued in all parts of the empire, and the wares were made for sale, and for the use of rich and poor alike. Under these circumstances, it was natural for the potters to mark their productions; but it was otherwise with the rarer efforts in illuminated books, lacquer ware, and the exquisite cloisonné enamels upon copper, which were produced by artists in the service of the nobles for the use of their patrons. Such works, especially those of the highest beauty, were seldom signed by the workman, who would naturally sink his own individuality in that of his prince.

A careful study of the marks in general, and of those upon pottery in particular, leads one to the conclusion that Japanese art is of more modern growth than is generally supposed.

From the early part of the fourteenth century the country was disturbed by incessant civil wars, which, with short intervals of peace, continued until the beginning of the seventeenth century, when the Tokugawa Shôgunate was founded, and the country became comparatively settled, but it was not until the time of the third Shôgun, 1623 to 1649 A.D., that order was firmly established, and the nation turned its thoughts to peaceful arts. All the information furnished by the marks goes to prove that the works produced prior to this period were of a rude and inartistic character. The stone ware vessels and figures made in Owari, Bizen, Chikuzen, and elsewhere, between the eighth century and the sixteenth, the earlier examples of raku ware, and the ancient works in lacquer, which are still preserved in Japan, were all rude in form, workmanship, and decoration; and although the earlier specimens of the porcelain known as Old Japan were produced during the sixteenth century, the designs and colours employed in its decoration were characteristic of Chinese and European, rather than of Japanese art.

Considerable progress appears to have been made during the seventeenth century; the potters of Satsuma first employed gold in the decoration of their wares in 1630 A.D.; and those of Kaga commenced its use in 1650 A.D. It was in the latter year that the celebrated Nonomura Ninsei originated the manufacture of decorated faience in Kioto, and it is probable that the earliest examples of pottery of an artistic character, other than Old Japan, date from this time. During the period of Genroku, towards the close of the century, a number of skilful artists appeared, and about this time the choicest works in lacquer were made, and the occurrence of a notable development in the art of painting may be traced by an examination of the illuminated books produced between the periods of Shotoku and Bunkwa (1711 to 1818, A.D.), from which several of the inscriptions are taken. Perhaps the most brilliant period of Japanese art was the last century, and the earlier years of the present one. The choicest Satsuma faience, the finest red and gold Kaga pottery, and the exquisite Mikawachi porcelain were all made during the last century; whilst the beautiful kinrande and sometsuke styles of decoration were first used by the Kioto and Owari potters during the early years of the present one.

The decadence of Japanese art coincides with the growth of the feeling which led to the opening of the country to intercourse with Western nations, and since then its character has entirely changed, and Japanese art is now, alas! almost a thing of the past.

JAMES L. BOWES.

LIVERPOOL, 1882.

MEIJI KI-BI.
The Year of the Sheep, in the Period of Meiji.
(1882.)

The marks upon the cloth cover of the book read ZEN-PEN, IN-SHO; MEIJI KI-BI; DAI NIPPON; meaning, *The whole volume of marks and seals; the year of the Sheep, the period of Meiji* (1882); *Great Japan.*

CONTENTS.

CONTENTS.

IN-SHO.
Marks or Seals.

MAP

OF

THE EMPIRE OF JAPAN,

SHOWING

SEATS OF VARIOUS MANUFACTURES,

RAILWAY, &c.

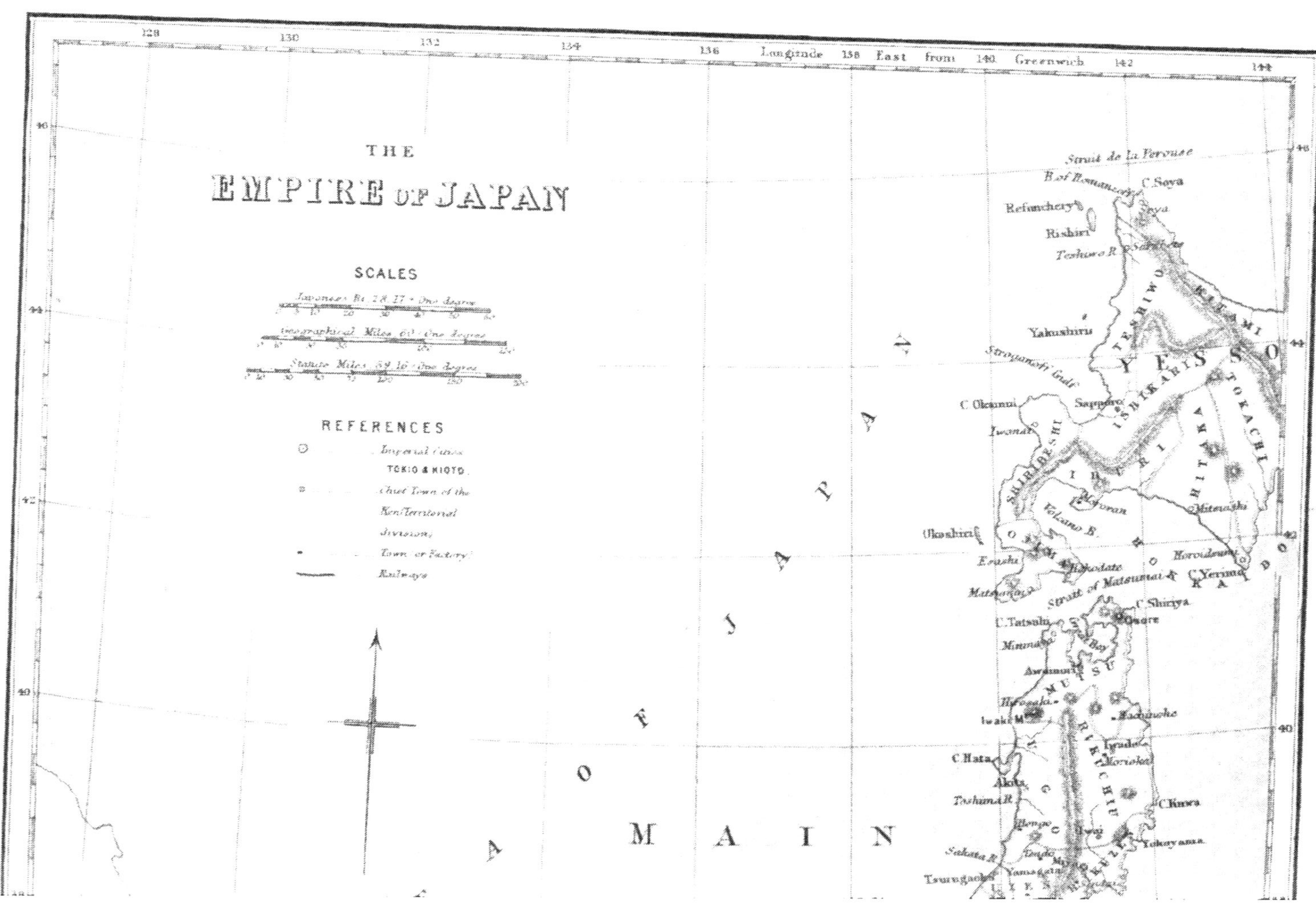

THE
EMPIRE OF JAPAN
SCALES
REFERENCES
TOKIO & KIOTO
Longitude East from Greenwich
SEA OF JAPAN
YESSO
TESHIWO
KITAMI
ISHKARI
TOKACHI
HITAKA
IBURI
SHIRIBESHI
OSHIMA
MUTSU
RIKUCHIU
Strait de La Perouse
C. Soya
Refunchery
Rishiri
Yakushiru
Strogonoff Gulf
C. Okamui
Sapporo
Volcano B.
Mitsuishi
Horoidzumi
C. Yerimo
Strait of Matsumai
C. Shiriya
C. Tatsupi
Okoshiri
Hakodate
C. Hata
Toshima R.
C. Kinwa
Yokoyama
Sakata R.
Tsurugaoka

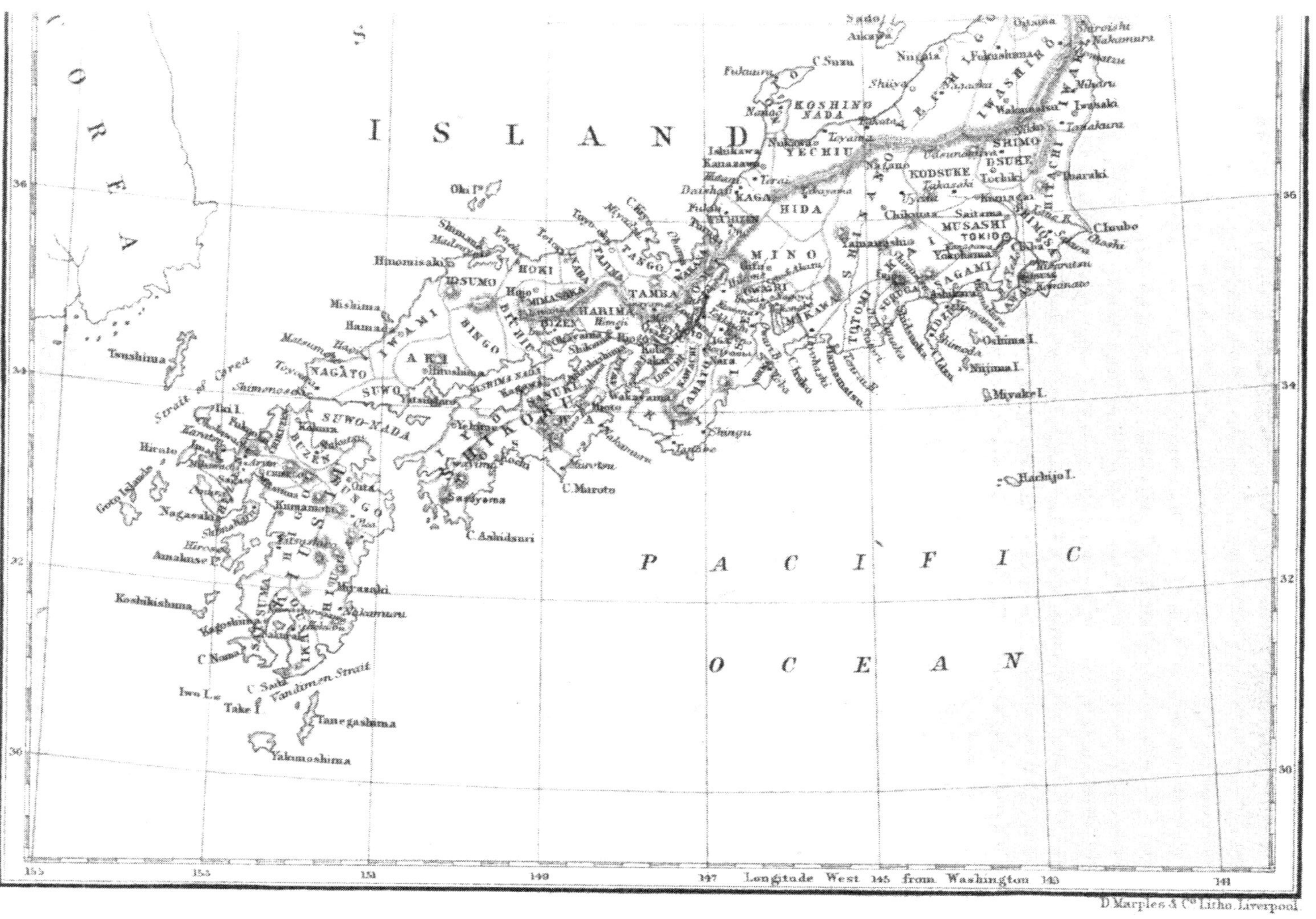
COREA
ISLAND
PACIFIC
OCEAN
Longitude West 145 from Washington
Strait of Corea
Tsushima
Oki I.
Hinomisaki
Mishima
Hamada
NAGATO
SUWO
SUWO-NADA
IWAMI
AKI
BINGO
IDSUMO
HOKI
TANGO
TAMBA
HARIMA
MINO
HIDA
KAGA
KOSHINO NADA
YECHIU
C. Suzu
Sado
Niigata
KODSUKE
MUSASHI
TOKIO
SAGAMI
SHIMO
Yokohama
Oshima I.
Nijima I.
Miyake I.
Hachijo I.
C. Maroto
C. Ashidsuri
Kumamoto
Nagasaki
Hirato
Goto Islands
Koshikishima
Miyasaki
Vandimen Strait
Iwo I.
Take I.
Tanegashima
Yakunoshima
D Marples & Co Litho. Liverpool

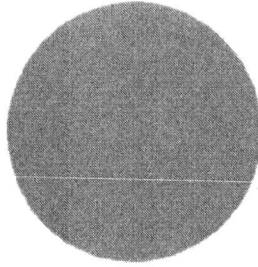

THE RED SUN OF JAPAN.

POTTERY.

MARKS AND SEALS ON POTTERY.

THE custom of painting or otherwise placing marks and seals upon the Keramic wares of Japan has been very general, although not universal. The marks differ in many and important respects from those found upon the productions of Chinese and European potters, which seldom give definite information regarding the names of the workmen or their residences. The circumstances under which the industry has been carried on in Japan, the wares being either the work of a single artist, or produced at one of the small factories which abound in that country, lead to the pieces being marked with the signature of the artist, or the seal of the factory of which he is a member, together with, in many cases, the name of the kiln, the town and province in which it is situated, and other information which renders the identification and classification of the varied productions of the Japanese potter an easy and interesting study.

Before entering upon the technical portion of the subject, it may be advisable to take a general view of the features which characterize the systems followed in the various provinces and cities of the Empire.

The earliest marks are those found upon the rude earthenware and stoneware vessels said to have been made in Bizen and Owari, during the 13th and 14th centuries; the authenticity of these is, however, not well established, and it is only necessary to give the following examples before proceeding to deal with those which are undoubted, the earliest of which date from the latter part of the 16th or the commencement of the 17th century.

ENGRAVED UPON OWARI STONEWARE.
Reputed 13th Century.

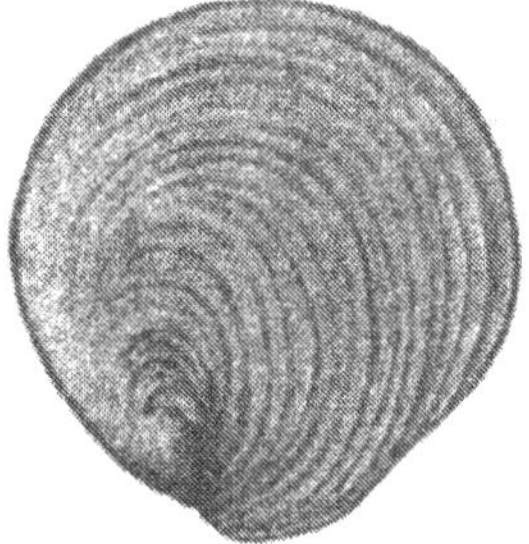

THE ITOGUIRI MARK, ENGRAVED UPON OWARI STONEWARE.
Reputed 14th Century.

ENGRAVED UPON BIZEN STONEWARE.
Reputed 13th Century.

The manufacture of porcelain was introduced into Japan by Gorodayu Shonsui, who settled in the province of Hizen upon his return from China in 1513 A.D., and there commenced the industry, which was brought to perfection a century later by a Corean potter named Risampei. The ware then produced is that decorated with red, blue, green, black, and gold, in the *nishikide* fashion, and known in Europe as Old Japan. The exportation commenced in 1641, and examples are to be found in all European countries, but the most important collection of this description of Japanese porcelain is that formed by August II, between the years 1698 and 1711, and now preserved in the Japanese Palace at Dresden.

Many of these works are marked underneath the

vessels with sprays of flowers, such as the *botan*, *kiku*, and *sakura*, painted in colours and gold, whilst upon others are found year-periods and symbolical ornaments, copied from Chinese wares, and, in exceptional cases, modifications of the *Kiku* crest of the Mikado. The mark given below is copied from one of the choicest specimens in the Dresden Collection.

PAINTED UPON HIZEN PORCELAIN, IN THE DRESDEN COLLECTION.

The use of Chinese year-periods upon Japanese porcelain appears to have been general from the earlier days of its manufacture, for numerous instances are to be found in the Dresden Collection. The following mark, of the Tch'ing-hoa period, 1465-1487 A.D., is copied from a dish in that collection bearing a representation of the baptism of Christ, a subject which could only have been used subsequently to the introduction of Christianity into Japan in 1549.

DAI MING, SEIKA, NEN SEI.
Made in the year of Seika, during the dynasty of Dai Ming, 1465-1487 A.D. A forgery of the Chinese mark of the Tch'ing-hoa period.

Forged Chinese marks are also frequently used by the modern Hizen potters, and large quantities of imitation Old Japan have been recently received in Europe, bearing the following marks or others of a similar character:—

DAI MING, KASEI, NEN SEI.
Made in the year of Kasei, during the dynasty of Dai Ming, 1522-1566 A.D. A forgery of the Chinese mark of the Kia-tsing period.

DAI THSING, KENRIU, NEN SEI.
Made in the year of Kenriu, during the dynasty of Dai Thsing, 1736-1795 A.D. A forgery of the Chinese mark of the Khien-long period.

The names of the makers do not appear upon any but comparatively modern Hizen work, and it would probably be correct to assume that this plan of marking has not been followed more than fifty years; it is, however, very generally pursued at the present time. The first of the two marks given below is taken from a good specimen of Nagasaki porcelain decorated in colours, and the second from an example of fine late period blue and white.

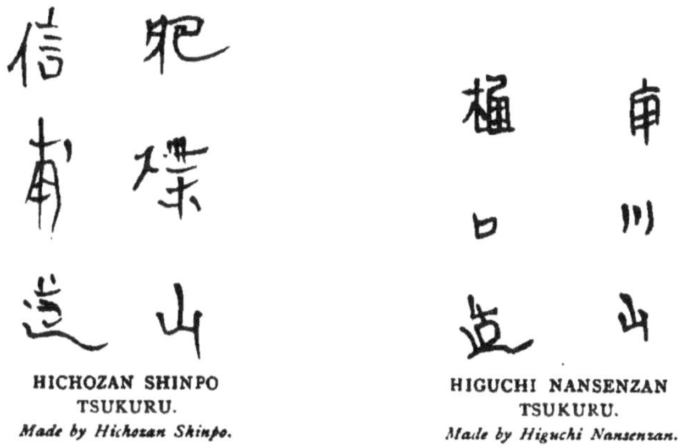

HICHOZAN SHINPO TSUKURU.
Made by Hichozan Shinpo.

HIGUCHI NANSENZAN TSUKURU.
Made by Higuchi Nansenzan.

Marks are very seldom used in the province of Satsuma, but occasionally the maker impresses or paints his signature, and in rare instances the crest or the name of the Prince appears.

IDE.
The name of the maker.

MATSUDAIRA, SATSUMA NO KAMI.
The name of the Prince of Satsuma.

RANZAN.
The name of the maker.

In the province of Kaga painted marks are almost invariably used; it is seldom that the word Kutani does not appear, either alone or in combination with the name of the potter and other information. Two representations of the word Kutani, which is the name of the district in which the earliest factories were established, are given as the frontispiece of this Work.

The more ancient examples of the ware bear the word Kutani alone, as shown below; this mark is copied from a specimen dating from about 1650 A.D., and belongs to the period before gold was used in the decoration of the ware.

KUTANI.

Nine Valleys.

Works of this character are also marked with Chinese year-periods, of which the following is an example:—

SEIKA, NEN SEI.

Made in the year of Seika. A forgery of the Chinese mark of the Tch'ing hoa period, 1465-1487 A.D.

Upon the finest examples of the early ware decorated with red and gold, the mark is generally written in gold upon a panel of red, but occasionally the characters are painted in red without the introduction of gold.

KUTANI.

Other examples of early date and great excellence show the characters in combination with the name of the maker, in the following manner:—

KUTANI, HOKUHO.

The seal is the maker's mark.

The same plan was followed by the makers of the finest middle period ware.

KUTANI, TOZAN.

In works of more recent date, the names of the factory, the painter, and other information is given.

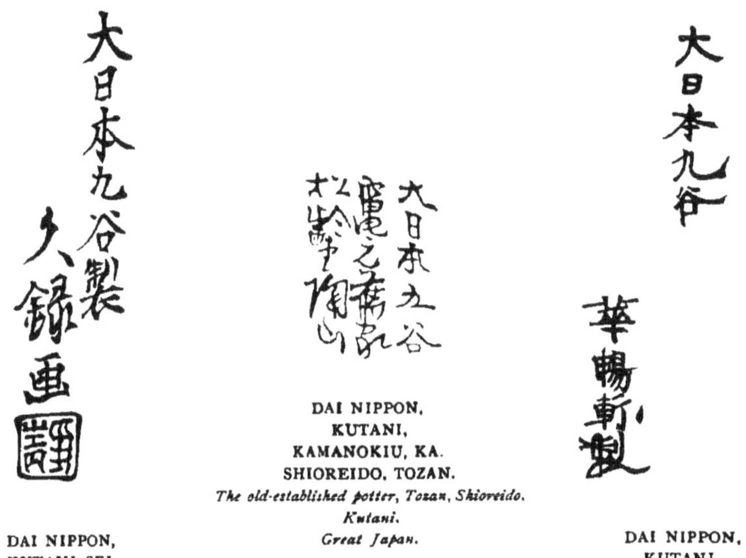

DAI NIPPON,
KUTANI SEI,
KUROKU, YEGAKU.
Made in Kutani, Great Japan; painted by Kuroku.

DAI NIPPON,
KUTANI,
KAMANOKIU, KA.
SHIOREIDO, TOZAN.
The old-established potter, Tozan, Shioreido. Kutani. Great Japan.

DAI NIPPON,
KUTANI,
KACHOKEN, SEISU.
Made by Kachoken, Kutani, Great Japan.

The mark at the foot of the first inscription is the painter's seal.

The *sometsuke* porcelain, ware decorated with blue under the glaze, made at Seto in the province of Owari, the manufacture of which dates from the earlier years of the present century, has nearly always the name of the maker painted upon it, together with the characters signifying Seto, Japan, in the fashion shown in the first mark on the following page.

In some instances fuller information than this is given; for example, the second inscription given on the next page is copied from a large plaque of *sometsuke* porcelain, in the Bowes Collection, which is decorated with a representation of mountainous scenery.

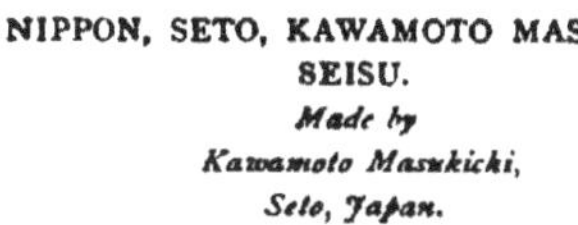

NIPPON, SETO, KAWAMOTO MASUKICHI, SEISU.
Made by Kawamoto Masukichi, Seto, Japan.

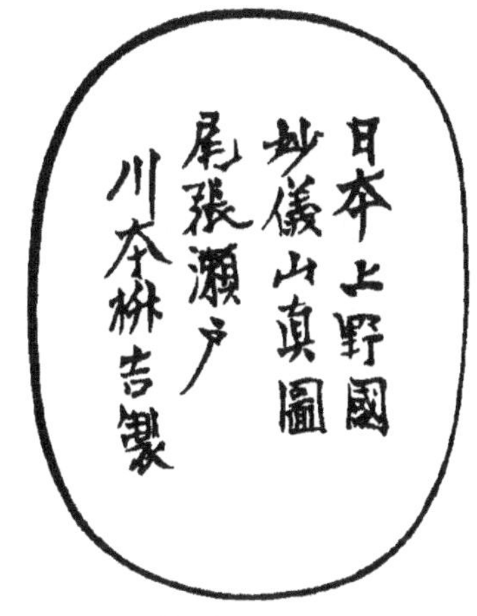

NIPPON, KOZUKE NO KUNI, MIOGI SAN, NO SHIN DZU; OWARI, SETO, KAWAMOTO MASUKICHI, SEISU.
A faithful view of the Miogi mountain in the province of Kozuke, Japan; made by Kawamoto Masukichi, Seto, Owari.

Another favorite method employed by the Seto potter is to decorate his wares with stanzas of Chinese poetry, as shown

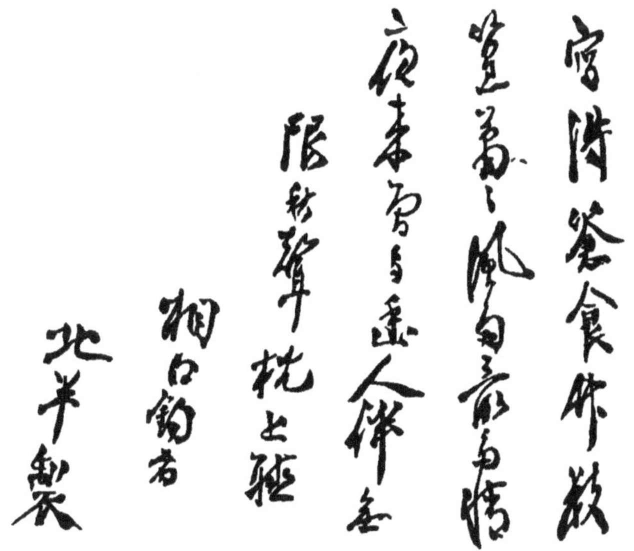

HOKU HAN, SEISU
Made by Hoku Han.

in the foregoing inscription, which appears upon the side of a *sake* bottle; the three marks to the left are the maker's name, and the other characters are the verses.

Impressed and painted marks are used by the Kioto potters; the former are generally applied to faïence and the latter to porcelain. The chief impressed marks are those of the potters Ninsei, Dohachi, Yeiraku, Taizan, and Kinkozan, of which examples are here given:—

NINSEI.

DOHACHI.

YEIRAKU.

TAIZAN.

KINKOZAN.

The signatures of Dohachi and Kozan are sometimes painted, and this mode is followed by Yeiraku in marking the porcelain for which he is so celebrated; when this is done, other information generally accompanies the signature; for example:—

NIPPON, KIOTO, KINKOZAN, TSUKURU. *Made by Kinkozan, Kioto. Japan.*

DAI NIPPON, YEIRAKU, TSUKURU. *Made by Yeiraku, Great Japan.*

DOHACHI. *The name of the maker.*

The impressed and painted marks are occasionally used together upon faïence, as shown by the inscription given on next page. The seal is impressed underneath the basin from which this mark is taken, and the panels form part of the internal decoration.

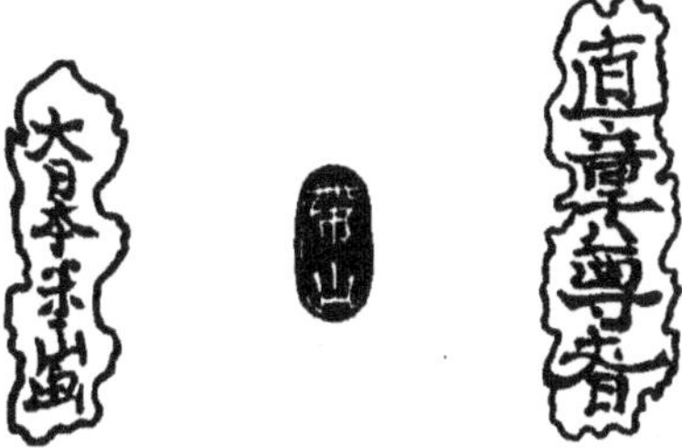

The mark in the centre is the impressed seal of Taizan; the characters on the right are *Chiokusho Songsha*, the former being the name and the latter the title of the priest depicted, and those on the left are *Dai Nippon*, *Bizan*, *yegaku;* meaning, Painted by Bizan, Great Japan.

Impressed marks are very seldom found upon porcelain, but Kitei, a maker of *sometsuke* ware in Kiomidzu, occasionally follows this plan; the mark given below is impressed in the undecorated part of the specimen from which it is copied.

NO IN
KITEI.
The Seal of Kitei.

The wares produced in the province of Ise are known by the name of Banko, which signifies "for ever," or, literally, ancient ten thousand; *ban*, ten thousand; *ko*, old or ancient. The character is found impressed, or in rare instances painted, upon nearly all the wares made in this province; it is written in various styles, of which examples are here given:—

BANKO. *Impressed.* BANKO. *Impressed.* BANKO. *Impressed.*

BANKO. *Impressed. Old style.* BANKO. *Painted.* BANKO. *Impressed. New style.*

The stamp is seldom used alone; it is generally shown in combination with marks of a similar meaning, or with the name of the maker, of the factory, or some other character.

BANKO. FUYEKI. *Banko ware. Unchanging.*

BANKO. TEKIZAN. *Banko ware. Tekizan, the maker.*

BANKO. YOFU KEN. SENSHU. *Banko ware. Yofu factory. A Thousand Autumns.*

BANKO. NIPPON. *Banko ware. Japan.*

The impressed characters are most frequently found upon the thin, hand-potted ware with which the name Banko is generally associated, but the faïence, which is also made in this province, is often decorated with painted characters of a similar meaning. These are sometimes so arranged as to form a favorite Japanese phrase, in the following manner:—

TAMOTS.
To enjoy.

SHIO.
Pine Tree.

JIU.
Longevity.

KAKU.
Stork.

REI.
Age.

SHIO JIU KAKU REI O TAMOTS.
To enjoy the longevity of the Pine Tree and the age of the Stork.

The character *Fuku*, as given below, signifying prosperity, happiness, and so forth, is also found upon Iśe faïence.

The employment of colours and gold in the inscription of the marks is very general, but it has no special significance, and as the examples already given are sufficient to furnish an idea of the colours used in the principal provinces, it is not necessary to increase the number, and the remainder of the marks in the work will be given in facsimile as regards size and drawing only.

The marks and seals are in nearly all instances written in Chinese characters, each of which signifies a word, the Japanese *Kata-kana* and *Hira-kana* letters being seldom used except as auxiliaries to connect or complete a sentence composed of Chinese words. These are written in four ways, known as the *Sosho*, *Giosho*, *Kaisho*, and *Reisho* styles; the first two are those in daily use for correspondence, but signatures are generally written in *Giosho* fashion; the *Kaisho* style is employed in the printing of books, and for writing titles and documents of a ceremonial nature, whilst stamps and seals are generally rendered in the *Reisho* characters.

All of these styles of writing are aptly illustrated by the following inscriptions copied from wares made by Kiso, a Hizen potter; they all have precisely the same meaning, namely, *Made by Kiso Toshikian;* the characters in these marks are identical, with the exception of the upper and lower words in the fourth inscription, which, although bearing the same interpretation as those employed in the others, are written in a different form.

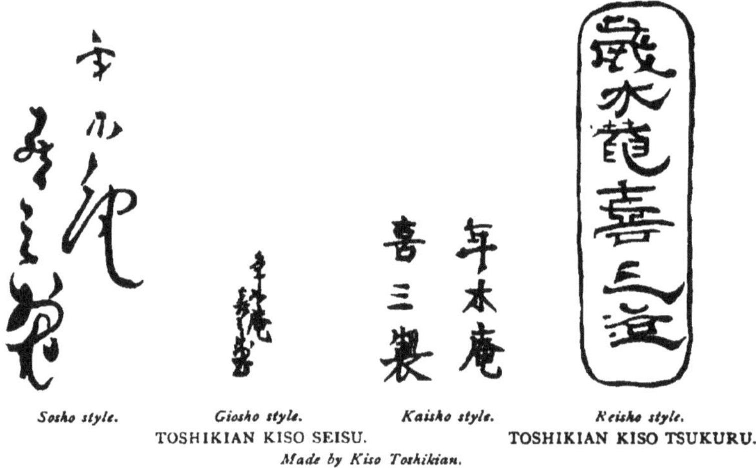

Sosho style. *Giosho style.* *Kaisho style.* *Reisho style.*
TOSHIKIAN KISO SEISU. TOSHIKIAN KISO TSUKURU.
Made by Kiso Toshikian.

With the view of facilitating the easier comprehension of the marks, it may be well to give examples of the characters most frequently used, and to show the different styles in which they are written.

Tsukuru, often read *Zo*, and *Sei*, or *Seisu*, all meaning *made by* or *made in*, are in general use wherever painted inscriptions are applied; *sei* is the correct reading when the word comes after the name of a place or year, whilst *seisu* is used when it follows proper names. These characters are seldom found in seal marks or stamps. The various forms in which the words are written in the different provinces are shown in the following examples:—

The word *Ko* is occasionally used in the place of *tsukuru*, but it is generally applied in connection with the painting rather than the manufacture of the ware.

KO.
Made by.

Tsukuru and *sei* are sometimes found in combination; when this is the case they are translated as following after the name of the maker instead of preceding it, and *zo* is used in place of *tsukuru*.

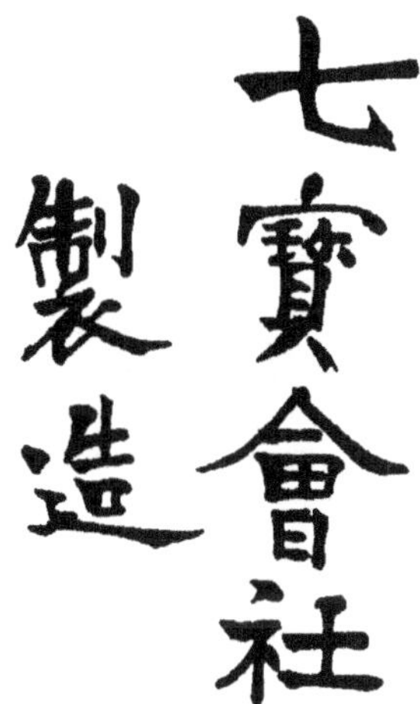

The characters to the left are *Sei-zo*, and those to the right are *Shippo kuwai-sha*, meaning that *the Shippo Company made* the ware from which the inscription was copied.

The word *sei* is frequently used with the character *kore*, meaning *this*, when the mark is read *Kore o seisu*. Various examples are given below.

Hizen. *Owari.*

Kioto.
KORE O SEISU.
Makes this.

Kioto. *Kaga.*

It is only in rare instances that the word *tsukuru* is used in this manner. The following inscription is taken from an old example of Kioto faience. The two upper characters are *tsukuru* and the lower ones are *kore* :—

KORE O TSUKURU.
Makes this.

When the maker desires to emphasize the beauty of his ware, he uses the characters *Sei sei*, to signify that it has been made with care.

Owari. *Kioto.* *Owari.*
SEI SEI.
Made with care.

Occasionally inscriptions appear signifying that the object was made at the request of some purchaser, or the words "respectfully made" are placed upon it by the manufacturer;

Kaga.
MOTOME NI OZITE.
For demand.

Kioto.
KINSAKU.
Respectfully made.

The words *Motome ni ozite* are only applied to articles made for distinguished personages or for personal friends of the manufacturer.

When two workmen join in the production of any specimen of pottery, they sometimes add the words *Narabini* (and) and *Sin* (together) to their names, as shown by the following inscription :—

GOROTA NARABINI SHOZUI SIN-ZO.
Made by Gorota and Shozui together.
Hizen.

Two characters are used to signify *painted by*, *Hitsu* or *Hitsusu*, a pencil or a pen, and *Ga* or *Yegaku*, to draw or delineate ; *yegaku* is the more correct rendering of the latter character when it is associated with the name of a painter.

When the decoration is in various colours, the character *Sai* is used to express this; when the latter is combined with *ga*, it signifies that the artist, whose name is given in the inscription, painted the example in colours.

Kaga. SAI. *Painted in colours* — *Tokio.* SAIGASU. *Painted in colours by.*

The word *Dzu*, meaning a drawing, picture, or sketch, is used alone or in combination with *No* (of), or *Shin* (real), as shown below :—

Ise. DZU. *A picture.* — *Owari.* NO DZU. *A portrait of.* — *Owari.* SHIN DZU *A faithful picture.*

When one maker copies the style of another, he occasionally couples the word *Utsusu*, meaning copied, with his name, but this character is often used by celebrated makers upon original works as an expression of humility, and of their inability to do otherwise than copy those of more skilful artists. The larger of the two marks below is taken from an example made by a very celebrated Kioto potter named Shisui Kenzan, who lived in 1745.

UTSUSU. *Copied.* — KENZAN UTSUSU. *Kenzan copies.*

The character *Zan*, meaning a mountain, is one which frequently forms part of the names of the potters and others in Japan ; the examples which are here given will show the manner in which it is used. When this character designates a place, it is also read as *San* or *Yama*, the latter being the Japanese, and the former the Chinese form.

ZAN, SAN, OR YAMA.

KIOKU-ZAN. *Painted. Kaga.*

HICHO-ZAN. *Painted. Hizen.*

TAN-ZAN. *Painted. Kioto.*

TO-ZAN. *Painted. Kaga.*

KEN-ZAN. *Painted. Kioto.*

TAI-ZAN. *Impressed. Kioto.*

MIOGI-SAN. *Miogi Mountain. Painted. Owari.*

AKAHADA-YAMA. *Name of a Place. Impressed. Akahada.*

The words *An*, *Tei*, *Ken*, *Ro*, *Yen*, *Sai*, *Do* and *Sha*, meaning house, temple, hall and so forth, are constantly found in conjunction with the names of the potters and painters, and the words thus formed might be supposed to be the name of the factory or workshop at which the wares were made or decorated. But this reading is seldom correct except in those cases where the characters *ni oite*, or *oite*, meaning in or at, are also used, or when the word *Shiujin* (the master) appears in the inscription. Occasionally, however, words terminating with *sha* may be taken as being the titles of factories, but in other cases it will generally be safer to accept the names as those which it is customary in Japan for the makers and painters to assume as their professional cognomen. Two of the examples of *oite* given below are written in the Chinese style, whilst in the third the Japanese *Kata-kana* characters *ni* and *te* are added:

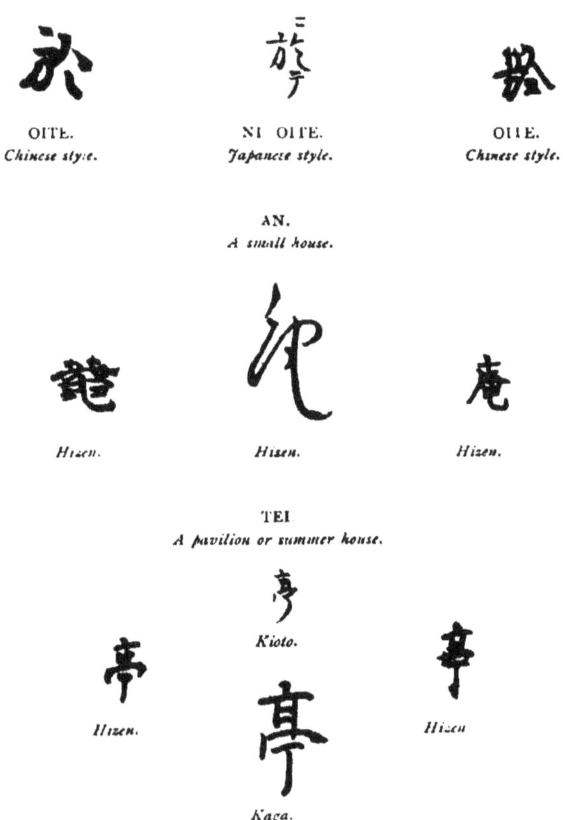

KEN.
A house.
Kioto. Kaga. Kaga. Kaga. Owari. Owari. Mutsu.
RO.
The upper story of a house.
樓
Kaga.
YEN.
A garden.
Tokio. Owari. Owari. Tokio.
SAI.
A study.
Kioto. Satsuma. Tokio. Tokio. Tokio.
DO.
A temple or hall.
Satsuma. Kaga. Kaga. Kaga. Kaga. Kaga. Hizen.
SHA.
A cottage.
Ise. Tokio. Kaga. Tokio.

found in conjunction with the names of the potters and painters, and the words thus formed might be supposed to be the name of the factory or workshop at which the wares were made or decorated. But this reading is seldom correct except in those cases where the characters *ni oite*, or *oite*, meaning in or at, are also used, or when the word *Shiujin* (the master) appears in the inscription. Occasionally, however, words terminating with *sha* may be taken as being the titles of factories, but in other cases it will generally be safer to accept the names as those which it is customary in Japan for the makers and painters to assume as their professional cognomen. Two of the examples of *oite* given below are written in the Chinese style, whilst in the third the Japanese *Kata-kana* characters *ni* and *te* are added:

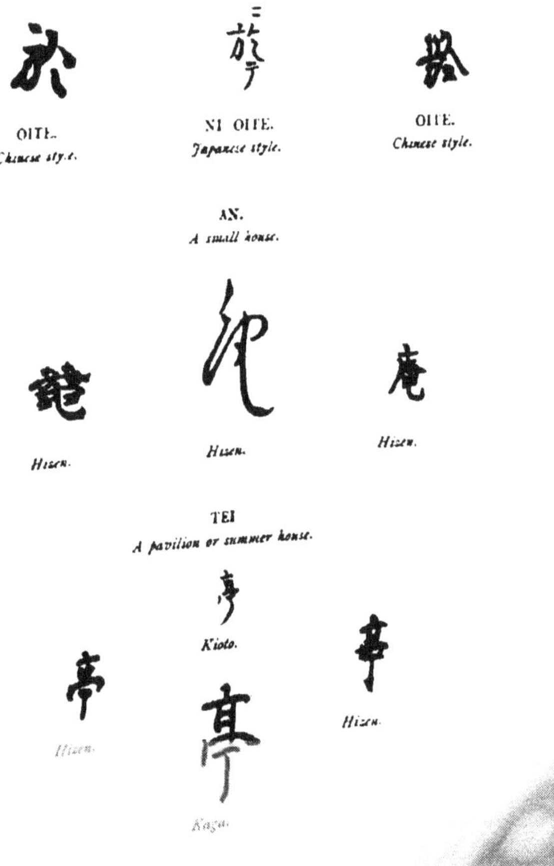

OITE. *Chinese style.* NI OITE. *Japanese style.* OITE. *Chinese style.*

AN. *A small house.*

Hizen. *Hizen.* *Hizen.*

TEI *A pavilion or summer house.*

Kioto. *Hizen.* *Hizen.* *Kaga.*

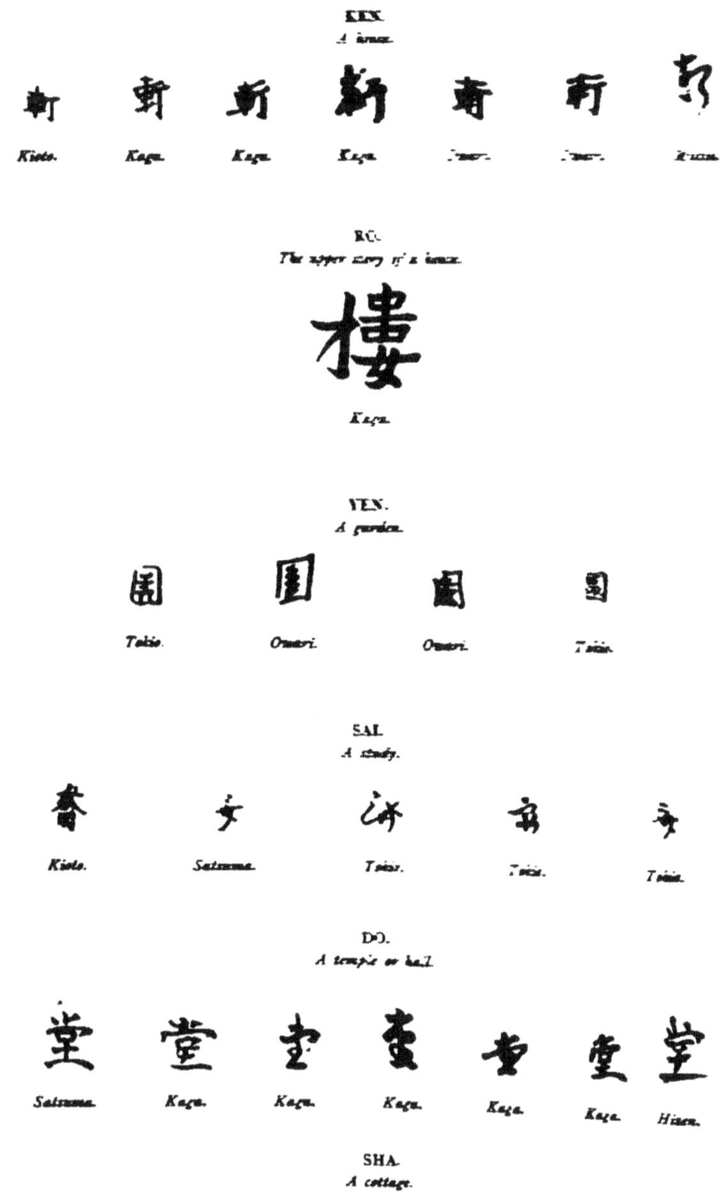
KEN.
A house.
Kioto.
Kaga.
Kaga.
Kaga.
RO.
The upper story of a house.
Kaga.
YEN.
A garden.
Tokio.
Owari.
Owari.
SAI.
A study.
Kioto.
Satsuma.
DO.
A temple or hall.
Satsuma.
Kaga.
Kaga.
Kaga.
Kaga.
Kaga.
Hizen.
SHA.
A cottage.

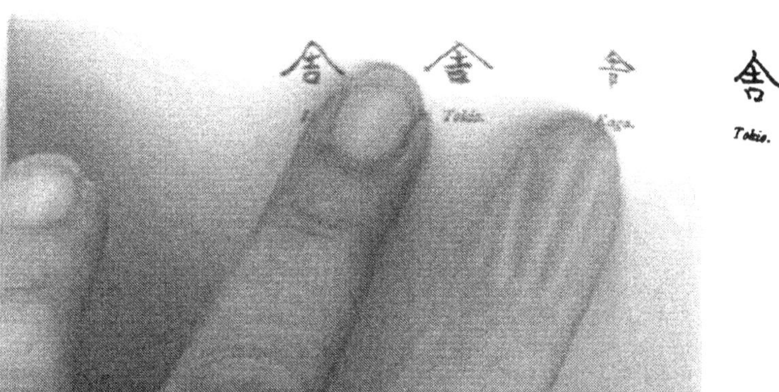
Tokio.
Tokio.

Combinations.

TOSHIKI-AN. *Hizen*

SOSEN-TEI. *Kaga.*

KIN-UN-KEN. *Kioto.*

HOGIUKU-YEN. *Owari.*

FU-WA SO-DO. *Satsuma.*

CHIUSEN-SAI. *Tokio.*

YENSO-SHA. *Yenso factory. Ise.*

KINKO-SHA, NI OITE. *At the Kinko factory. Tokio.*

KINKO-SHA. *Kinko factory. Tokio.*

KINTO-SHA. *Kinto factory. Kaga.*

In rare instances the word *Ko* (a kiln) is used. The following inscription is copied from a specimen of Hizen porcelain :—

KUWAN KO.
Government kiln.

Two characters are generally used together to signify the word Company, *kuwai*, a meeting or assembly, and *sha*, an association, but sometimes the word *sha* is found alone. The following inscription is that of the Shippo Company of Owari :—

KUWAI-SHA.
Company.

NIPPON, SHIPPO KUWAI-SHA, SEI-ZO.
The Shippo Company, Japan, made THE WARE.

In connection with this subject it is only necessary to notice two other words, *san* (the product), and *shiujin* (the master), which are occasionally used.

SAN.
The product.

HIRATO, SAN, YEDAMATS TSUKURU.
Made by Yedamats; the product of Hirato.

SHIUJIN.
The master.

KIYEN, SHIUJIN.
The master of Kiyen factory.

The Japanese *Nengo*, or year-period, is rarely found upon pottery, and only four instances occur in our list of

D

marks. It has, however, long been the custom in Hizen to make use of Chinese year-marks, which have been applied without regard to the date at which the ware was made. Upon many of the choicest examples of Old Japan porcelain, produced early in the 17th century, the mark of the Tching-hoa period, 1465-1487 A.D., is found, and dates even earlier than this are used; such forged marks are also found upon the earliest wares made in Kaga. The practice has been recently revived in Hizen, and ancient marks are freely used upon the imitation Old Japan which is now being produced in large quantities for sale in Europe and America; in Owari, also, such marks are found upon the modern porcelain coated with *cloisonné* decoration.

The character *Nen* (year or period) occurs in most of these marks, and as it is written in various styles, a few examples may be given:—

NEN.
Year or period.

The word *Sai* is occasionally used in the same sense.

SAI.
Year or period.
Hizen.

The following Japanese *Nengo* are those which occur in the list of marks upon pottery. It would, of course, be possible to increase the number by adding those found upon other art works, but it is not advisable to introduce any marks into this chapter, except those taken from Keramic wares. A list of year periods is given at the end of the Volume.

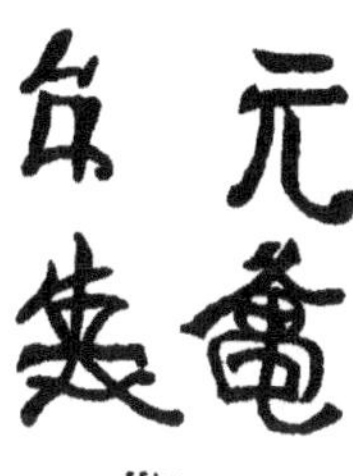

Hizen.

GENKI NEN SEI, meaning, *Made in the period of Genki,* 1570-1573 A.D.

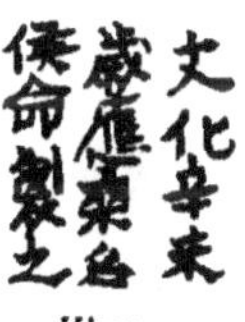

Hizen.

BUNKWA, SHIN-BI NO TOSHI, KUWA-NA KO NO MEI NI OZITE KORE O SEISU, meaning, *This is made by command of the Prince of Kuwana, in the period of Bunkwa, the Zodiac year of the Sheep,* 1804-1818 A.D. The upper characters on the right are Bunk-wa.

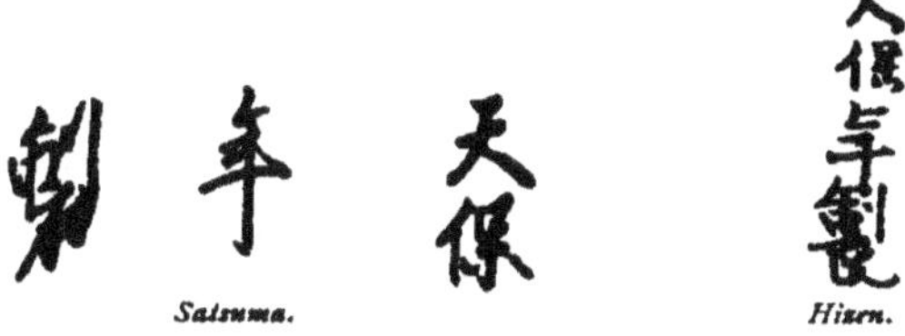

Satsuma. *Hizen.*

Both the inscriptions given above read TEMPO, NEN SEI, meaning, *Made in the period of Tempo,* 1830-1844 A.D.

Kioto.

KAYEI, SHII, SHO-SHIU, meaning, *The seventh month of the fourth year of the period of Kayei.* This period commenced in 1848 and ended in 1854 A.D.; therefore the example from which the mark is copied was made in 1851. The two upper characters on the right are Ka-yei.

Kioto.

MEIJI, ROKUSAI, meaning, *The sixth year of the period of Meiji.* This period commenced in 1868, and still continues. The example from which the mark is copied was made in 1873. The two upper characters are Mei-ji.

Tokio.

MEIJI, KUNEN, KUGATSU, meaning, *The ninth month of the ninth year of the period of Meiji.* The specimen from which this mark is copied was made in 1876. The two upper characters are Mei-ji.

The Chinese year-marks generally contain six characters, two of which indicate the dynasty:

DAI, *i.e.*, Great.

MING, The dynasty which reigned from 1368 to 1643 A.D.

DAI, *i.e.*, Great.

THSING, The dynasty which commenced in 1643 and still reigns.

The characters for the Dai Thsing dynasty are often given in seal form as follows:—

DAI, *i.e.*, Great.

THSING.

In some inscriptions these characters are omitted, and those denoting the period, and the words *nen* and *sei*, only are given.

The following periods have been forged upon Japanese wares :—

永樂	Yei-raku.	Yeiraku; or in Chinese, Yong-lo, 1403-1424 A.D.
成化	Sei-ka.	Seika; or in Chinese, Tch'ing-hoa, 1465-1487 A.D.
嘉清	Ka-sei.	Kasei; or in Chinese, Kia-tsing, 1522-1566 A.D.
萬曆	Man-reki.	Manreki; or in Chinese, Wan-li, 1573-1619 A.D.
康熙	Ko-ki.	Koki; or in Chinese, Khang-hi, 1662-1722 A.D.
乾隆	Ken-riu.	Kenriu; or in Chinese, Khien-long, 1736-1795 A.D.

The characters *nen* and *sei* having been given already, it is not necessary to repeat them here, and a single complete mark of each period will show how the various words are used in combination:—

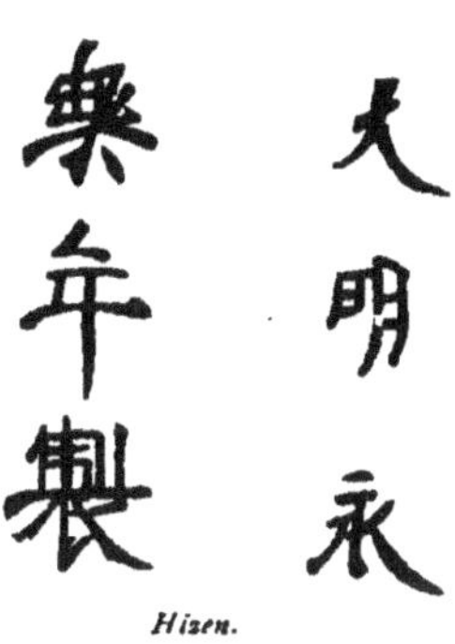

Yeiraku or Yong-lo period.

Seika or Tch'ing-hoa period.

Kasei or Kia-tsing period.

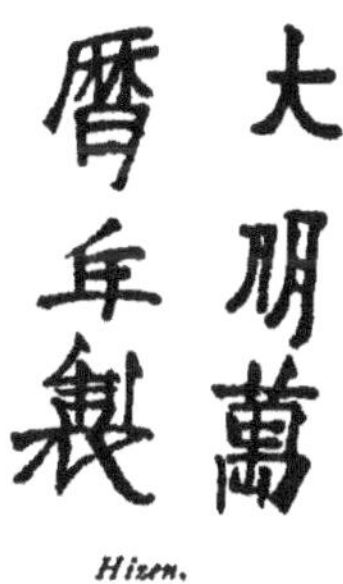

Manreki or Wan-li period.

Koki or Khang-hi period.

Kenriu or Khien-long period.

Dai Nippon, Great Japan, is a favourite inscription, and is used almost universally by the potters of Kaga and Owari, and in a lesser degree by those of other provinces, as a portion of their marks. Upon Owari porcelain the name of the principal town, Seto, is generally given, and few inscriptions upon Kaga ware are found without the word Kutani being used. Examples of these and other words of a similar character are given below.

DAI NIPPON. *Great Japan.*

NIPPON. *Japan.*

KIOTO. *The Western Capital.*

MAKUZUHARA. *A district in Kioto.*

KIOMIDZU. *A quarter in Kioto.*

AWATA. *A district in Kioto.*

KUTANI.

KUTANI. *A district in the province of Kaga.*

KUTANI.

KASHU.
Another name of the province of Kaga.

KAYO.
Another name of the province of Kaga.

KINJIO OR KANASAWA.
A town in Kaga.

HIZEN.
A province.

HIRATO.
An island near Hizen.

ARITA.
A town in Hizen.

AWAJI.
An island.

MIKAWACHI.
A town in Hizen.

TOKIO.
The Eastern Capital.

SATSUMA.
A province.

YOKOHAMA.
A town near Tokio.

TOYOURAZAN.
A town in the province of Nagato.

OWARI.
A province.

AICHI KEN KA.
The political division of Japan in which Owari is situated.

NAGOYA.
A town in Owari.

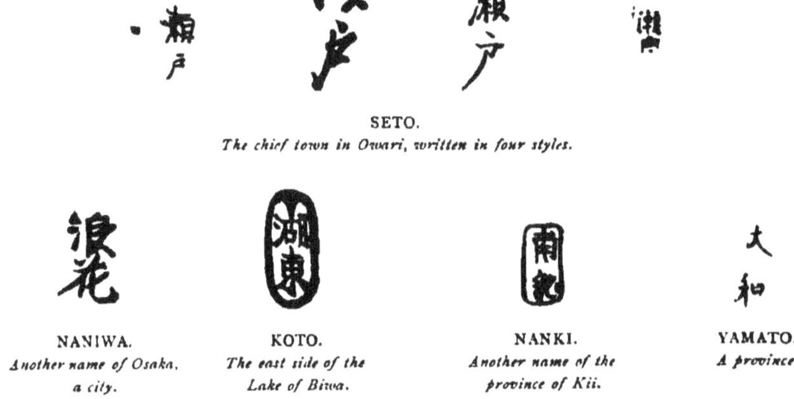

SETO.
The chief town in Owari, written in four styles.

NANIWA. *Another name of Osaka, a city.*

KOTO. *The east side of the Lake of Biwa.*

NANKI. *Another name of the province of Kii.*

YAMATO. *A province.*

In some cases the names by which the ware is known are given, occasionally with the word *Yaki*, meaning ware, added; these marks are nearly always stamped:—

MINATO YAKI.

SOMA.

RAKU.

ASAHI.

AKAHADA.

BANKO.

It appears to have been a custom of the princes in Japan to honor distinguished potters with whose efforts they were pleased, by presenting to them seals bearing some device with which to mark their productions. The most notable incident of this nature upon record is the presentation by Taico Sama of a gold seal bearing the character *Raku*, signifying Enjoyment, to Chojiro, the son of a Corean potter named Ameya, who settled in Kioto in 1550 A.D., and originated the manufacture of the ware afterwards known as *raku*, which, although rude in form and devoid of decoration, has always been held in the highest esteem by the *Chajin*, especially during the period when the ceremony of tea drinking, known as *Chanoyu*, flourished. For eleven generations the Chojiro family has pursued the manufacture of this ware, and marked it with the *raku* seal, but, as the second Chojiro lost the seal presented by Taico Sama, each succeeding generation has used a stamp of its own, differing in drawing and size no doubt, but all bearing the same word. The names of the eleven generations are as follows:—1, Chojiro; 2, Chojiro; 3, Nonko; 4, Ichiniu or Sahei; 5, Soniu; 6, Saniu; 7, Choniu; 8, Tokoniu; 9, Riyoniu; 10, Tanniu; 11, Kichizayemon, who is now living.

The examples of the seal here given appear to comprise those of eight out of the eleven generations, and include all that occur in the list of marks, and probably all that have reached Europe.

THE SEAL RAKU.
Enjoyment. Used by the Chojiro family.

Another well-known seal is that used by the Yeiraku family of Kioto. Although this family is now represented by the thirteenth in descent from Zengoro, its founder, the use of the seal dates only from the commencement of the present century, when Riozen, the tenth in descent, invented the beautiful decoration in red and gold known as *kinrande*, and received as a reward from a member of the Tokugawa family a seal bearing the characters *Yeiraku*, which signify Everlasting enjoyment. The examples given below probably represent all the seals used by Riozen and his successors.

THE SEAL YEIRAKU.
Everlasting enjoyment. Used by the Yeiraku family.

Native reports state that during the feudal times several of the principal factories were conducted under the direction of the Daimios of the provinces in which they were situated, but it is not clear whether the kilns were the property of the princes or were merely favoured with their patronage. It will probably be correct to assume that the connection of the prince of Satsuma with the factory at which the ware of that name was made was of the former character, and his crest, as drawn below, is copied from a bowl of faience, upon which it occupies the position in which the mark of the maker is usually found.

CREST OF THE PRINCE OF SATSUMA.

The factory of Ohokawachi, in Hizen, was founded by the prince of that province, who reserved all the wares produced for his own use, or for presentation to the rulers and nobles of the country. Probably many of these were decorated with the crests of those who received them, and the following badge of the Tokugawa family appears upon a plate of porcelain, in the Bowes Collection, identified as having been made at this factory for presentation to a member of that family who filled the office of Shôgun.

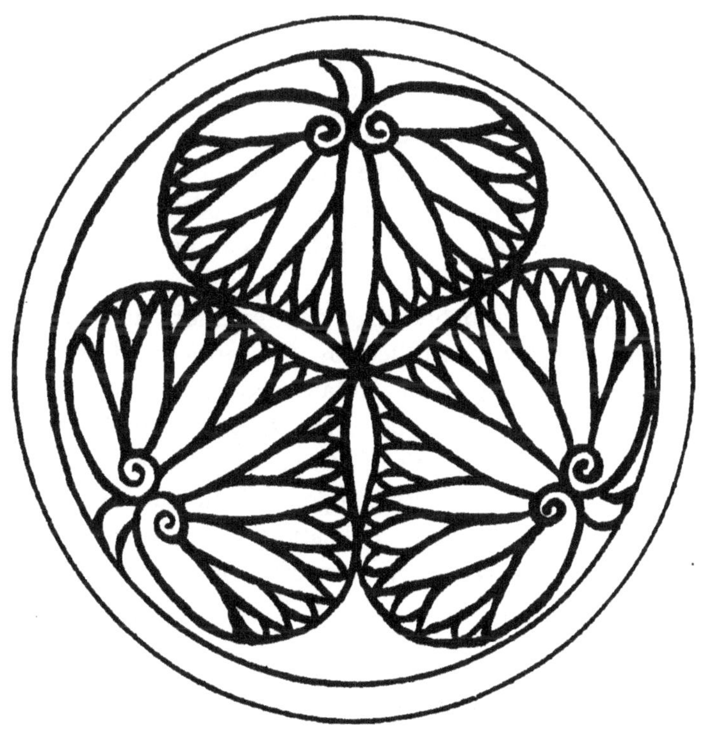

CREST OF THE TOKUGAWA FAMILY.

Another distinguishing feature of the decoration employed at the Ohokawachi factory was the use upon the lower edges of the plates and saucers made there of the mark shown on next page; it was painted in blue, and the articles so marked were known as *Kushide* ware, or ware marked after the style of a comb.

KUSHI-DE MARK.
Comb style mark.

Another factory in the same province, that of Mikawachi, was established by the prince of Hirato; the ware made at this kiln, in its best days, was porcelain of the choicest quality, decorated in the *sometsuke* fashion. The pieces were all of small size and were reserved by the princes for their own use or for presentation to their friends, but we are not aware that crests or other distinguishing marks were placed upon them. The favorite subject for decoration was groups of boys; on the finest specimens there are seven and five boys, but only three appear upon less perfect examples.

It is highly probable that one or more of the Kutani kilns were directly controlled by the princes of Kaga, for several choice examples of Kutani ware received in Europe have been accompanied by the statement that they had been made at the prince's factory, and there is a covered jar in the Bowes Collection upon which the crest of the prince of Bizen appears, indicating that the example was presented to him by the prince of Kaga.

CREST OF THE PRINCE OF BIZEN.

The use of crests for decorative purposes is not customary; it was indeed a common practice during the 17th century for the makers of Old Japan ware to introduce modifications of the *kiku* crest of the Mikado into their decoration, and occasionally to paint the crest, properly displayed, either as a mark or as an ornament. But this practice was a contravention of the law which prohibited the use of the imperial crests by any subject, and it was probably discontinued after the principal offender, Tomimura Kanyemon, was compelled to commit the *hara kiri*, as described in *Keramic Art of Japan.*

The crest was drawn in various ways, sometimes entire, whilst in other instances only a portion of the figure was shown; the number of petals also varied, the correct number of sixteen being occasionally shown, as in the example given below, but upon specimens of Old Japan in the Dresden Collection the number of petals varies from twelve to thirty-one. The following marks are copied from authenticated specimens:—

THE KIKU CREST.
Used as a mark upon Old Japan in the Dresden Collection.

THE KIKU CREST.
A PORTION. THE WHOLE.
Used as a decoration upon a tea bowl of Old Japan in the Bowes Collection.

Instances, however, occur where the crests of the Mikado have apparently been used by authority, for they appear upon articles made in Kioto at a time when it is highly improbable that the stringent laws forbidding their use would have been disregarded. An example of this is seen upon a perfume box in the Bowes Collection; it was made by Nonomura Ninsei, a distinguished potter, who settled at Kioto in 1650 A.D., and originated the manufacture of artistic pottery. The *kiku* and *kiri* crests are rendered in white and gold upon the black enamel ground of the cover of the box, as shown in the drawing given below; the variation in the number of petals in the *kiku* crest and the substitution of five and three leaves in the sprays of the *kiri*, for the correct number of seven and five, may indicate that the example was made for a member of the imperial family and not for the Mikado himself.

THE KIKU AND KIRI CRESTS.
From a perfume box made by Nonomura Ninsei.

The decoration of a small box, in the form of a *famaguri* shell, in the same collection, affords another example of this treatment; upon one side both crests appear, whilst the *kiku* alone is given on the reverse.

THE KIKU AND KIRI CRESTS.
From a perfume box made by Yusetsu, of Kioto.

The rudely formed tea bowls made in the province of Iwaki, known as Soma ware, are generally decorated with one or both of the crests of the prince from whom the ware takes its name. Both the crests are shown in the drawing given below; the principal one is a horse, which is drawn alone or tethered to stakes, and the subsidiary crest consists of a central ball surrounded by eight smaller ones.

THE CRESTS OF THE PRINCE OF SOMA.

HIZEN POTTERY.

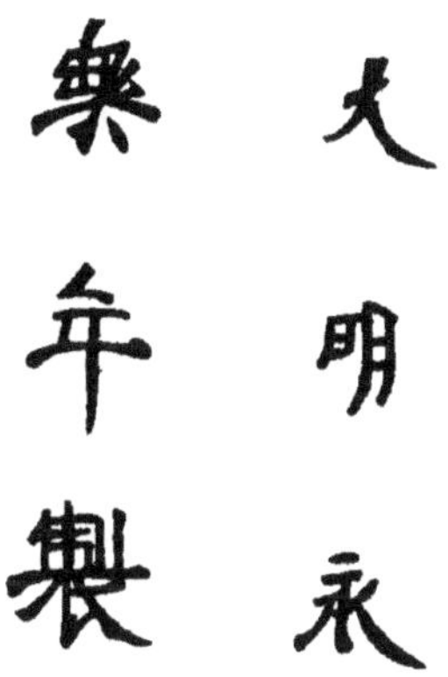

No. 1.

Painted in blue upon a Bowl of Old Japan in the Dresden Collection. DAI MING, YEI-RAKU, NEN SEI. *Made in the year of Yeiraku, during the dynasty of Dai Ming,* 1403–1424 A.D. A forgery of the Chinese mark of the Yong-lo period.

No. 2.

Painted in blue upon a Bowl of Old Japan in the Dresden Collection. DAI MING, SEI-KA, NEN SEI. *Made in the year of Seika, during the dynasty of Dai Ming,* 1465–1487 A.D. A forgery of the Chinese mark of the Tch'ing-hoa period.

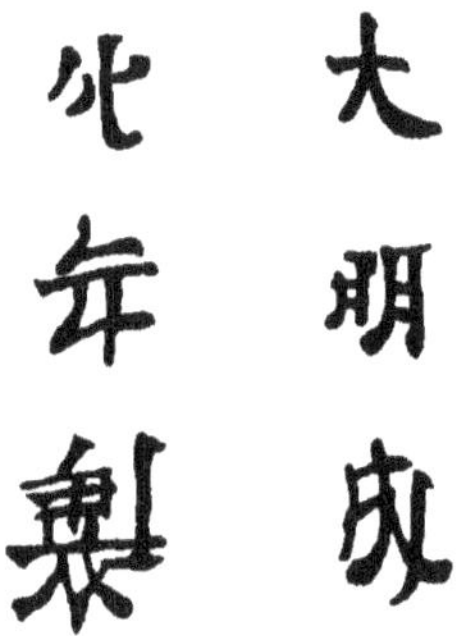

No. 3.

Painted in blue upon a Saucer of fine Old Japan. DAI MING, SEI-KA, NEN SEI. *Made in the year of Seika, during the dynasty of Dai Ming*, 1465-1487 A.D. A forgery of the Chinese mark of the Tch'ing-hoa period.

No. 4.

Another forgery of the Chinese mark of the Tch'ing-hoa period. Painted in blue upon a large Dish, in the Dresden Collection, of Old Japan, bearing a representation of the baptism of Christ, a subject which could only have been used subsequent to 1549, when Christianity was introduced into Japan.

No. 5.

Another forgery of the Chinese mark of the Tch'ing-hoa period. Painted in blue upon a Cup of Old Japan in the Dresden Collection, with five spur-marks as shown above.

No. 6.

Another forgery of the Chinese mark of the Tch'ing-hoa period. Painted in blue upon a Plate of Old Japan of fair age.

No. 7.

Another forgery of the Chinese mark of the Tch'ing-hoa period. Painted in blue upon a Dish of modern Old Japan; this example also shows five spur-marks.

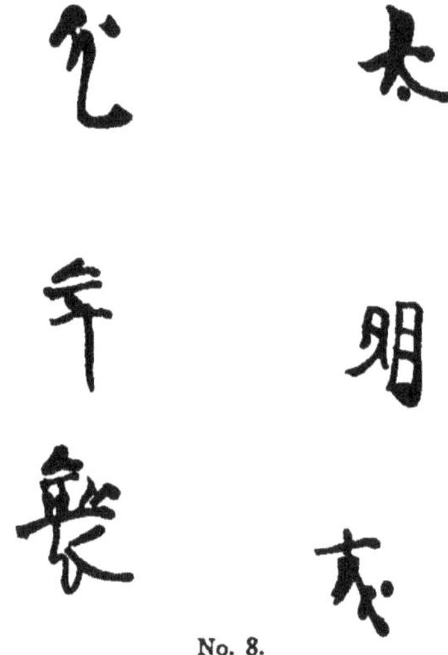

No. 8.

Another forgery of the Chinese mark of the Tch'ing-hoa period. Painted in blue upon a Dish of Old Japan of fair age.

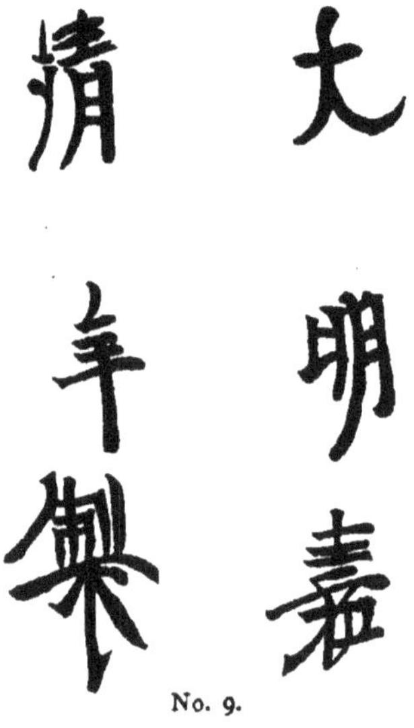

No. 9.

Painted in blue upon a Dish of Old Japan in the Dresden Collection. DAI MING, KA-SEI, NEN SEI. *Made in the year of Kasei, during the dynasty of Dai Ming*, 1522–1566 A.D. A forgery of the Chinese mark of the Kia-tsing period.

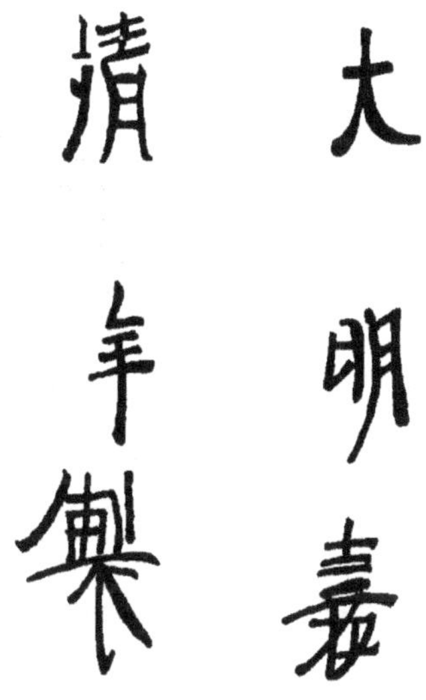

No. 10.

Another forgery of the Chinese mark of the Kia-tsing period. Painted in blue upon a Dish in the Dresden Collection.

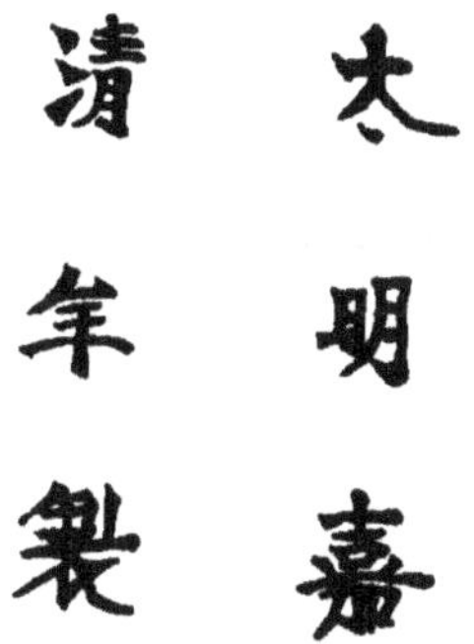

No. 11.

Another forgery of the Chinese mark of the Kia-tsing period. Painted in blue upon a Dish of Old Japan of modern work. This example bears five spur-marks.

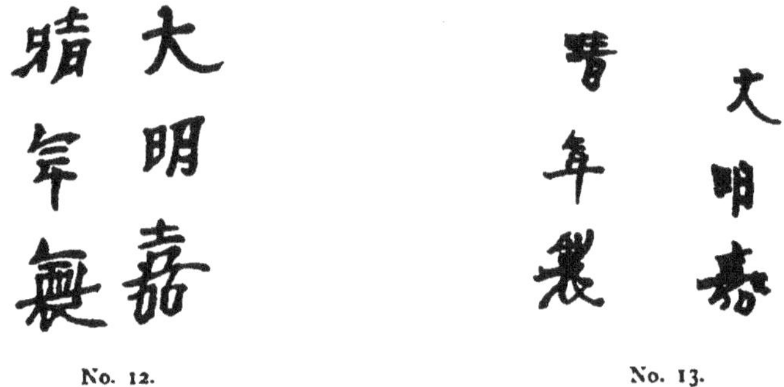

No. 12. No. 13.

Forgeries of the Chinese mark of the Kia-tsing period. Painted in blue upon Plates of old Japan.

No. 14.

Painted in blue upon a Covered Bowl of fine Old Japan. KA-SEI, NEN SEI. A forgery of the Chinese mark of the Kia-tsing period.

No. 15.

Painted in blue upon a Bowl of Old Japan in the Dresden Collection. DAI MING, MAN-REKI, NEN SEI. *Made in the year of Manreki, during the dynasty of Dai Ming*, 1573–1619 A.D. A forgery of the Chinese mark of the Wan-li period.

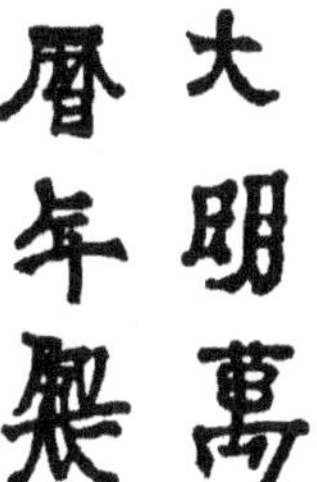

No. 16.

Another forgery of the Chinese mark of the Wan-li period. Painted in blue upon a Bowl of fine Old Japan.

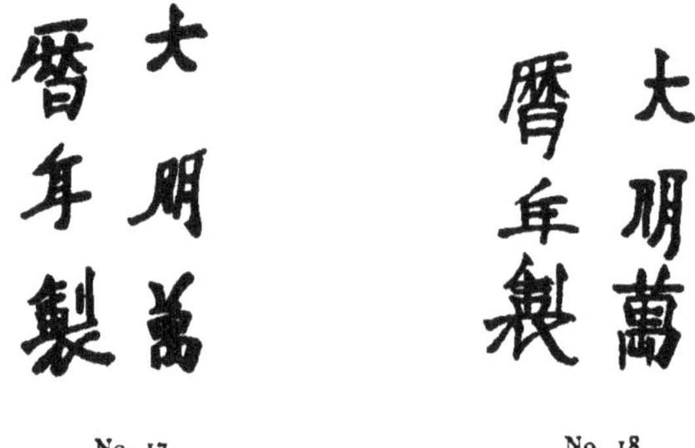

No. 17. No. 18.

Forgeries of the Chinese mark of the Wan-li period. Painted in blue upon Bowls of the finest Old Japan.

No. 19.

Another forgery of the Chinese mark of the Wan-li period. Painted in blue upon a Bowl of Old Japan in the Dresden Collection.

No. 20.

Painted in blue upon a Bowl of very fine Old Japan. DAI MING, MAN-REKI, NEN SEI. *Made in the year of Manreki, during the dynasty of Dai Ming*, 1573–1619 A.D. A forgery of the Chinese mark of the Wan-li period.

No. 21.

Painted in blue upon a Bowl of Old Japan, of comparatively modern workmanship. DAI THSING, KO-KI, NEN SEI. *Made in the year of Koki, during the dynasty of Dai Thsing*, A.D. 1662–1722. A forgery of the Chinese mark of the Khang-hi period

No. 22.

Painted in blue upon a modern imitation of Old Japan. Dai Thsing, Ken-riu nen sei. *Made in the year of Kenriu, during the period of Dai Thsing*, A.D. 1736–1795. A forgery of the Chinese mark of the period of Khien-long.

No. 23.

Another forgery of the Chinese mark of the Khien-long period. Painted in blue upon a circular Jar of Old Japan, of comparatively modern workmanship.

No. 24.

Painted in black upon a Bowl of Old Japan, of comparatively modern workmanship. Dai Thsing, Ken-riu. A forgery of the Chinese mark of the Khien-long period.

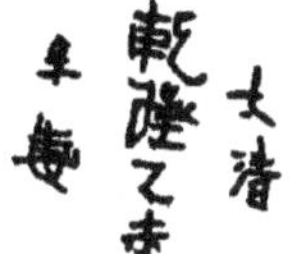

No. 25.

Painted in blue upon a circular Jar of Mikawachi porcelain decorated in blue. DAI THSING, KEN-RIU, ITSU-BI, NEN SEI. *Made in the year of Kenriu, in the Zodiac year of the Sheep, during the dynasty of Dai Thsing.* A forgery of the Chinese mark of the Khien-long period.

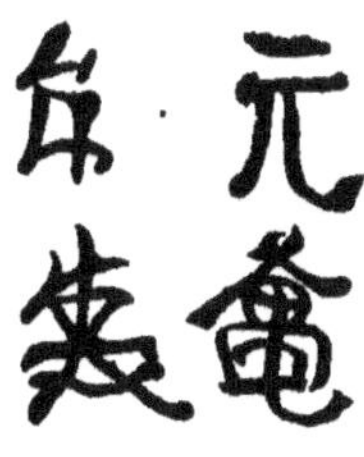

No. 26.

Painted in blue upon a Basin of fine Old Japan. GEN-KI, NEN SEI. *Made in the year of Genki;* a Japanese period dating from 1570 to 1573 A.D.

No. 27.

Painted in blue upon a Jar of Old Japan in the Dresden Collection. FU-KI CHO-SHUN. Fuki Choshun, a phrase signifying *Fortune and Longevity.* Fuki means wealth, prosperity, or luck, and Choshun means Long spring.

No. 28.

Painted in blue upon a Saucer of Old Japan in the Dresden Collection. FUKI CHOSHUN. *Fortune and Longevity.*

No. 29.

Painted in blue upon a Bowl of Old Japan in the Dresden Collection. FUKI CHOSHUN. *Fortune and Longevity.*

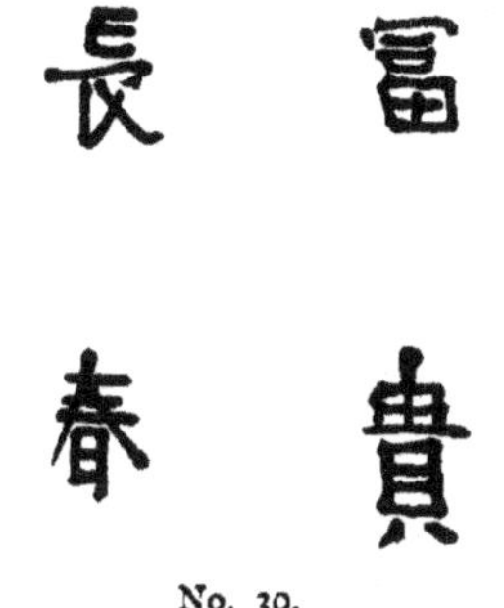

No. 30.

Painted in blue upon a Bowl of Old Japan of fair age. Fuki Choshun.

No. 31.

Painted in blue upon a Bowl of porcelain made in 1830, and decorated in the Old Japan fashion. Fuki Choshun.

No. 32. No. 33.

Painted in blue upon Bowls of Old Japan of modern workmanship. Fuki Choshun.

No. 34.

Painted in red upon a Bowl of imitation Old Japan. Fuki Choshun.

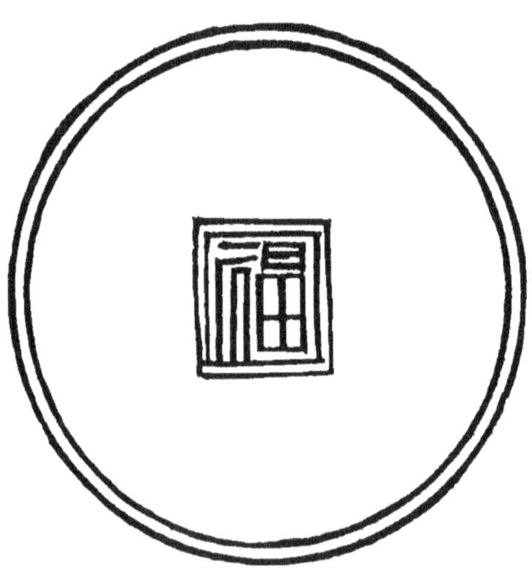

No. 35.

Painted in blue upon a Bowl of Old Japan in the Dresden Collection. Fuku, meaning Prosperity, luck, and so forth.

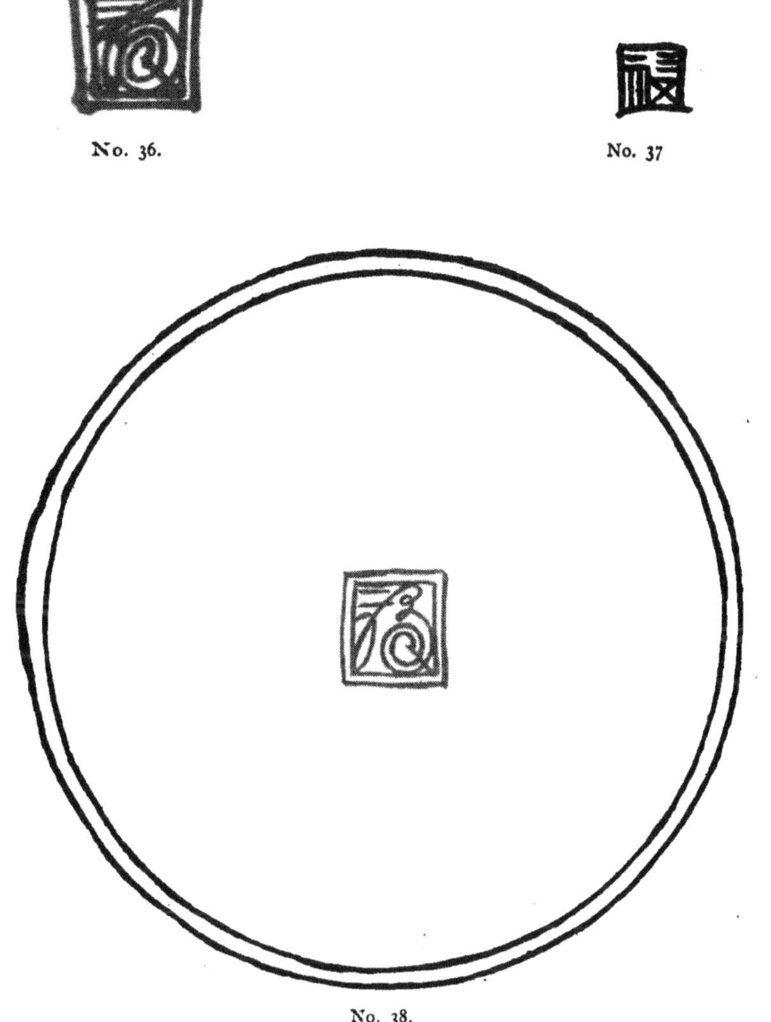

No. 36. No. 37

No. 38.

No. 36.—Painted in blue upon a Dish of Old Japan of fair age. No. 37.—Painted in blue upon a Cup of Old Japan in the Dresden Collection. No. 38.—Painted in blue upon a Bowl of Old Japan in the Dresden Collection. FUKU. *Prosperity.*

No. 39.

Painted in blue upon a Saucer of Old Japan in the Dresden Collection. TAMA, meaning *A Gem.*

No. 40.

Painted in blue upon a Cup of Old Japan in the Dresden Collection. KI-CHIN, TAMA NO GOTOSHI. *Like the rareness of a Gem.*

No. 41.

A Snail and leaves, painted in blue upon a Saucer of Old Japan in the Dresden Collection.

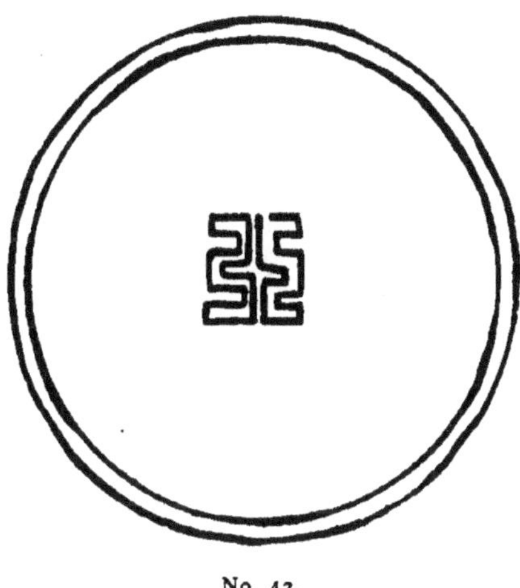

No. 42.

Painted in blue upon a Cup of Old Japan in the Dresden Collection. A Chinese symbol, probably the Sacred Axe.

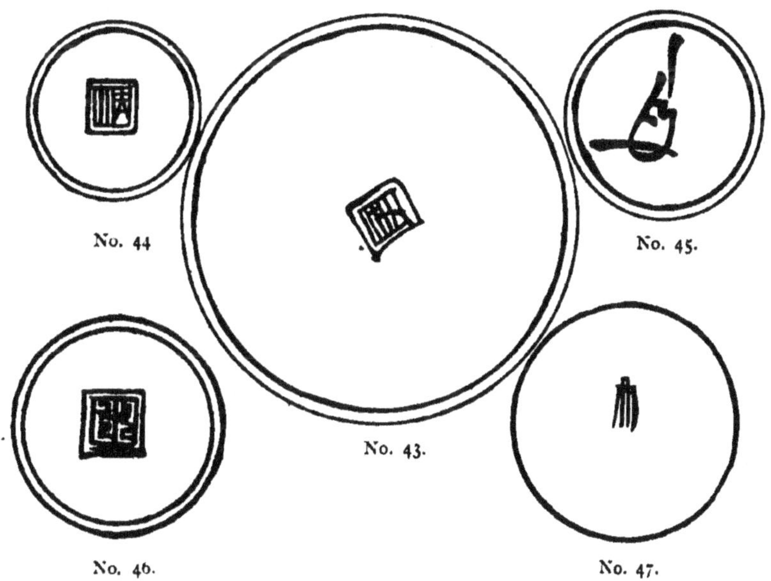

No. 44 No. 45. No. 43. No. 46. No. 47.

Makers' marks. Painted in blue upon examples of Old Japan in the Dresden Collection.

No. 48.

No. 49.

No. 50.

No. 51.

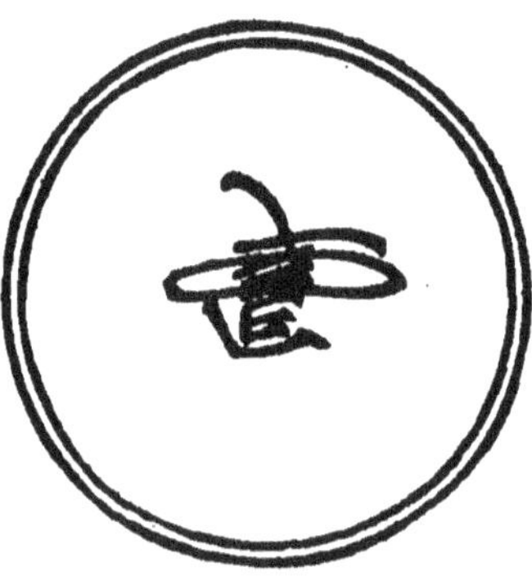

No. 52.

Makers' marks. Painted in blue upon examples of Old Japan in the Dresden Collection.

No. 53.

No. 54.

Painted in colours and gold upon Old Japan in the Dresden Collection. No. 53.—The OUMAI. No. 54.—The SAKURA.

No. 55.

Painted in red and gold upon a Dish of Old Japan in the Dresden Collection. The flower to the right is the SUISEN, a species of hyacinth, and that to the left is the KIKU, or chrysanthemum. These are the favourite flowers of the *Chajin*, connoisseurs in the ceremony of *Chanoyu* or tea drinking.

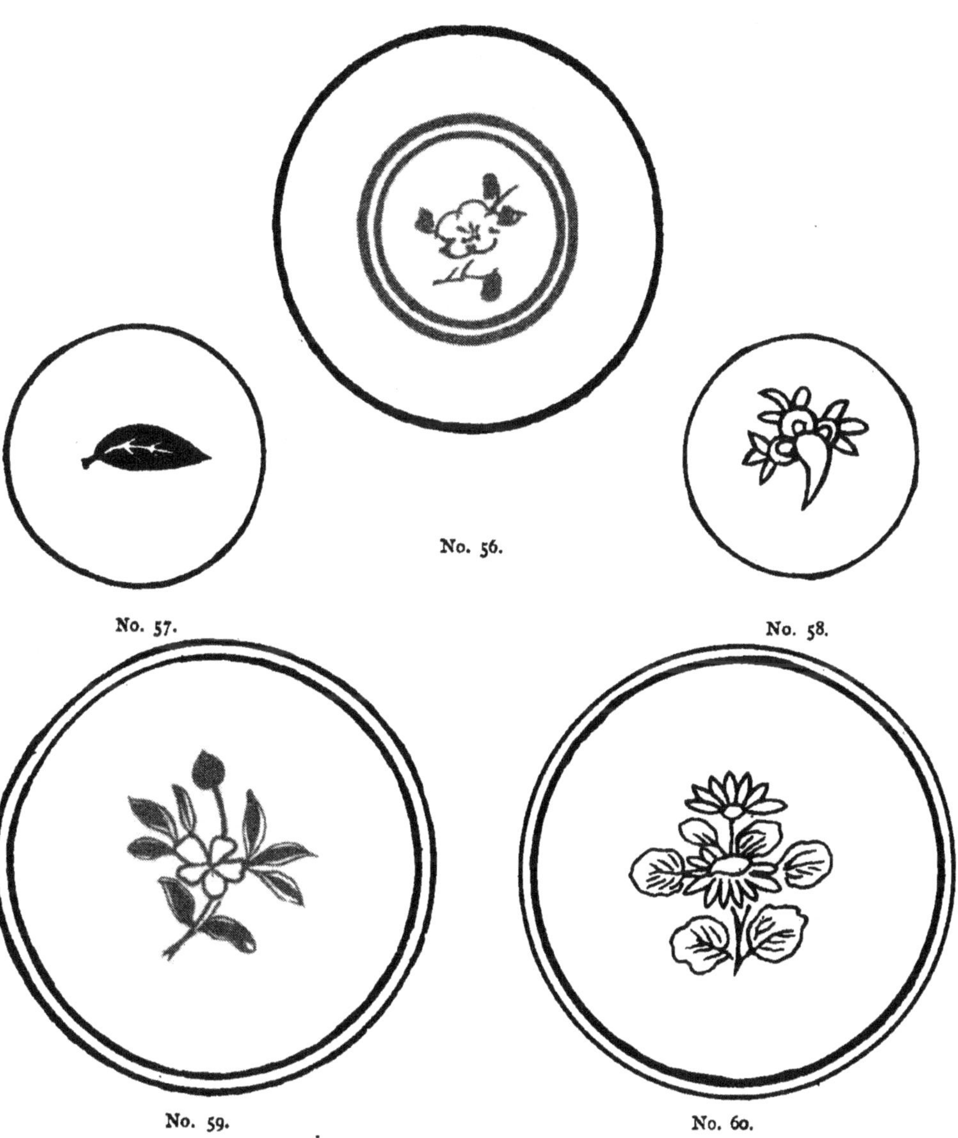

Painted upon Old Japan. No. 56.—The OUMAI. No. 57.—A leaf of the MOMO, or peach. No. 58.—The CHOJI, or clove. No. 59.—The SAKURA, or cherry. No. 60.—The KIKU, or chrysanthemum.

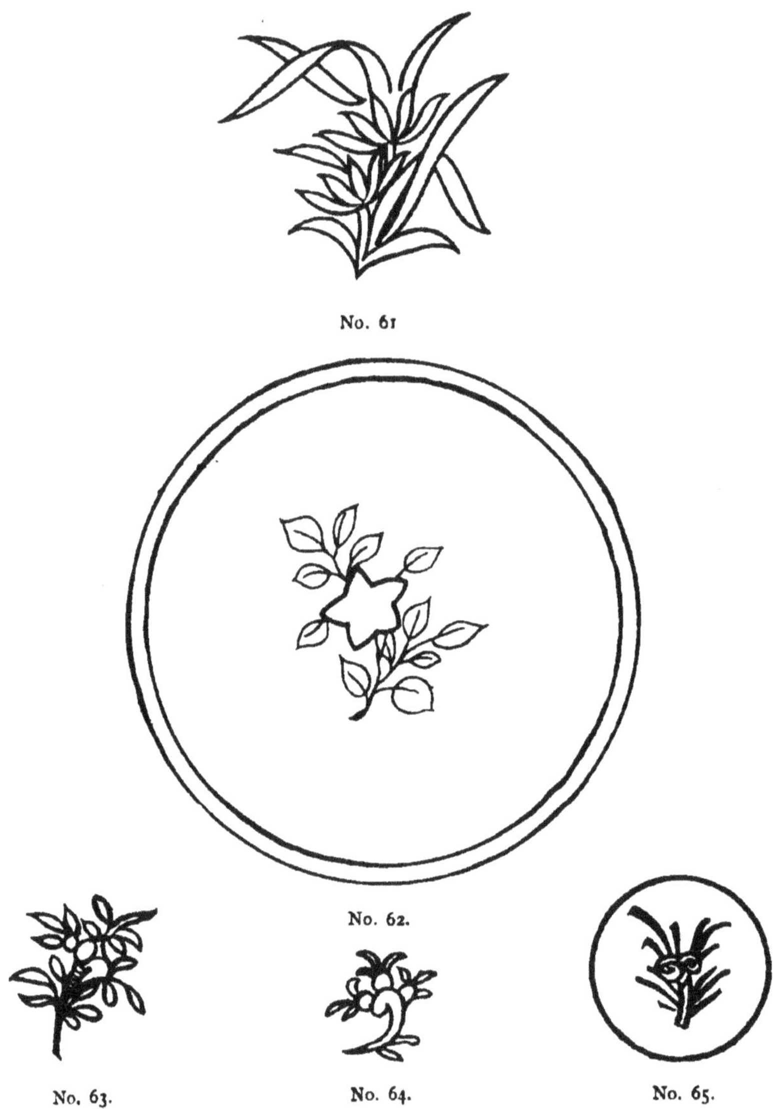

No. 61

No. 62.

No. 63. No. 64. No. 65.

Painted upon Old Japan. No. 61.—The RAN, a flower found in secluded valleys. No. 62.—The KIKO. No. 63.—Probably the leaves of the CHOJI, or clove. No. 64.—The CHOJI, or clove; the clove is one of the Seven precious things known in Japan as SHIPPO. No. 65.—Probably the SAIDAKE, or Happy Mushroom.

No. 66.

Painted in red and gold upon a Dish of Old Japan in the Dresden Collection. The leaves are those of the Ran, and the flower is that of the Botan, or peony.

Flowers and other marks painted upon Old Japan.

No. 74.

No. 75.

Modifications of the Kiku crest painted upon Old Japan in the Dresden Collection. No. 74.—Painted in red and gold, within a circle of blue, upon a Bowl. No. 75.—Painted in red and gold upon a Saucer.

No. 76.

A maker's mark. Painted in blue upon a modern imitation of Old Japan.

No. 77.

Painted in red upon a Vase of modern porcelain. NISHIAMA SEISU. *Made by Nishiyama.*

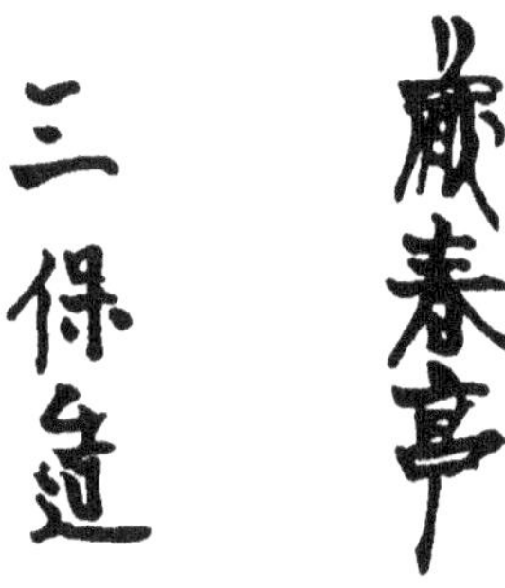

No. 78.

Painted in red upon a Dish of porcelain, made at Arita about 1820 A.D. ZO-SHUN-TEI SAN HO TSUKURU. *Made by Zoshuntei San Ho.*

No. 79.

Painted in blue upon a Cup of egg-shell porcelain. ZO-SHUN-TEI SAN HO TSUKURU. *Made by Zoshuntei San Ho.*

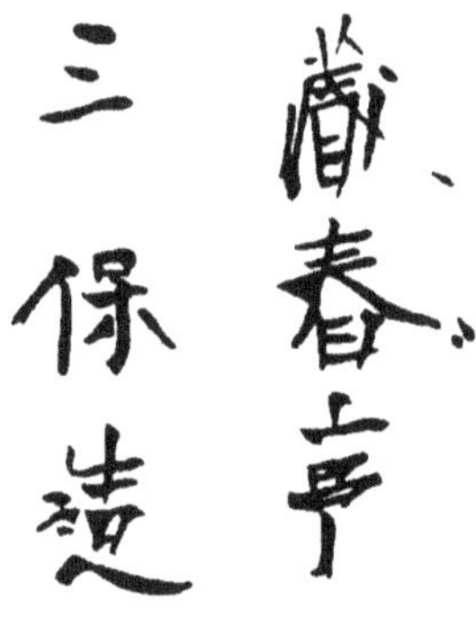

No. 80.

Painted in red upon a Bottle of porcelain. ZO-SHUN-TEI SAN HO TSUKURU. *Made by Zoshuntei San Ho.*

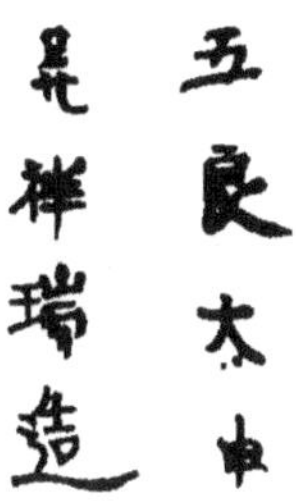

No. 81.

Painted in blue upon a Dish of porcelain, made at Arita about 1820 A.D. GO-RO-TA NARABINI SHO-ZUI SIN-ZO. *Made by Gorota and Shozui together.*

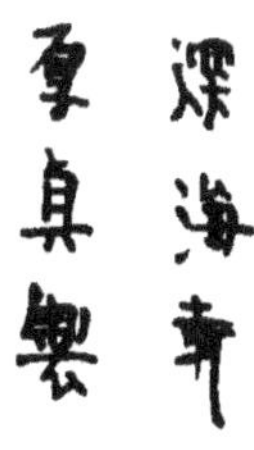

No. 82.

Painted in blue upon a Saucer of porcelain, decorated in blue. SHIN-KAI-KEN AT-SUSADA SEISU. *Made by Atsusada at the Shinkai factory.*

No. 83.

Painted in red upon a Saucer of porcelain, partially lacquered. SAI-SIN-TEI SISI SEISU. *Made by Saisintei Sisi.*

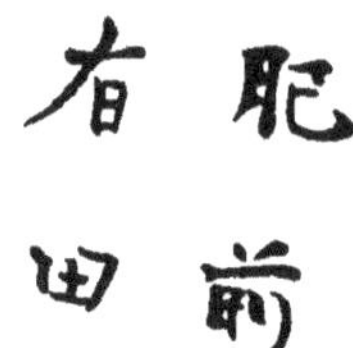

No. 84.

Painted in black upon a Vase of porcelain made at Arita. HI-ZEN, ARI-TA.

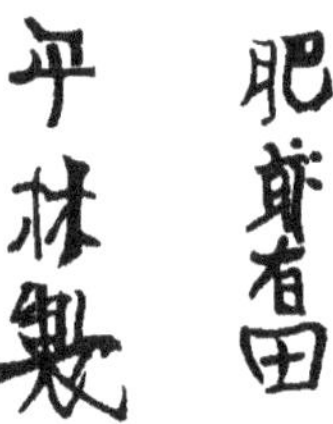

No. 85.

Painted in red upon a Vase of Porcelain; modern, of inferior workmanship. HI-ZEN, ARI-TA, HIRA-BAYASHI SEISU. *Made by Hirabayashi, Arita, Hizen.*

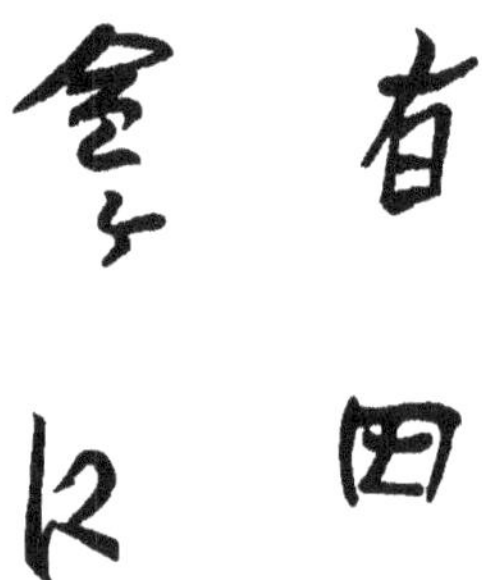

No. 86.

Painted upon a Vase of porcelain, of fair workmanship. ARITA, KANAGA-YE. *Kanagaye*, the name of the maker, and the town in which he resides.

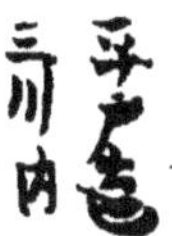

No. 87.

Painted in red upon a Cup of egg-shell porcelain. HIRA-TO ZO, MI-KAWA-CHI. *Made in Hirato* at the *Mikawachi* factory.

No. 88.

Painted in red upon a Cup of egg-shell porcelain. HIRA-TO SEI, MI-KAWA-CHI. *Made in Hirato* at the *Mikawachi* factory.

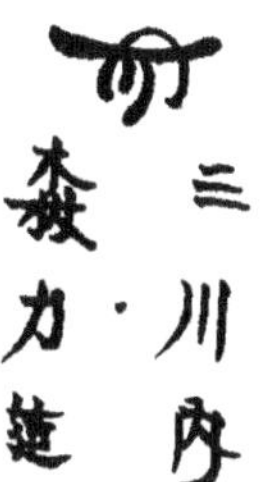

No. 89.

Painted in red upon a Tea Cup of egg-shell porcelain, made in 1875 A.D. MI-KAWA-CHI, MORI CHIKARA TSUKURU. *Made by Mori Chikara, Mikawachi.* The figure at the top of the inscription, an ornament, is painted in gold.

No. 90.

Upon a Flower Vase of porcelain of modern workmanship; the circular mark is impressed, and the characters at the side are painted in red. DAI NIP-PON. MI-KAWA-CHI SEI, KORAN-SHA NI OITE NISHI-YAMA SEISU. *Made by Nishiyama in the Koransha* (Koran factory). *Mikawachi manufacture. Great Japan.*

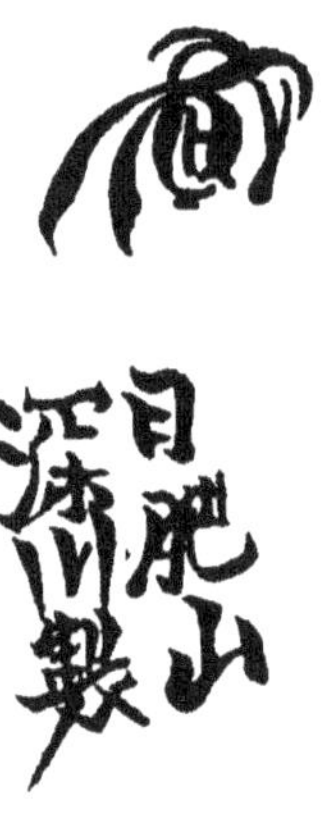

No. 91.

Painted in gold upon a Flower Vase of celadon ware made at Ohokawachi in 1875 A.D. NICHI-HI-ZAN, FUKA-GAWA SEISU. *Made by Fukagawa of Nichihizan.* The figure at the top is an ornament.

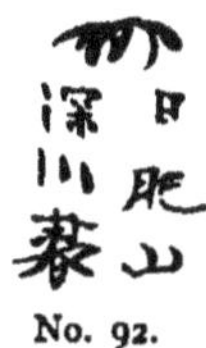

No. 92.

The characters painted in red, the ornament in gold; upon a Cup and Saucer of modern egg-shell porcelain. NICHI-HI-ZAN, FUKA-GAWA SEISU. *Made by Fukagawa of Nichihizan.*

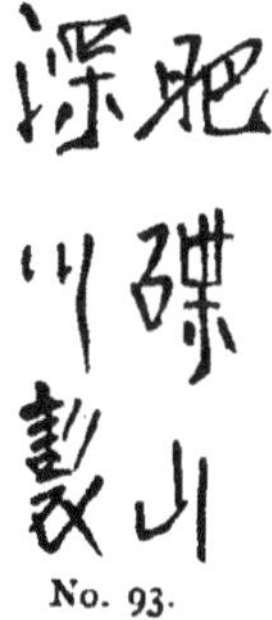

No. 93.

Painted in red upon a Dish in the shape of the fish Koi. HI-CHO-ZAN FUKA-GAWA SEISU. *Made by Hichozan Fukagawa.*

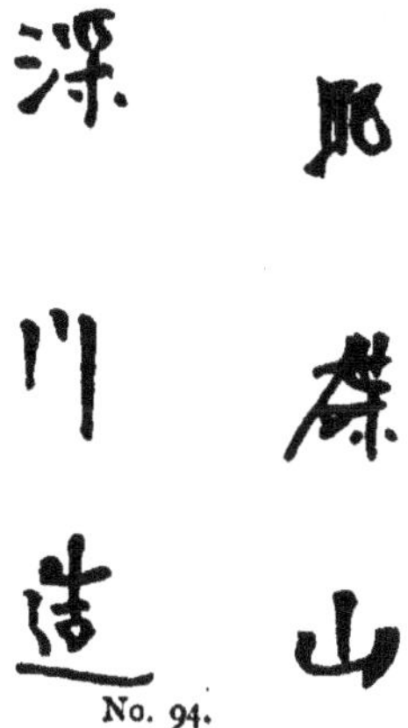

No. 94.

Painted in red upon a Dish of common modern porcelain. HI-CHO-ZAN FUKA-GAWA TSUKURU. *Made by Hichozan Fukagawa.*

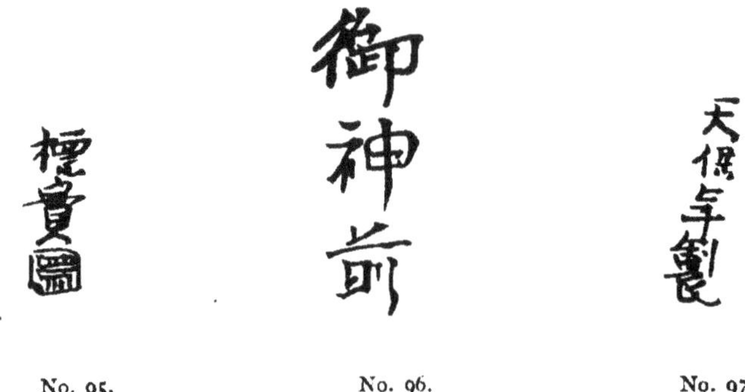

No. 95. No. 96. No. 97.

The three inscriptions given above are painted in blue upon a small Temple Lamp of Mikawachi porcelain. No. 95.—HIO-ZITSU; the maker. The seal is his mark. No. 96.—GO-SIN-ZEN, a phrase used upon articles devoted to religious uses; it signifies Before the God, or Offered to the Shrine. No. 97.—TEM-PO NEN SEI. *Made in the period of Tempo;* 1830–1844 A.D.

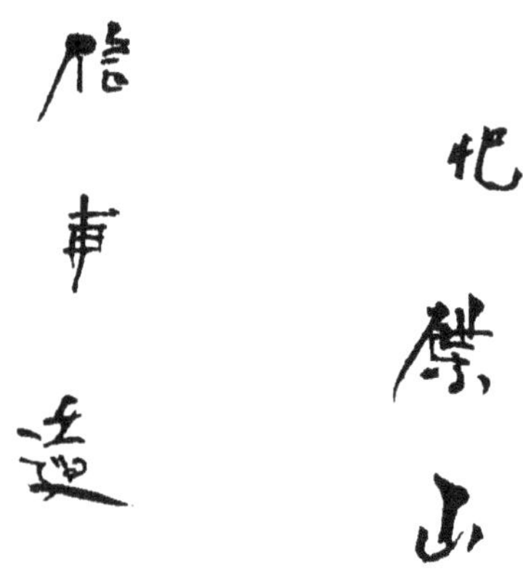

No. 98.

Painted in red upon a large Bowl of porcelain of good workmanship. HI-CHO-ZAN SHIN-PO TSUKURU. *Made by Hichozan Shinpo.*

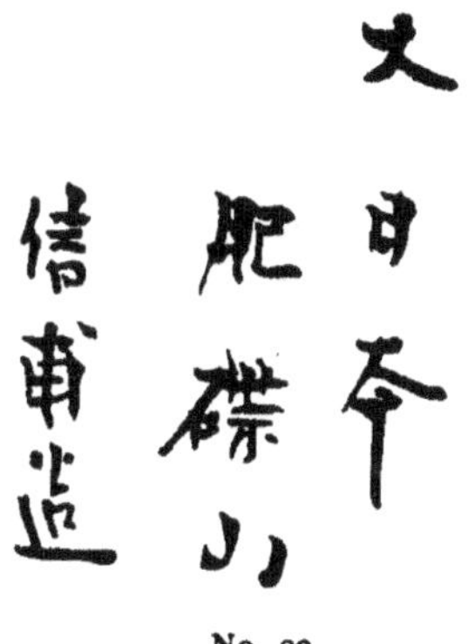

No. 99.

Painted in red upon a Vase of porcelain, decorated with *cloisonné* enamel, of modern manufacture. DAI NIP-PON, HI-CHO-ZAN SHIN-PO TSUKURU. *Made by Hichozan Shinpo, Great Japan.*

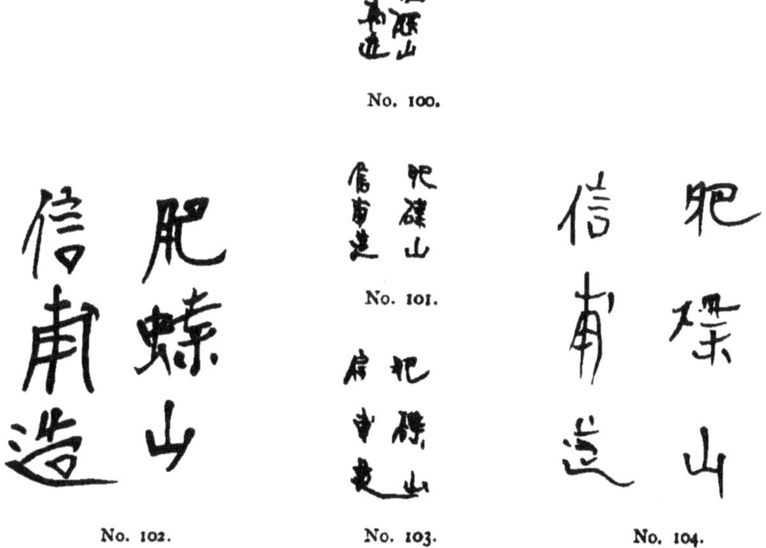

No. 100.

No. 101.

No. 102. No. 103. No. 104.

Nos. 100 to 104. Painted upon modern porcelain of ordinary character. HI-CHO-ZAN SHIN-PO TSUKURU. *Made by Hichozan Shinpo.*

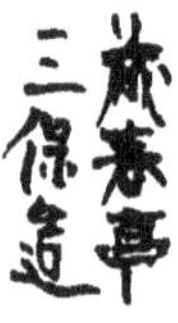

No. 105.

Painted in red upon a Cup and Saucer of egg-shell porcelain; probably an early specimen of this ware, the manufacture of which was originated at the Mikawachi factory in 1837 A.D. ZO-SHUN-TEI SAN HO TSUKURU. *Made by Zoshuntei San Ho.*

No. 106.

Painted in blue upon an octagonal Cup of *sometsuke* porcelain of choice quality. The inscription is the same as that given above.

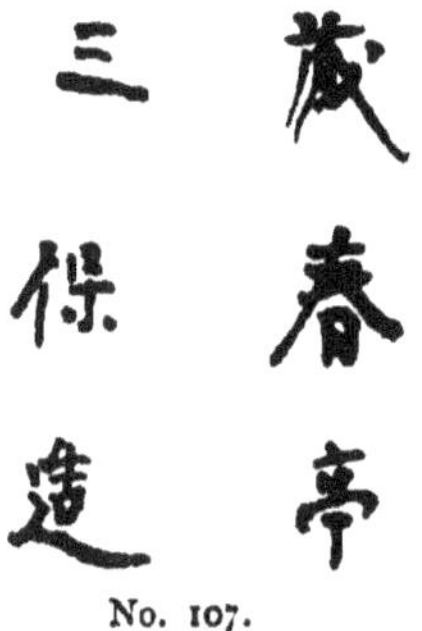

No. 107.

Painted in red upon a Saucer of imitation Old Japan. The inscription is the same as those given above.

No. 108.

Painted in red upon a Vase of porcelain covered with a crackled glaze; modern work. YAMA-KA SEISU. *Made by Yamaka.*

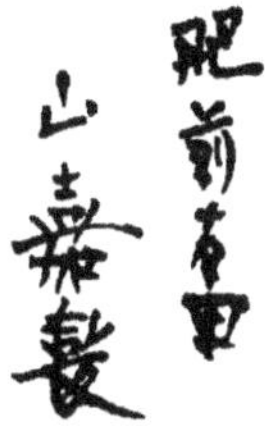

No. 109.

Painted in red upon a Vase of porcelain, of modern work. HI-ZEN, ARI-TA, YAMA-KA SEISU. *Made by Yamaka, Arita, Hizen.*

No. 110.

Painted in blue upon a Perfume Burner of the choicest Mikawachi porcelain, decorated in blue with groups of Chinese boys; made in the period of Bunkwa, 1804-1818 A.D., for presentation to the Prince of Kuwana. U-KAWA, the name of the painter; HO-GAN, a title of honour given to distinguished painters; the lower character is the mark of the painter.

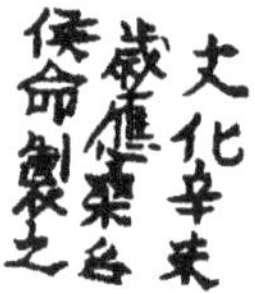

No. 111.

Painted in blue upon a Perfume Burner of choice Mikawachi porcelain. BUNK-WA, SHIN-BI NO TOSHI KUWA-NA KO NO MEI NI OZITE KORE O SEISU. *This is made by command of the Prince of Kuwana in the period Bunkwa, the Zodiac year of the Sheep,* 1804-1818 A.D.

No. 112.

Painted in blue upon a Dish of porcelain decorated in blue. NAN-SEN-ZAN HI-GUCHI TSUKURU. *Made by Nansenzan Higuchi.*

No. 113.

The KUSHIDE mark, used upon porcelain, decorated in blue, made at the Ohokawachi factory subsequent to its removal from Iwayagama to its present position, in the neighbourhood of Arita, in 1710 A.D. Examples marked in this manner are known as comb-teeth ware.

No. 114.

Painted in blue upon a covered Cup of *sometsuke* porcelain, made at Arita. Toshi-ki-an Ki-so seisu. *Made by Kiso Toshikian.*

No 115.

Painted in blue upon a choice example of modern *sometsuke* porcelain. Toshi-ki-an Ki-so seisu. *Made by Kiso Toshikian.* This inscription is written in the *Sosho* style; the one above it, having the same meaning, is in the *Kaisho* style.

No. 116.

Painted in blue upon a Cup of porcelain, covered with chocolate glaze. The characters to the right are HI-ZEN, KUWAN KO. Made at the *Government Kiln, Hizen;* those to the left are TOSHI-KI-AN KI-SO SEISU, written in the *Giosho* style.

No. 117.

Painted in blue upon a Dish of porcelain decorated with blue and brown. TOSHI-KI-AN KI-SO TSUKURU, written in the *Reisho* style. Refer to Nos. 114, 115, 116.

No. 118.

Painted in red upon modern Nagasaki porcelain of inferior quality. A maker's mark.

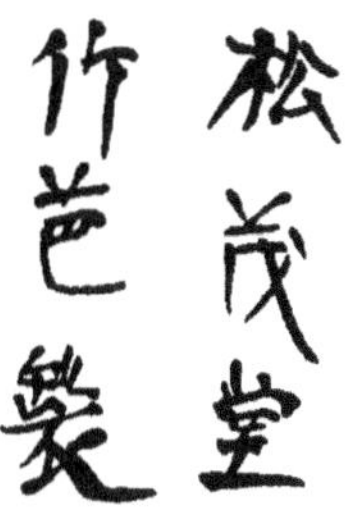

No. 119.

Painted in blue upon a Plate of modern *sometsuke* porcelain made at Arita. SHIO-MO-DO TIKU-BA SEISU. *Made by Tikuba Shiomodo.*

No. 120.

Painted in red upon modern porcelain of ordinary quality. HI-CHO-ZAN JIO-SEN TSUKURU. *Made by Hichozan Jiosen.*

No. 121.

Painted in red upon a Cup of porcelain of ordinary work. HIRA-TO, SAN YEDA-MATS TSUKURU. *Made by Yedamats; the product of Hirato.*

No. 122.

Painted in blue upon a Cup of Arita *sometsuke* porcelain. GO-KEI TSUKURU. *Made by Gokei.* The seal mark is the professional name of the maker, ATSU-SADA.

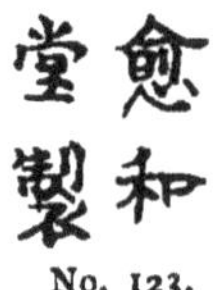

No. 123.

Painted in red upon egg-shell porcelain. YUWA-DO SEISU. *Made by Yuwado.*

No. 124.

Painted in blue upon a Vase of porcelain of fair age. SU-YE. *Suye*, the name of the maker.

No. 125.

Scratched upon a Flower Pot of old Hirato stoneware. The mark of the maker.

No. 126.

Scratched upon a Water Jar of stoneware made at Karatzu about 1800 A.D. HICHI-JIU-NI SAI NI-RAKU TSUKURU. *Made by Niraku, 72 years old.*

The kiln of Karatzu is situated in the northern part of the province of Hizen; it is said to have been founded in the seventh century, and it was here that glazed pottery was first made. So closely is this ancient factory associated with the manufacture of pottery, that its name has given rise to the use, in the southern part of Japan, of the term *Karatzumono*, to signify pottery in general, just as *Setomono* is used in other parts of the country. The latter word is derived from Seto, a town in Owari, where most of the wares of that province are manufactured, and *mono*, which signifies articles or things. —*Keramic Art of Japan, 8vo. edition, pp. 117 and 154.*

SATSUMA POTTERY.

No. 127

The crest of the prince of Satsuma. Rendered in slight relief, in gold and red, upon a Tea Bowl of choice faience.

No. 128.

Painted in gold upon a small Tray of choice faience. MATSU-DAIRA SATSU-MA NO KAMI. *Matsudaira Satsuma no Kami*, the name of the prince of Satsuma.

No. 129.

Engraved upon a Figure of good faience of fair age. TO-GAN. *Togan*, the name of the maker.

M

No. 130.

Impressed upon a Vase of excellent work and considerable age. GIOKU-ZAN. *Giokuzan*, the name of the maker.

No. 131.

Painted in red upon the preceding example. JU-RAKU-SAI SHIO-HO YEGAKU. *Painted by Shioho Jurakusai.* The seal is the painter's mark.

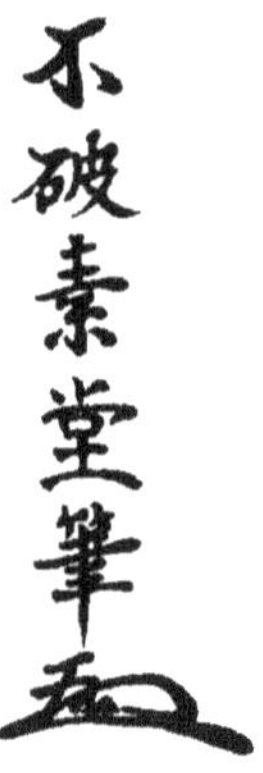

No. 132.

Painted in black upon a Tray of faience decorated with great skill. FU-WA SO-DO HITSUSU. *Painted by Fuwa Sodo.* The mark at the foot of the inscription is the seal of the painter.

No. 133.

Painted in gold upon the face of a small Tray of choice faience. I-DE. *Ide*, the name of the maker or painter.

No. 134.

Painted in gold upon the face of a small Tray of choice faience. RAN-ZAN. *Ranzan*, the name of the maker or painter.

No. 135.

Painted in black upon the backs of the Trays from which the marks given above are copied. TEM-PO, NEN SEI. *Made in the period of Tempo*, 1830–1844 A.D.

No. 136.

Painted in gold upon a covered Tea Jar of very early ware. The upper character is KAI, the name of the artist by whom the lacquer decoration of the vessel was executed; the lower character is his mark.

No. 137.

Painted in red upon a Saucer of modern faience. SHIO-ZAN. *Shiozan*, the name of the maker.

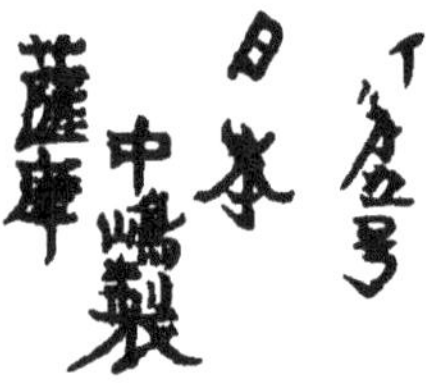

No. 138.

Painted in red upon a Flower Vase made in 1875 A.D. The character at the top of the first column to the right is the first letter of the Japanese alphabet, I, and those below it are DAI-GO-GO, *No. 5*, the whole meaning *I, No. 5*. The other characters are NIP-PON, NAKA-JIMA SEISU, SATSU-MA. *Made by Nakajima, Satsuma, Japan.*

KAGA POTTERY.

No. 140.

No. 139.

No. 141.

No. 142.

The characters shown above are KU-TANI. *Kutani* is the name of the district in the province of Kaga in which the ware of that name was first made. No. 139.—Painted in blue upon a Teapot of ancient pottery. No. 140.—Painted in red upon a Bowl of early ware. No. 141.—Painted in gold, upon a panel of red, on a Bowl of early ware. No. 142.—Painted in black, upon a panel of dark green, on a Dish of early polychromatic ware.

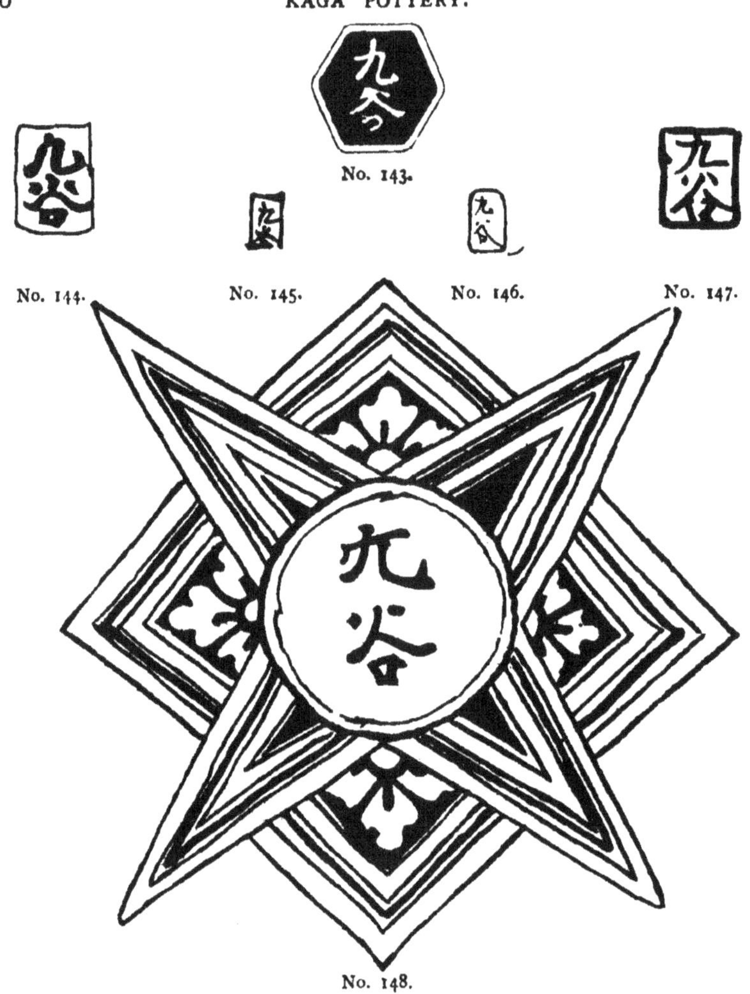

No. 143. No. 144. No. 145. No. 146. No. 147. No. 148.

KUTANI. No. 143.—Impressed upon a Flower Vase of modern ware; an unusual method of applying the mark. No. 144.—Painted in gold, upon a panel of red, on a Bowl of early ware. No. 145.—Painted in gold, upon a panel of red, on a Teapot. No. 146.—Painted in red upon a Teapot of modern porcelain. No. 147.—Painted in black, upon a yellow panel, on a Tazza. No. 148.—Painted in red upon a Vase of middle period polychromatic ware; the ornamental work which surrounds the mark is executed in various colours, but it has no practical significance.

No. 149.

Painted in black upon a Plate of ancient ware decorated with green and yellow, made before gold was used. SEI-KA, NEN SEI. *Made in the period of Seika;* a forgery of the Chinese mark of the Tch'ing-hoa period, 1465-1487 A.D.

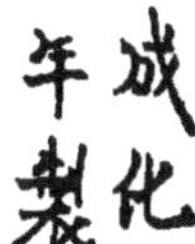

No. 150.

Painted in red upon a Saucer of similar ware to example No. 149. The mark is the same as that above.

No. 151.

Painted in gold, upon a panel of red, on a Bowl of early ware. KU-TANI, KIOKU-ZAN. *Kutani, Kiokuzan;* the name of the maker and the place where the piece was made. The characters are written in the old style.

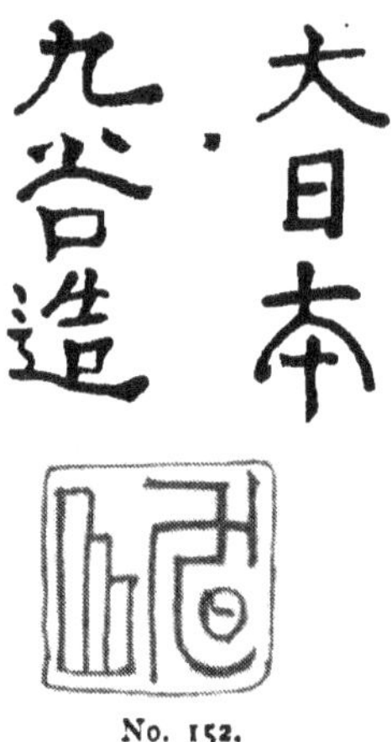

No. 152.

Painted upon a Dish of middle period ware; the inscription in red, and the seal in gold upon red. DAI NIP-PON, KU-TANI TSUKURU. *Made in Kutani, Great Japan.* The seal is that of KIOKUZAN, the maker.

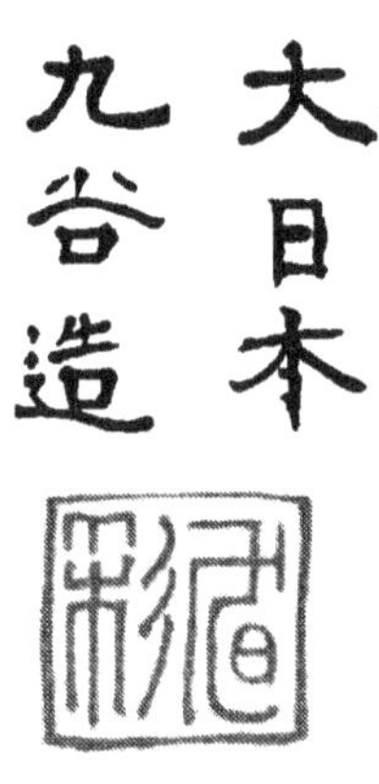

No. 153.

Painted upon a Dish similar to the foregoing example. DAI NIP-PON, KU-TANI TSUKURU. *Made in Kutani, Great Japan.* The character to the right of the seal is KIO-KU, the remainder of the name of KIOKUZAN being omitted; the characters to the left are SAI, meaning *Painting in colours.*

No. 154.

Painted in red upon a Teapot of early ware. KU-TANI, KIOKU-ZAN TSUKURU. *Made by Kiokuzan, Kutani.*

No. 155.

Painted in blue upon a Flower-pot. KUTANI SEI. *Made in Kutani.*

九谷

No. 156.

Painted in gold, upon a red ground, on a Bowl of middle period ware. KU-TANI, FUKU. *Kutani, Fuku;* the latter word signifies Happiness.

No. 157.

Painted in black upon a Flower-pot of polychroı ware. KU-TANI TSUKURU. *Made in Kutani.*

No. 158.

Painted in red upon a Bowl of polychromatic KU-TANI TSUKURU. *Made in Kutani.*

No. 159.

Painted in blue upon a Bowl of semi-porcelain. TANI SEI. *Made in Kutani.*

No 160.

Painted upon a Bowl of early ware; the upper characters in red, and the seal mark in gold upon a panel of red. KU-TANI, FUKU. *Kutani, Fuku.*

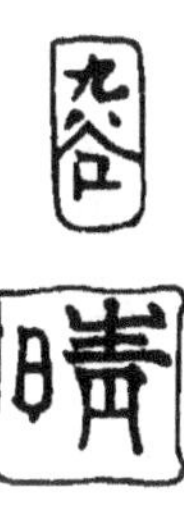

No. 161.

Painted in gold, upon red grounds, on a Bowl of early ware. KU-TANI, SEI. The lower mark, *Sei*, is the mark of the maker, probably a contraction of the name of Seiundo.

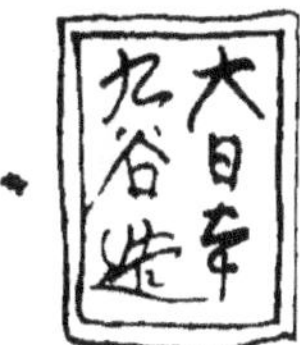

No 162.

Painted in black, upon a panel of green, on a Bowl of modern polychromatic ware. DAI NIP-PON, KU-TANI TSUKURU. *Made in Kutani, Great Japan.*

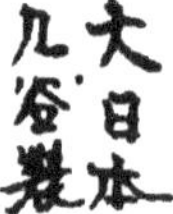

No. 163.

Painted in red upon a Cup of modern egg-shell porcelain. DAI NIP-PON, KU-TANI SEI. *Made in Kutani, Great Japan.*

No. 164.

Painted in red upon a Basin of middle period ware. KU-TANI. YU-ZAN. *Kutani. Yuzan,* the name of the maker.

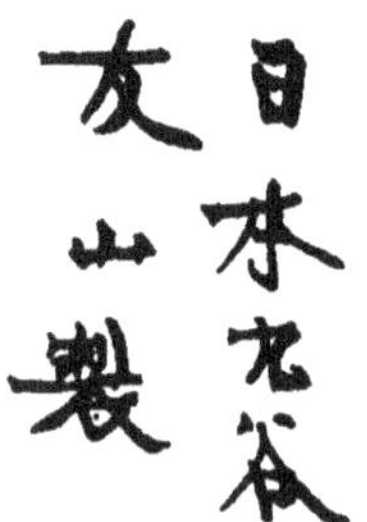

No. 165.

Painted in brown upon a Teapot of middle period ware. NIP-PON, KU-TANI YU-ZAN SEISU. *Made by Yuzan in Kutani, Japan.*

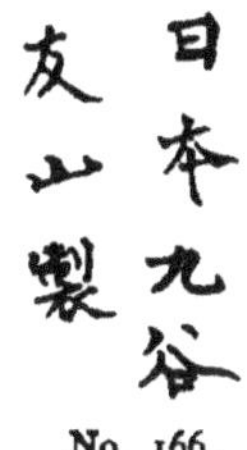

No. 166.

Painted in red upon a Teapot of modern ware. The inscription is the same as the preceding. one.

No. 167.

Painted in red upon a Cup of modern ware. KUTANI, YUZAN, the latter being the name of the maker.

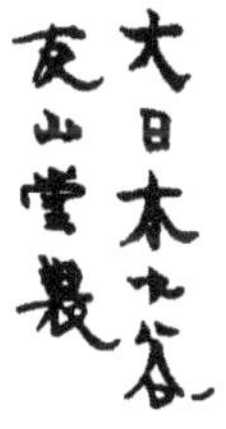

No. 168.

Painted in red upon a Teapot of modern ware. DAI NIP-PON, KU-TANI, YU-ZAN-DO, SEISU. *Made by Yuzando* (the professional name of the maker), *Kutani, Great Japan.*

No. 169.

Painted in red upon a Cup of modern ware. KU-TANI, YU-ZAN-DO. *Kutani, Yuzando.*

No. 170. No. 171. No. 172.

Painted upon late period ware of fair excellence. KU-TANI SEI. KA-CHO-KEN. *Kutani manufacture. Kachoken*, the professional name of the maker.

No. 173.

Painted in gold, upon a panel of red, on a Teapot of similar ware to the preceding example. KA-CHO-KEN SEISU. *Made by Kachoken.* It will be noticed that the word Ka-cho is rendered by characters different to those used in the Marks Nos. 170 to 172.

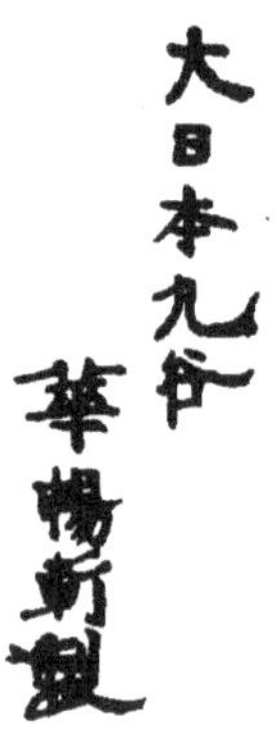

No. 174.

Painted in red upon a Bowl of good late period ware. DAI NIP-PON, KU-TANI, KA-CHO-KEN SEISU. *Made by Kachoken, Kutani, Great Japan.*

No. 175.

Painted in red upon a Dish of late period ware, decorated in red, gold and brown, with great skill. DAI NIP-PON, KU-TANI, KA-CHO-KEN SEISU. *Made by Kachoken, Kutani, Great Japan.*

No. 176. No. 177. No. 178.

No. 176.—Painted in red upon a Cup. No. 177.—Painted in brown upon a Bowl. No. 178.—Painted in red upon a Cup. All of modern ware. DAI NIP-PON, KU-TANI, KA-CHO-KEN SEISU. *Made by Kachoken, Kutani, Great Japan.*

No. 179.

Painted in black, upon a panel of green, on old ware. FUKU—*Happiness.* This character is also frequently used upon modern imitations of the old green and yellow ware.

No. 180.

Painted in gold, upon red, on a Bowl of early ware. KA-YO, KU-TANI. *Kutani, Kayo,* the latter being one of the names by which the province of Kaga is known.

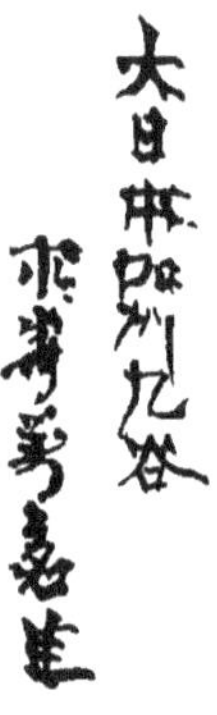

No. 181.

Painted in black upon a Vase of modern porcelain. DAI NIP-PON, KA-SHU, KU-TANI, KI-SAKI MAN-KI TSUKURU. *Made by Kisaki Manki, Kutani, Kashu, Great Japan.* Kashu is another name for Kaga.

大日本加州九谷木崎造

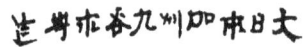

No. 182.

Painted in gold upon a Teapot of late period ware. DAI NIP-PON, KA-SHU, KU-TANI, KI-SAKI TSUKURU. *Made by Kisaki, Kutani, Kashu, Great Japan.*

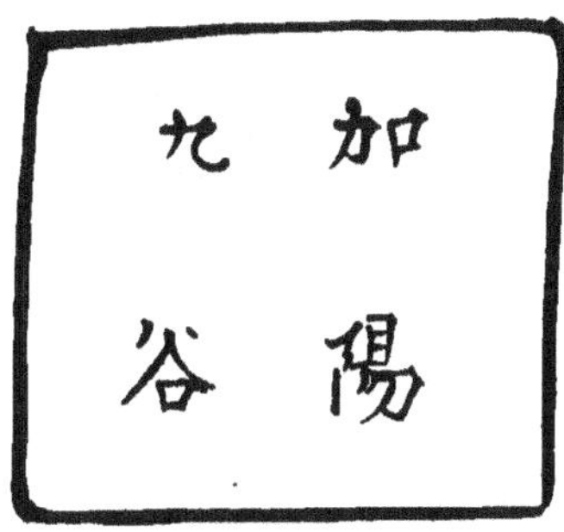

No. 183.

Painted in gold upon a panel of red, surrounded by a gold line, upon a covered Bowl of choice middle period polychromatic ware. KA-YO KU-TANI. *Kutani*, *Kayo*, another name for Kaga.

No. 184.

Painted in red upon a Basin of choice middle period ware. TO-ZAN. *Tozan*, the name of the maker.

No. 185.

Painted in red upon a Bowl of choice middle period polychromatic ware. KU-TANI, TO-ZAN. *Tozan*, *Kutani*.

No. 186.

Painted in red, upon a shaded lozenge, on a Bowl of choice middle period ware. KU-TANI, TO-ZAN SEISU. *Made by Tozan, Kutani.*

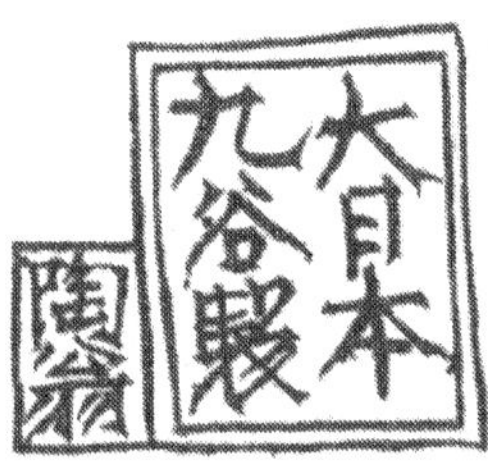

No. 187.

Painted in black, upon a yellow ground, on a Dish of common polychromatic ware. DAI NIP-PON, KU-TANI SEI *Made in Kutani, Great Japan.* The characters to the left are To-o, meaning *Tozan*, the *o* being used in place of *zan*, because the member of the family who made the specimen was an old man—*The old man Tozan.*

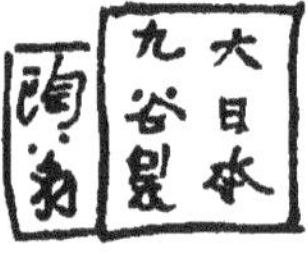

No. 188.

Painted in red upon a Vase of common ware. The inscription has the same meaning as No. 187.

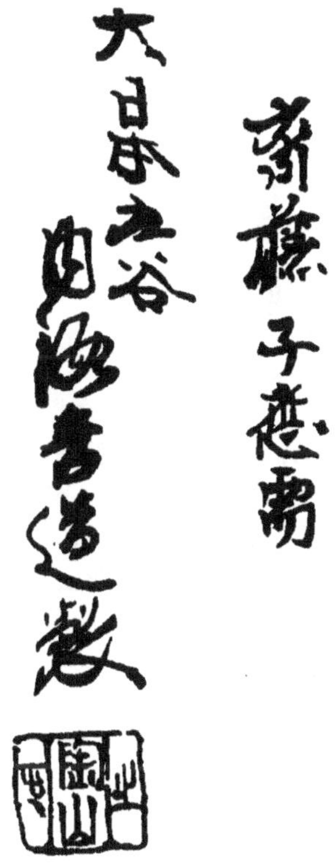

No. 189.

Painted in red upon a large Dish of choice middle period ware. The three upper characters to the right are SAI-TO SI, *Mr. Saito;* the two lower ones are MOTOME NI OZITE, *For demand;* those in the centre of the inscription are DAI NIP-PON, KU-TANI; the four upper characters to the left are WUCHI-MI KICHI-ZO, one of Tozan's names, and the lower one is SEISU. The whole reads, *Made by Wuchimi Kichizo, Kutani, Great Japan, by order of Mr. Saito.* The square mark is the seal of TOZAN, the centre mark being his name, and the side characters, NO IN, *The seal of.*

No. 190.

This inscription appears upon the face of the Dish, No. 189; the written characters are painted in black, and the seals are painted in gold upon red grounds. SHIO-REI-DO. *Shioreido*, the professional name of Tozan. The characters in the seals are TOZAN.

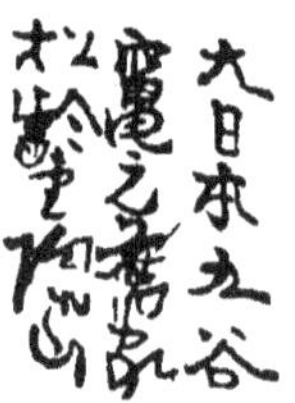

No. 191.

Painted in gold upon a Vase of good modern work. DAI NIP-PON, KU-TANI, KAMANOKIU KA, SHIO-REI-DO, TO-ZAN. *Tozan, Shioreido, the old-established potter, Kutani, Great Japan.*

No. 192.

Painted in red upon a Teapot of middle period ware. KU-TANI, IWA-ZO. *Iwazo* being the maker.

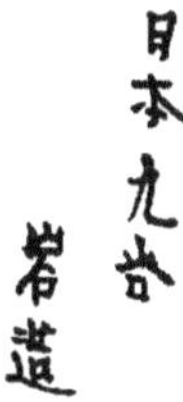

No. 193.

Painted in red upon a Cup and Saucer of modern porcelain. NIP-PON, KU-TANI, IWA-ZO. *Iwazo, Kutani, Japan.* The lower character to the left of the inscription is read as zo, being part of the maker's name, and not as TSUKURU, as it generally is when found in this position.

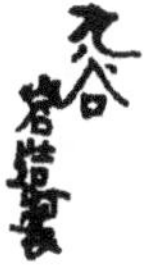

No. 194.

Painted in red upon a covered Jar of good modern polychromatic ware. KU-TANI, IWA-ZO SEISU. *Made by Iwazo, Kutani.*

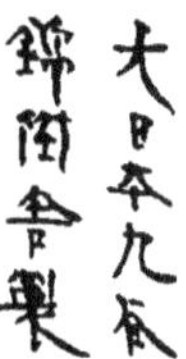

No. 195.

Painted in red upon a Spill Pot of modern porcelain. DAI NIP-PON, KU-TANI, KIN-TO-SHA SEI. *Made at the Kinto factory, Kutani, Great Japan.*

No. 196.

Painted in gold, upon a panel of red, on a shallow Basin of choice early ware. KU-TANI, HAN-YEI. *Hanyei* being the name of the maker.

No. 197.

Painted upon a Bowl of choice early ware; the inscription in red, the seal gold upon red. KU-TANI, HOKU-HO, *Hokuho* being the name of the maker; the seal is his mark.

No. 198.

Painted in gold, upon red panels, on a Cup of fine modern ware. KU-TANI, SEI-KAN TSUKURU. *Made by Seikan, Kutani.*

No. 199.

Painted in red upon a Cup of modern ware. Ku-tani, Sei-kan. *Seikan* being the maker's name.

No. 200.

Painted upon a Bowl of semi-porcelain; the central mark in blue under the bowl, and outer inscription in gold around the bowl. The mark in the centre reads: Dai Nip-pon, Yei-raku tsukuru. *Made by Yeiraku, Great Japan.* The inscription in the circle is Ku-tani, So-sen-tei Ichi-go yegaku. *Painted by Ichigo Sosentei, Kutani.*

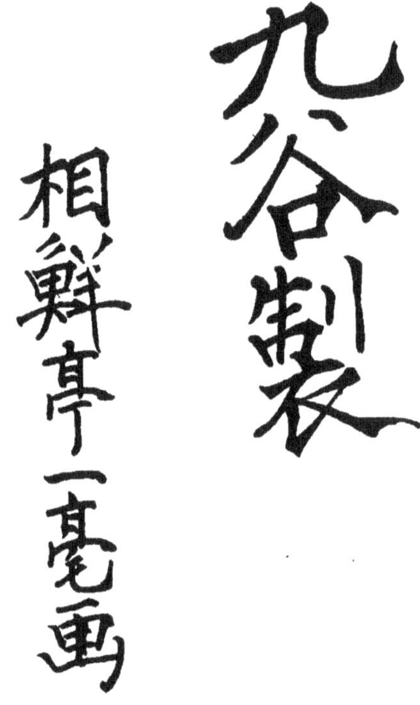

No. 201.

Painted in red upon a Dish decorated in a bold and most satisfactory fashion. KU-TANI SEI; SO-SEN-TEI ICHI-GO YEGAKU. *Made in Kutani; painted by Ichigo Sosentei.*

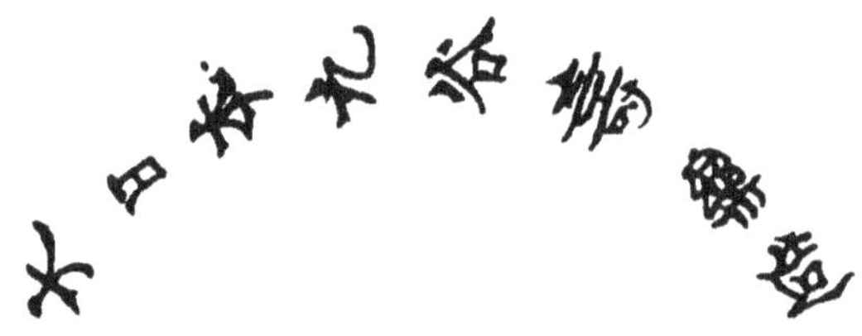

No. 202.

Painted in blue upon the stand of a Vase of modern porcelain. DAI NIP-PON, KU-TANI, JU-RAKU TSUKURU. *Made by Juraku, Kutani, Great Japan.*

No. 203.

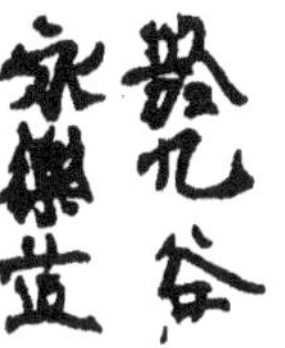

No. 204.

No. 203.—Painted in gold, upon red panels, on a Teapot of late period ware. DAI NIP-PON, KU-TANI NI OITE YEI-RAKU TSUKURU. *Made by Yeiraku in Kutani, Great Japan.* A member of the Yeiraku family of Kioto settled in Kutani about twenty years ago and introduced various improvements into the decoration of the ware. No. 204.—Painted in red upon a Bowl of late period ware. NI OITE YEI-RAKU KU-TANI TSUKURU. *Made by Yeiraku in Kutani.*

No. 205.

Painted in blue upon a Dish of late period ware. The inscription is the same as that on No. 203.

No. 206.

No. 207.

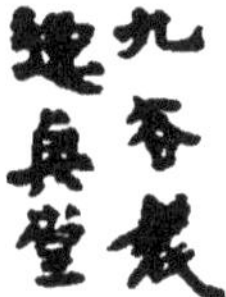

No. 208.

No. 206.—Painted in red upon a Cup. No. 207.—Painted in red upon a Plate. No. 208.—Painted in brown upon a Vase; all modern ware. The inscriptions are the same; KU-TANI SEI, ITSU-KIO-DO. *Made in Kutani, Itsukiodo,* the latter being the name of the maker.

No. 209.

Painted in red upon a Teapot of modern ware. KU-TANI, ITSU-KIO-DO SEISU. *Made by Itsukiodo, Kutani.*

No. 210.

Painted in red upon a Vase of very good modern ware. KU-TANI, ITSU-KIO-DO. The seal is the maker's mark, and gives his second name; the characters to the left are NO IN, and those to the right are RIN-KO, meaning *The seal of Rinko.*

No. 211.

Painted in black upon a Dish of modern ware. Ku-tani, Shio-zo. *Shiozo* being the maker.

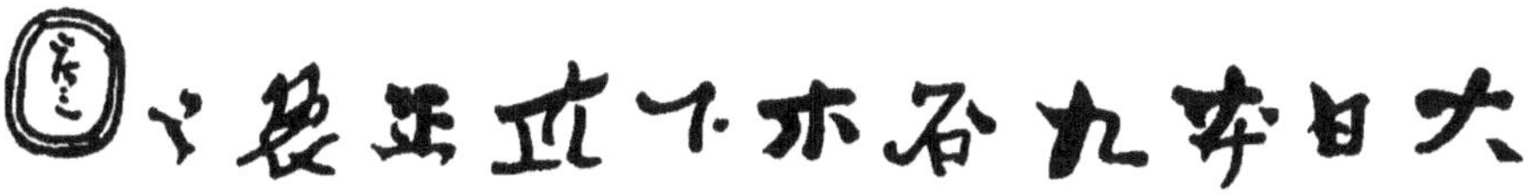

No. 212.

Painted upon a Tazza of modern porcelain; the inscription in black, and the seal in gold upon red. Dai Nip pon, Ku-tani, Ki-no-shita Nao-masa kore o seisu. *Kinoshita Naomasa, Kutani, Great Japan, makes this.* The seal is that of *Shiozo*, which is the maker's second name.

No. 213.

Painted in red upon a Bowl of early ware. Ku-tani, Sei-un-do. *Seiundo* being the name of the maker.

No. 214.

Painted in blue upon a Vase of modern porcelain. DAI NIP-PON, KU-TANI, JU-RAKU TSUKURU. *Made by Juraku, Kutani, Great Japan.*

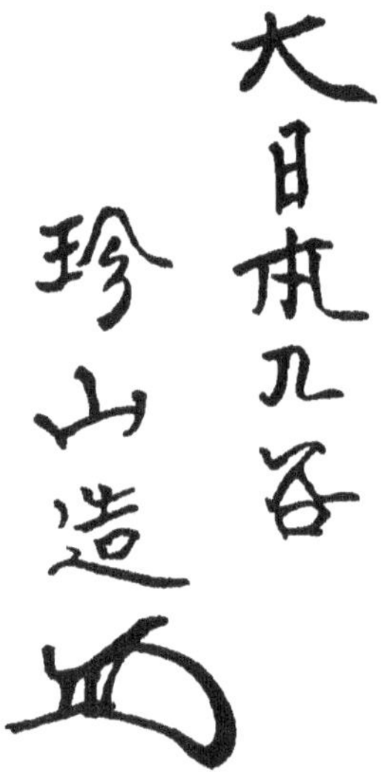

No. 215.

Painted in black upon a Dish of ware made about 1879. DAI NIP-PON, KU-TANI, TIN-ZAN TSUKURU. *Made by Tinzan, Kutani, Great Japan.* The lower mark is Tinzan's monogram.

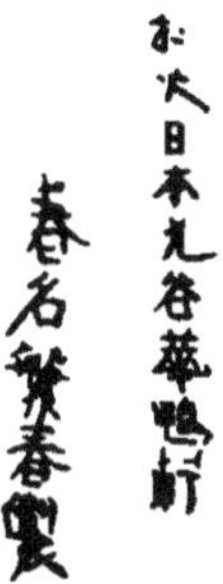

No. 216.

Painted in red upon a Vase of good modern porcelain. DAI NIP-PON, KU-TANI, KA-CHO-KEN NI OITE HARU-NA SHIGI-HARU SEISU. *Made by Haruna Shigiharu in the Kacho factory, Kutani, Great Japan.*

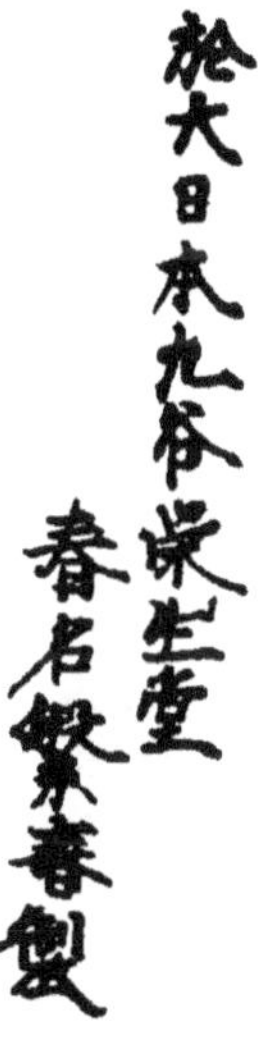

No. 217.

Painted in red upon a Plate of good modern porcelain. DAI NIP-PON, KUTANI, YEI-SEI-DO NI OITE HARU-NA SHIGI-HARU SEISU. *Made by Haruna Shigiharu in the Yeisei factory, Kutani, Great Japan.*

No. 218.

Painted in red upon a Medicine Box of porcelain. KIN-JIO, TO-KA SEI, SAI-UN-RO. *Made by Saiunro at the pottery of Kinjio*, which is the scholastic name of Kanaşawa, a town in Kaga. The lower mark is the seal of *Kiokuzan*, the maker's second name.

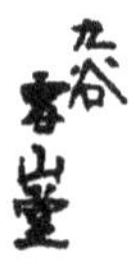

No. 219.

Painted in red upon modern ware. KUTANI, SETSU-ZAN-DO. *Setsuzando* being the name of the maker.

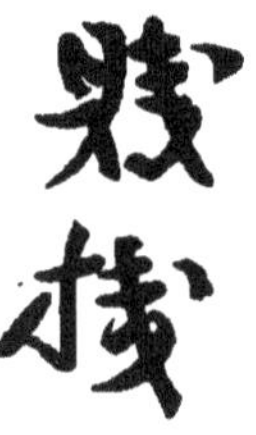

No. 220.

Scratched upon common pottery, called Ohi ware, made near Kanasawa about 1820 A.D. SEN-KI, meaning *A poor thing*, an affectation of humility.

No. 221.

No. 222.

Inscriptions, painted in gold within red borders, upon Dishes of good late period ware; they describe the scenes which are painted on the dishes. No. 221.—NANI-WA, NO IKU-DAMA NO SHA. *The temple of Ikudama, of Naniwa.* Naniwa is another name for Osaka. No. 222.—NANIWA, NO SAKURA MIYA. *Sakura no Miya* is the name of a picturesque place in Osaka.

No. 223.

Painted in red upon a Dish of choice middle period ware. DAI NIP-PON, KU-TANI SEI, KU-ROKU YEGAKU. *Made in Kutani, Great Japan. Painted by Kuroku.* The seal, which reads SEI, is the mark of Kuroku.

KIOTO POTTERY.

No. 224.

Impressed upon a Tea Bowl of *Raku* ware made by a descendant of AMEYA, the founder of the Chojiro family, who settled at Kioto in 1550 A.D., and originated this manufacture, as related in the introduction. This example is taken from a tea bowl said to have been made by Chojiro, the 2nd in descent from Ameya, or by Nonko; 1630 or 1650 A.D.

No. 225.

The seal RAKU, impressed upon a Tea Bowl said to have been made by SANIU, the 6th in descent from Ameya; 1730 A.D.

No. 226.

The seal RAKU, impressed upon a Tea Bowl said to have been made by RIYONIU, the 9th in descent from Ameya; 1790 A.D.

No. 227.

The seal RAKU, impressed upon a Tea Bowl said to have been made by TANNIU, the 10th in descent from Ameya; 1810 A.D.

No. 228.

The seal used by KICHIZAYEMON, the 11th in descent from Ameya, and the present representative of the family. Impressed upon a Tea Bowl said to have been made in 1840 A.D. The upper character is the RAKU seal; the other mark reads KAI-RAKU-YEN SEISU, or *Made by Kairakuyen*, this probably being the professional name of Kichizayemon.

No. 229.

Another example of the seal used by Kichizayemon. Impressed upon a Napkin Holder of faience.

No. 230.

The seal RAKU, impressed upon a Tea Bowl of considerable age and great beauty.

No. 231.

The seal RAKU, impressed upon a Tea Bowl of considerable age.

No. 232.

The seal RAKU, impressed upon a Flower Vase of comparatively modern date. Note: Information concerning the Chojiro family will be found on page 35.

No. 233

The seal used by NONOMURA NINSEI, who established himself at Kioto about 1650 A.D., and originated the manufacture of faience in Awata, a district of that city. The productions of this artist occupy the foremost place amongst the works of the Japanese potter. This seal, which reads NIN-SEI, is impressed upon the Perfume Box of faience mentioned on page 40.

No. 234.

The seal of NINSEI impressed upon a Tea Bowl of similar ware to the foregoing example.

No. 235.

The seal of NINSEI, impressed upon a Tea Bowl of faience, decorated with groups of figures painted in colours. This example, like all those of which the decoration consists of figures, is probably of modern manufacture.

No. 236.

The seal of NINSEI, impressed upon a Tea Bowl of faience, decorated with figures and unquestionably of recent date. The seal is frequently forged upon ware made in the present day.

No. 237.

Painted in brown upon a Tea Jar of pottery, decorated with inlaid and other ornamentation of an exquisite character. KEN-ZAN, the mark of *Shisui Kenzan*, a distinguished potter who lived in Kioto about 1745 A.D., and produced clever imitations of the works of Ninsei as well as original examples which have always been held in high esteem by the *Chajin*.

No. 238.

Painted in black upon a Tea Bowl made by *Shisui Kenzan.* KEN-ZAN.

No. 239

Painted in brown upon a Perfume Box made by *Shisui Kenzan.* KEN-ZAN.

No. 240

Painted in brown upon a Teapot made by *Shisui Kenzan.* KEN-ZAN UTSUSU MAKU-ZU SEI. *Kenzan copies the Makuzu manufacture.*

No. 241.

Impressed upon a small Perfume Box, of faience, modelled in the form of an *Okame* woman, made by TAKAHASHI DOHACHI about 1820 A.D. This maker was celebrated for his skill in making figures and *raku* ware. DO-HACHI, the maker's name.

No. 242.

Painted in black upon a Dish of *raku* ware made by Takahashi Dohachi. DO-HACHI, the maker's name.

No. 243.

Scratched upon a Flower Vase of pottery made by a descendant of the above-named maker in 1875 A.D. DAI NIP-PON, DO-HACHI SEISU. *Made by Dohachi, Great Japan.*

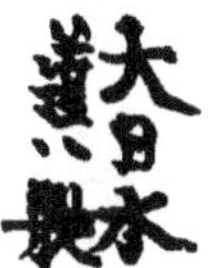

No. 244.

Painted in blue upon an Oil Jug of modern porcelain. DAI NIP-PON, DO-HACHI SEISU. *Made by Dohachi, Great Japan.*

No. 245.

Painted in blue upon a Covered Box of porcelain. KI-TEI, the maker's name. WAKA KITEI was one of the originators of the manufacture of porcelain, decorated in the *sometsuke* fashion, in Kiomidzu and Gojozaka, districts of Kioto, in 1800 A.D.

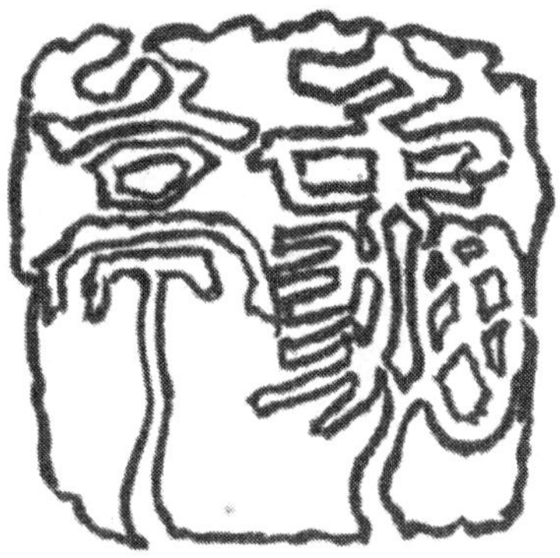

No. 246.

Painted in blue upon a Basket of porcelain. KI-TEI, the maker's name.

No. 247.

Impressed upon a Covered Box of porcelain decorated in blue. KI-TEI, NO IN. *The seal of Kitei.*

No. 248.

Painted in black upon a Flower Pot of modern faience. KI-TEI KORE O SEISU. *Kitei makes this.*

No. 249.

Painted in black upon a Coffee Pot of modern faience. KI-TEI KORE O SEISU. *Kitei makes this.*

No. 250.

The seal of the YEIRAKU family referred to in the introduction, page 36. Impressed upon a Tea Bowl of faience. YEI-RAKU, the name of the maker.

No. 251.

Impressed upon a Koro of faience. YEI-RAKU, the name of the maker.

No. 252.

Impressed upon a Bottle of faience. YEI-RAKU, the name of the maker.

No. 253.

Impressed upon a Tea Bowl of faience. YEI-RAKU, the name of the maker.

No. 254

Impressed upon a Saucer of porcelain. YEI-RAKU, the name of the maker.

No. 255.

Painted upon a small Cup of porcelain decorated with red and gold in the *kinrande* style, which was invented in 1800 A.D. by RIOZEN, the tenth in descent from ZENGORO the founder of the Yeiraku family. DAI NIP-PON, YEI-RAKU TSUKURU. *Made by Yeiraku, Great Japan.* The inscription is in gold, and is surrounded by a circle of blue.

No. 256.

Painted upon a Saucer of porcelain decorated in the *kinrande* fashion; the inscription, which is in red in a blue circle, is the same as that given above.

No. 257.

Painted in red upon a Wine Cup of porcelain. The inscription is the same as those given above.

No. 258.

Painted in red upon a Cup of faience. YEI-RAKU, the name of the maker.

No. 259.

Painted in blue upon a Cup of porcelain. DAI NIP-PON, YEI-RAKU. *Yeiraku, Great Japan.*

No. 260.

Painted in red upon a Cup of porcelain. YEIRAKU.

No. 261.

Painted in red upon a Cup of porcelain. DAI NIP-PON, YEI-RAKU TSUKURU. *Made by Yeiraku, Great Japan.*

No. 262.

Impressed upon a circular Jar of modern Awata faience. KIN-UN-KEN. *Kinunken*, the name of the maker or the factory.

No. 263.

The impressed mark of TAIZAN, one of the most extensive manufacturers of faience in Awata. The mark given above is taken from a Hibatchi of choice workmanship and some age.

No 264.

Another example of the same mark, taken from a Hibatchi of choice quality.

No. 265.

Another example of the same mark, taken from a Hibatchi of considerable age.

No. 266.

No. 267.

No. 268.

Examples of the same mark, taken from modern faience of common quality.

No. 269.

Impressed upon a Hibatchi of faience, of choice quality. The upper characters are AWA-TA, and the lower ones TAI-ZAN; the name of the maker, and the district in which he resides.

No. 270.

Taken from a Tea Bowl of faience made by Taizan, and probably decorated at Tokio. The mark of the maker is impressed underneath the bowl; the other marks are painted in gold upon the interior of it, and refer to the subject of the decoration. The characters to the right are CHIOKU-SHO SONG-SHA, meaning *The Priest Chiokusho.* Those to the left are DAI NIP-PON, BI-ZAN YEGAKU. *Painted by Bizan, Great Japan.*

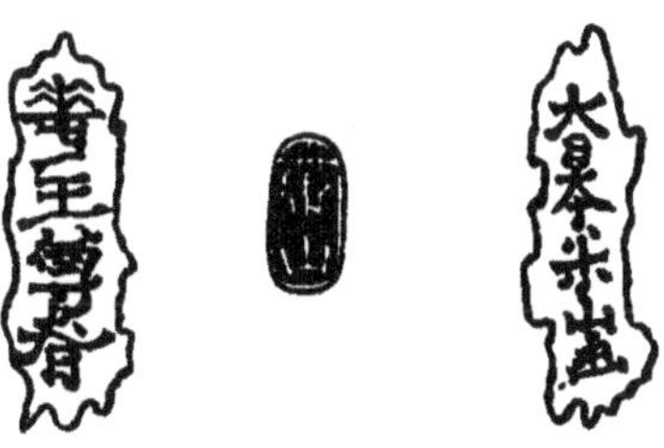

No. 271.

Taken from a Tea Bowl of similar character to that named above. The inscriptions read DAI NIP-PON, BI-ZAN YEGAKU. KUA-O SONG-SHA. *The Priest Kuao, painted by Bizan, Great Japan.*

No. 272.

The mark of TANZAN, one of the most extensive makers of faience in Awata; he also makes some porcelain. Painted in gold upon a Teapot of modern faience; TANZAN.

No. 273.

Another example of the same mark. Painted in blue upon a Teapot of pottery.

No. 274.

Another example of the same mark. Painted in red upon a Vase of porcelain.

No. 275.

Another example of the same mark. Painted in brown upon a Dish of faience.

No. 276.

Another example of the same mark. Painted in red upon a Vase of faience.

No. 277.

Painted in black upon a Dish of faience. NIP-PON, TAN-ZAN. *Tanzan, Japan.*

No. 278.

Painted in black upon a Dish of faience. NIP-PON, TAN-ZAN. *Tanzan, Japan.*

No. 279.

Painted in black upon a Dish of faience. NIP-PON, TAN-ZAN SEISU. *Made by Tanzan, Japan.*

No. 280.

The mark of KINKOZAN, another of the large producers of faience in Awata. This example is impressed upon a Water-pot of considerable age and beautiful decoration. KIN-KO-ZAN.

No. 281.

Impressed upon a Tea Bowl of choice faience. KINKOZAN, the maker's name.

No. 282.

Impressed upon a small circular Jar of choice faience. The mark is the same as those above.

No. 283.

Impressed upon a Flower Pot of modern faience of good style. The mark is the same as those above.

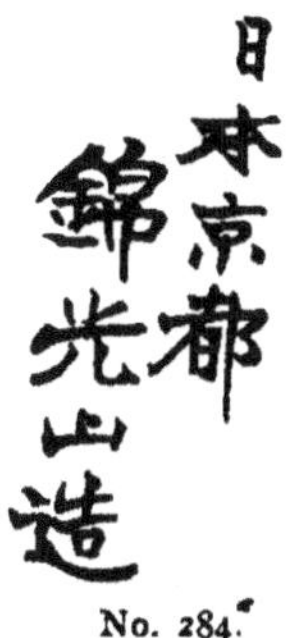

No. 284.

Painted in gold upon a Flower Pot of faience of inferior quality, and decorated with ornamentation in relief of a debased character. NIP-PON, KIO-TO, KIN-KO-ZAN TSUKURU. *Made by Kinkozan, Kioto, Japan.*

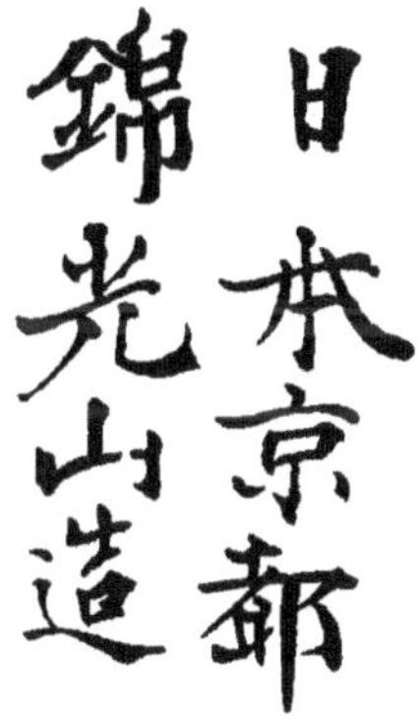

No. 285.

Painted upon a Vase of modern faience decorated with *cloisonné* enamel. The inscription is the same as that given above.

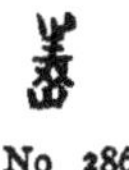

No 286.

Impressed upon modern faience of delicate workmanship and careful decoration. BI-ZAN. *Bizan*, the name of the maker.

No. 287.

Impressed upon a Cup of pottery. Zo-roku. *Zoroku*, the name of the maker.

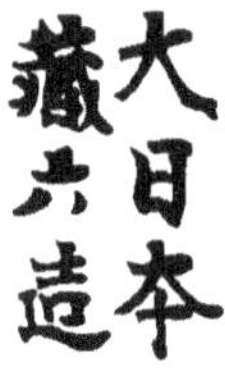

No. 288.

Painted in blue upon a Saucer of modern porcelain. Dai Nip-pon, Zo-roku tsukuru. *Made by Zoroku, Great Japan.*

No. 289.

Painted in blue upon a Vase of modern porcelain. The inscription is the same as that given above.

No. 290.

Impressed upon modern Awata faience. Matsu-moto. *Matsumoto*, the name of the maker.

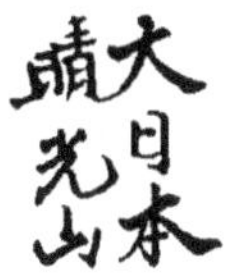

No. 291.

Painted in blue upon a Teapot of porcelain decorated in the *kinrande* style in imitation of the ware made by the Yeiraku family. DAI NIP-PON, SEI-KO-ZAN. *Seikozan, Great Japan.*

No. 292.

Painted in blue upon a covered Jar of ware similar to the foregoing example. SEI-KO-ZAN, KICHI-ROKU TSUKURU. *Made by Seikozan Kichiroku,* the latter being the professional name of the maker.

No. 293.

Painted in black upon a Vase of pottery. DAI NIP-PON, SHU-HEI TSUKURU. *Made by Shuhei, Great Japan.*

No. 294.

Impressed upon a Teapot of porcelain. The seal of KANZAN, the maker.

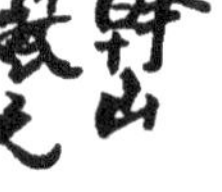

No. 295.

Painted in red upon a Teapot of porcelain, decorated in the *kinrande* style. KAN-ZAN KORE O SEISU. *Kanzan makes this.*

No. 296.

Painted upon a Cup of porcelain, decorated in the *kinrande* style. KAN-ZAN SEI SEI. *Kanzan's best make.*

No. 297.

Painted in blue upon a Spill Pot of modern porcelain. DAI NIP-PON, KAN-ZAN SEISU. *Made by Kanzan, Great Japan.*

No. 298.

No. 299.

Painted in blue upon a *sake* Bottle and a Teapot of porcelain. HICHI-BE-YE TSUKURU. *Made by Hichibeye.*

No. 300.

Painted in blue upon a Cup of porcelain. HICHI-BE-YE TSUKURU. *Made by Hichibeye.*

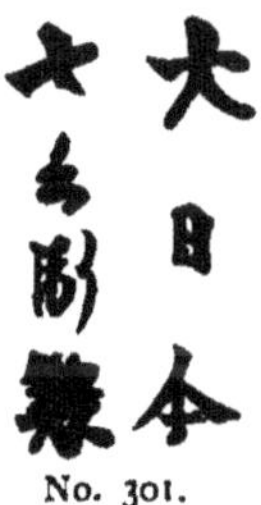

No. 301.

Painted in blue upon a Vase of porcelain. DAI NIP-PON, HICHI-BE-YE SEISU. *Made by Hichibeye, Great Japan.*

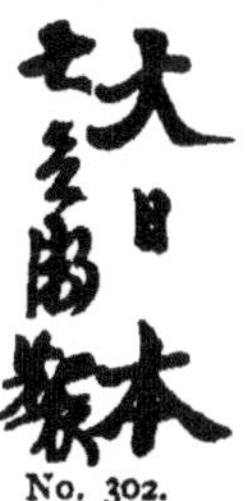

No. 302.

Painted in blue upon a Plate of porcelain. The inscription is the same as the foregoing one. This potter is a large maker of modern porcelain; his name is often read SHICHIBEI, but the spelling given above is the more correct one.

T

No. 303.

Painted in blue upon a Vase of choice Kiomidzu porcelain, decorated in *sometsuke* style. RAN-TEI TSUKURU. *Made by Rantei.*

No. 304.

Impressed upon a Teapot of porcelain. RAN, an abbreviation of *Rantei*, the name of the maker.

No. 305.

Painted in blue upon a *sake* Cup of porcelain, decorated in the *kinrande* style. SA-HEI. *Sahei*, the name of the maker.

No. 306.

Painted in blue upon a *sake* Cup of similar ware SA-HEI TSUKURU. *Made by Sahei.*

No. 307.

Painted in blue upon a Covered Pot of porcelain. SEI-FU. *Seifu*, the name of the maker.

No. 308.

Impressed upon a Saucer of faience of good style. The seal of SEIFU.

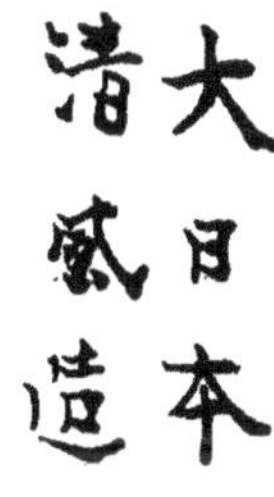

No. 309.

Painted in blue upon a Plate of modern porcelain. DAI NIP-PON, SEI-FU TSUKURU. *Made by Seifu, Great Japan.*

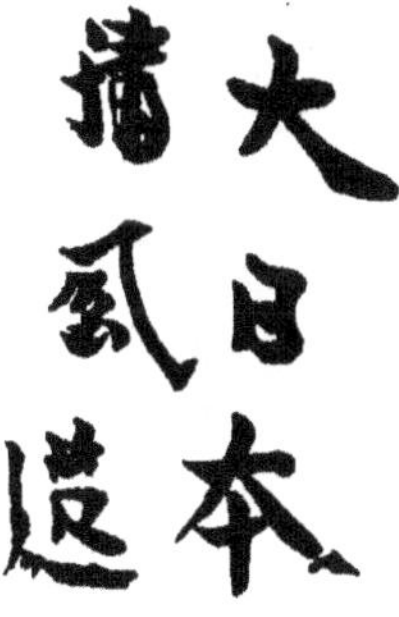

No. 310.

Painted in blue upon a Flower Vase of modern porcelain. The inscription is the same as the foregoing one.

No. 311.

Impressed upon a Dish of unglazed faience. MAKU-ZU-HARA DON-IU. *Doniu*, the name of the maker; *Makuzuhara*, the district in which he resides.

No 312.

Impressed upon a Cup of stoneware. KIOMIDZU, one of the principal districts in Kioto where pottery is made.

No. 313.

Impressed upon a Vase of fine pottery. The upper mark reads, KAHIN YEDA SUZUSHI, a phrase, meaning *Under the shade of a tree by the bank of the river.* The lower mark is the stamp of SEINEN, the maker.

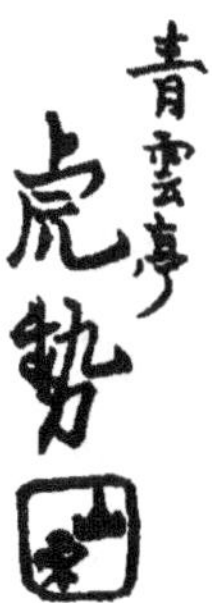

No. 314.

Painted upon a Teapot of faience. SEI-UN-TEI, KO-SEI, *Kosei Seiuntei*, the name of the maker; the seal is his mark.

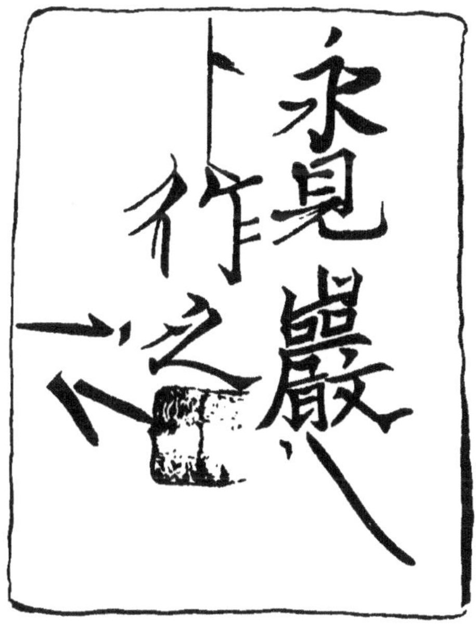

No. 315.

Engraved upon a Stag, modelled with great skill in faience. NAGA-MI IWAO KORE O TSUKURU. *Nagami Iwao makes this.*

No. 316.

Painted upon a Tea Bowl of faience. SES-SEN-SAI, SHUN-ICHI HITSUSU. *Painted by Shunichi Sessensai;* the seal is the mark of the painter.

No. 317.

Impressed upon a Tea Bowl of modern faience. HOZAN, the name of the maker.

No. 318.

Impressed upon a Hibatchi of good faience. OSI-NO-KO-ZI. *Osinokozi* being the name of the maker.

No. 319.

Impressed upon a Flower Vessel of good faience, NAGANO, the name of the maker.

No. 320.

Impressed upon a Flower Vase of good faience. KIURAKU, the name of the maker.

No. 321.

Impressed upon an Incense Burner of pottery. SEI-KAN-JI. *Seikanji* being the name of the maker, or of the district in which it was made.

No. 322.

Impressed upon a *sake* Bottle of good faience. SHA-WA, the name of the maker.

No. 323.

Impressed upon a Perfume Box of choicest faience. YUSETSU, the name of the maker.

No. 324.

Impressed upon a Cup of pottery. SEI, the mark of the maker.

No. 325.

Impressed upon a Cup of porcelain. SEI, the mark of the maker, partially stamped.

No. 326.

Impressed upon a Tea Bowl of choice faience and beautiful decoration. IWA-KURA-ZAN. *Iwakurazan*, the name of the maker.

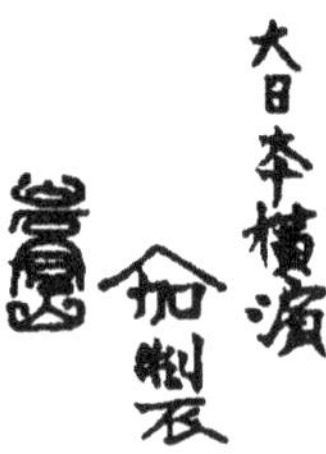

No. 327.

The written characters are painted in red, and the stamp is impressed, upon a Fruit Box of faience. The mark to the left is the stamp of IWAKURAZAN, the maker, of Kioto; the other characters are DAI NIP-PON, YOKO-HAMA YAMA-KA SEISU. *Made by Yamaka, Yokohama, Great Japan.* Probably, however, Yamaka only decorated the article.

No. 328.

Engraved upon a Figure of *Kiyohime* in faience of choice quality and beautiful decoration. SHA-ZAN TSUKURU. *Made by Shazan.* The seal mark is illegible.

No. 329.

Impressed upon a Cup of faience. The letter B, probably the initial of the maker.

No. 330.

Impressed upon a Perfume Box of choice pottery. To-RITSU-ZAN. *Toritsuzan*, the name of the maker.

No. 331.

Painted upon a Cup of porcelain decorated after the *kinrande* fashion. SHIO-FU-TEI TSUKURU. *Made by Shiofutei.*

No. 332.

No. 333.

These marks are impressed upon a Leaf-shaped Dish of pottery of considerable age, and modelled with great skill. The inscription reads—HOSAI SANZIN, the maker's name; the shell is his mark.

No. 334.

Painted in blue upon a Cup of porcelain. KI-RAKU. *Kiraku*, the name of the maker.

No. 335.

Painted in red, upon a brown medallion, on a Teapot of semi-porcelain. KAI-RO SHIU-HEI. *Kairo Shiuhei*, the name of the maker.

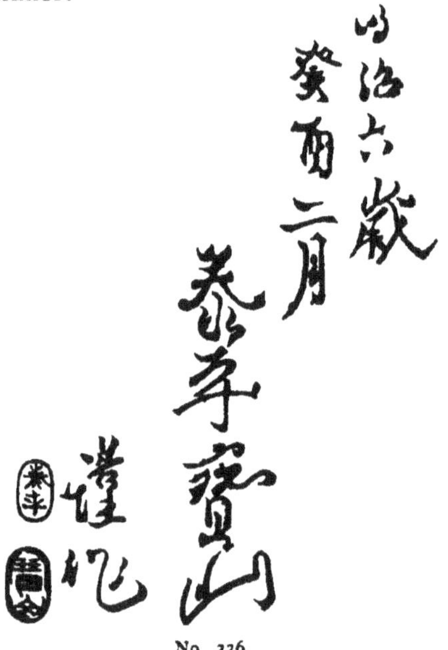

No. 336.

Engraved upon a Figure of faience. MEI-JI, ROKU-SAI, KI-YU NI-GAT-SU, TAI-HEI HO-ZAN, KIN-SAKU. *Respectfully made by Taihei Hozan, in the 2nd month of the 6th year of the period of Meiji;* February, 1873. The seals are the marks of the maker.

No. 337.

Impressed upon a Saucer of modern pottery. KICHI-KO. *Kichiko*, the name of the maker.

No. 338.

Impressed upon a Vase of faience. The left hand character is the word SEI, an abbreviation of the maker's name, and that to the right is his mark.

No. 339.

Painted in blue upon a Teapot of porcelain. SHIO-GETSU-TEI SEISU. *Made by Shiogetsutei.*

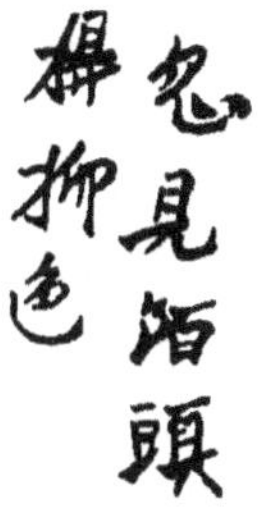

No. 340.

A phrase painted upon a Teapot of Kiomidzu porcelain. TACHIMACHI MIRU HAKUTO YORIU NO IRO. It refers to the spring-time, and tells of the bursting forth of the foliage of the willow trees by the roadside.

衆鳥高飛盡
孤雲獨去閑
相看兩不厭
只有敬亭山

No. 341.

A verse of Chinese poetry, painted in blue upon the of a Furnace of faience.

SHIU CHIO TAKAKU TOBI TSUKUSU.
KO-UN HITORI SATTSUTE KANNARI.
AI MITE FUTATSUNAGARA ITOWA-ZU.
TADA ARI KEITEI-ZAN.

Mr. Kawakami renders the verse into English follows:—

Many birds are flying high up into the air.
A cloud has quietly gone, and none remains.
What I can view without fatigue is only M
Keitei.
Nor is the Mount ever weary of me!

No. 342.

Painted in red upon a Dish of faience. TO-KIU YEGAKU. *Painted by Tokiu.* The lower character is the mark of the maker.

錦窯舎

No. 343.

Painted in red upon a Cup of pottery, decorated in Tokio. KIN-KO-SHA. *The Kinko factory.*

No. 344.

Painted in blue upon a Teapot of porcelain. KI-SUI TSUKURU. *Made by Kisui.*

No. 345.

Incised upon a Perfume Box of pottery. KA-YEI SHI I SHO-SHU. *The seventh month of the fourth year* [the zodiac year of the wild boar] *of the period of Kayei;* the time the ware was made—July, 1851 A.D.

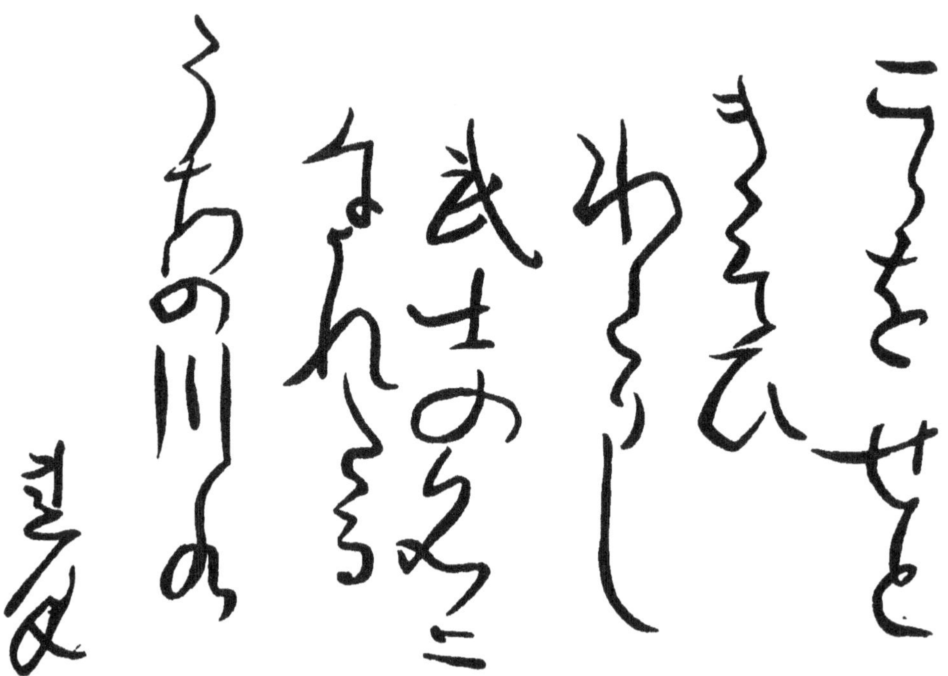

No. 346.

Incised upon a Flower Holder of pottery, made by RENGETSU, a poetess and potter now living in Kioto. The three characters to the left are her signature, and the others are the verses with which the piece is covered. They are written in *Hira-kana* characters, with two or three Chinese words, and run as follows: KOKO O SETO KISOI WATARISHI MONONOFU NO NATO NAGARETARU UZI NO KAWA MIZU.

Mr. Kawakami renders this historic ode into English thus:—

It is with the names of two rival warriors,
Who strove, in crossing its current,
To be the first in the field,
That the waters of the river of Uji have ever flown.

OWARI POTTERY.

No. 347.

Engraved upon a Tea Jar of brown stoneware, said to have been made in the 13th century. The mark of the maker.

No. 348.

Engraved upon a Tea Jar of brown stoneware, said to have been made in 1360 A.D. The ITOGUIRI mark.

No. 349.

Painted in blue upon a *sake* Bottle of porcelain, with *sometsuke* decoration. MASU-KICHI SEISU. *Made by Masukichi.* KAWAMOTO MASUKICHI is the most extensive manufacturer of porcelain in Owari.

No. 350.

Painted in blue upon a Vase of porcelain, decorated as above. The mark reads the same as the preceding one.

X

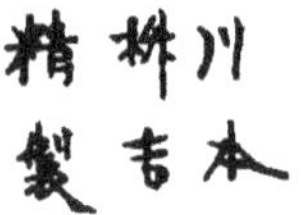

No. 351.

Painted in blue upon a gourd-shape Vase of porcelain, with *sometsuke* decoration. KAWA-MOTO MASU-KICHI; SEI SEI. *Kawamoto Masukichi; made with care;* or *Kawamoto Masukichi's best make.*

No. 352.

Painted in blue upon a Fruit Stand of porcelain, decorated as above. NIP-PON, SE-TO, KAWA-MOTO MASU-KICHI TSUKURU. *Made by Kawamoto Masukichi, Seto, Japan.* Seto is the town in which the principal factories are situated.

No. 353.

Painted in blue upon a Candlestick of porcelain, decorated as above. NIP-PON, SE-TO, KAWA-MOTO MASU-KICHI SEISU. *Made by Kawamoto Masukichi, Seto, Japan.*

No. 354.

Painted in blue upon a Vase of porcelain, decorated with various colours. NIP-PON, SE-TO, KAWA-MOTO MASU-KICHI SEISU. *Made by Kawamoto Masukichi, Seto, Japan.*

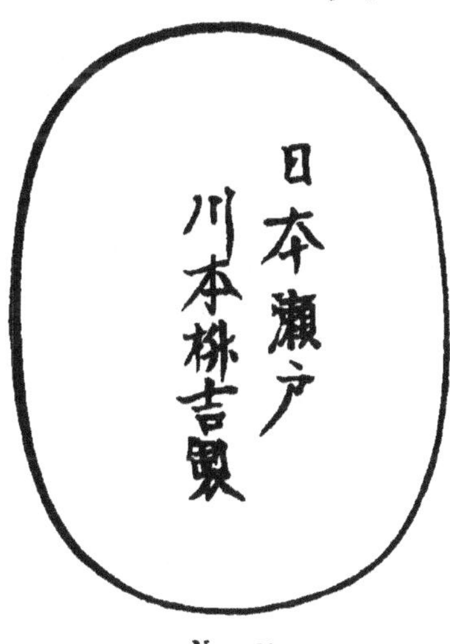

No. 355.

Painted upon a large Plaque of porcelain, decorated *sometsuke* fashion; a perfect example, in size and decoration, of the skill of *Masukichi;* it is illustrated in *Keramic Art of Japan.* The inscription reads the same as that given above.

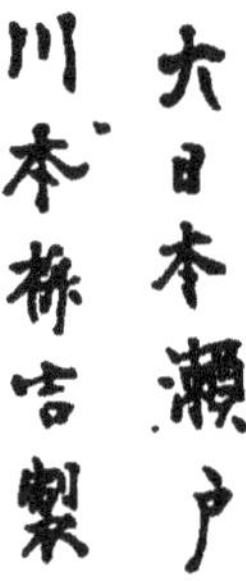

No. 356.

Painted in blue upon a Covered Jar of porcelain, with *sometsuke* decoration. DAI NIP-PON, SE-TO, KAWA-MOTO MASU-KICHI SEISU. *Made by Kawamoto Masukichi, Seto, Japan.*

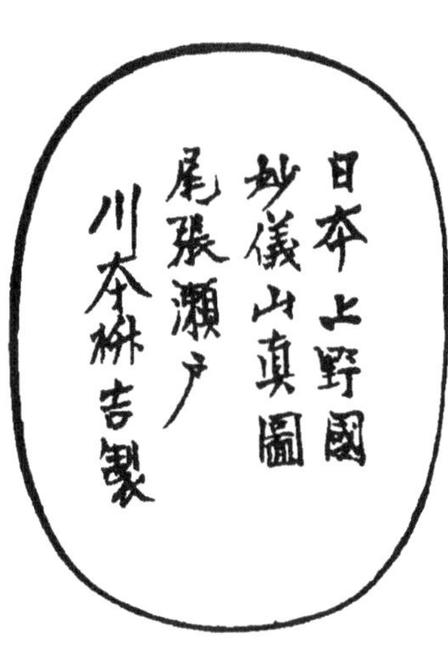

No. 357.

Painted in blue upon a large Plaque of porcelain, with *sometsuke* decoration of great beauty. NIP-PON, KOZUKE NO KUNI, MIO-GI SAN, NO SHIN DZU. O-WARI, SE-TO, KAWA-MOTO MASU-KICHI SEISU. *Made by Kawamoto Masukichi, Seto, Owari. A faithful view of the Miogi mountain in the province of Kozuke, Japan.*

No. 358.

Painted in blue upon the side of a Vase of porcelain, decorated *sometsuke* fashion. The characters to the left are KAWA-MOTO MASU-KICHI SEISU. *Made by Kawamoto Masukichi.* The other characters are a Japanese ode: KAZE KITATTSUTE KOYE RUI RUI AME SUGITE IRO SAN SAN. It refers to a grove of bamboos, and means *When the wind rises the sound is pleasant! When the rain falls the colour is lovely!*

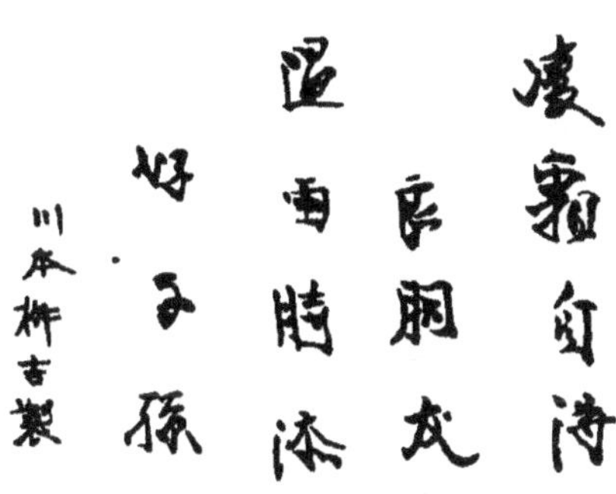

No. 359.

Painted upon a Vase similar to the foregoing example; the characters to the left are the same as above. The ode is RIO SO ONOZUKARA URU RIO HO YU KA U TOKINE SO KO SHI SON. *The severe frost naturally secures good friends. The passing rain sometimes adds fine offsprings.*

No. 360.

Painted in blue upon porcelain. KAWA-MOTO HAN-SUKE. *Kawamoto Hansuke* is one of the most celebrated potters now living at Seto.

No 361.

Painted in blue upon an Incense Burner of porcelain decorated *sometsuke* fashion. NIP-PON, SE-TO, KAWA-MOTO HAN-SUKE SEISU. *Made by Kawamoto Hansuke, Seto, Japan.*

No. 362.

Painted in blue upon a Bowl of porcelain, the exterior of which is covered with *cloisonné* enamel. Made since 1870 A.D., probably at Nagoya, the chief port in Owari. DAI MING, MAN-REKI NEN SEI. *Made in the period of Manreki, during the dynasty of Dai Ming.* A forgery of the Chinese mark of the Wan-li period, 1573-1619 A.D.

No. 363.

Impressed upon a covered Bowl of rough pottery. HO-RAKU. *Horaku*, the name of the maker.

No. 364.

Painted in blue upon a *sake* Cup, exquisitely painted in the *sometsuke* style. NIP-PON, SE-TO, FUJI SHIU-BEI SEISU. *Made by Fuji Shiubei, Seto, Japan.*

No. 365.

Painted in black upon a Vase of porcelain, decorated in various colours. DAI NIP-PON, ROKU-BE-YE SEISU. *Made by Rokubeye, Great Japan.*

No. 366.

In relief upon a circular Flower Pot of porcelain, covered with deep blue enamel glaze. SHIU-FU-YEDA NI KOYE ARI. A phrase meaning *When the autumn winds blow there are sounds in the branches of the trees.*

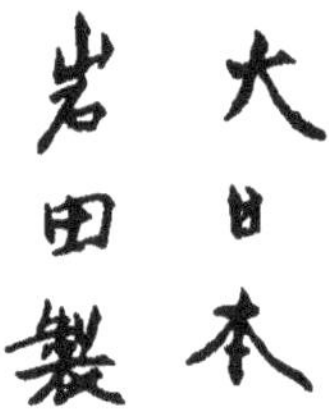

No. 367.

Painted in red upon a Cup of porcelain, with inferior decoration in various colours. DAI NIP-PON, IWA-TA SEISU. *Made by Iwata, Great Japan.*

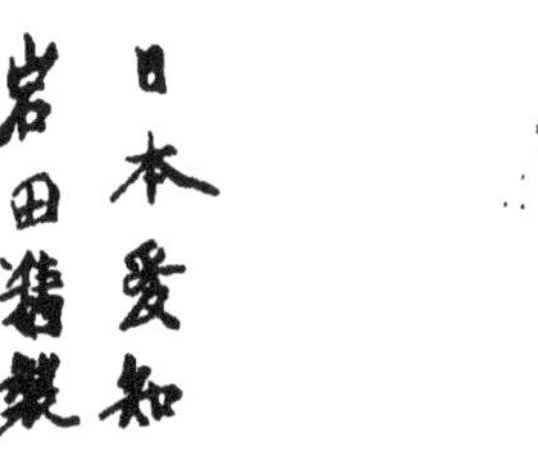

No. 368.

Painted in red upon a Plate of similar ware to the foregoing piece. NIP-PON, AI-CHI, IWA-TA, SEI SEI. *Iwata's best make; Aichi, Japan.* Aichi is the political division of Japan in which Owari is situated.

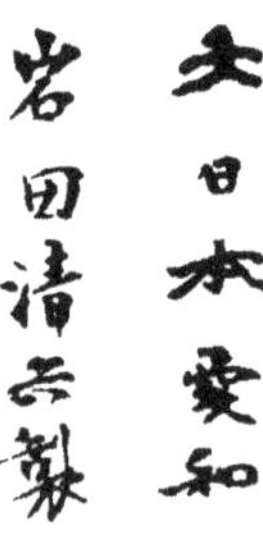

No. 369.

Painted in red upon a Teapot of similar ware to those named above. DAI NIP-PON, AI-CHI, IWA-TA SEI-BEI SEISU. *Made by Iwata Seibei, Aichi, Great Japan.*

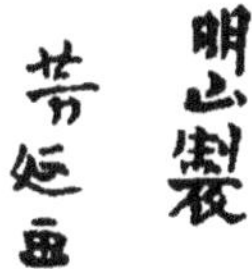

No. 370.

Painted in red upon a Vase of porcelain, made in Owari and decorated in Tokio. MEI-ZAN SEISU; HO-YEN YEGAKU. *Made by Meizan; painted by Hoyen.*

No. 371.

Painted in blue upon a Cup of porcelain; common ware, coated with brown glaze. TO-O-YEN, GO-SUKE SEISU. *Made by Tooyen Gosuke.*

No. 372.

Painted in blue upon ware similar to the foregoing example. KO-BOKU CHIKU SEKI. SO-DATSU; *Sodatsu*, the name of the maker. *Koboku chiku Seki*, a favourite phrase expressive of a Winter scene—a dead tree with the fallen leaves, and a bamboo with rocks around its graceful stem. The square character is the seal of the maker.

No. 373.

Painted in gold upon a covered Jar of porcelain, decorated in colours. NIP-PON, SE-TO, SHUN-KOW YEGAKU. *Painted by Shunkow, Seto, Japan.*

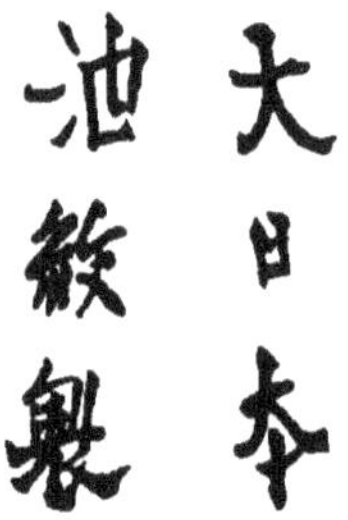

No. 374.

Painted in blue upon a Water Pail of porcelain, with *sometsuke* decoration. DAI NIP-PON, ABRA-SHIME SEISU. *Made by Abrashime, Great Japan.*

No. 375.

Painted in blue upon a Cup of porcelain, with *sometsuke* decoration of inferior character. DAI-O-KEN TAKA-MUNE SEISU. *Made by Daioken Takamune.*

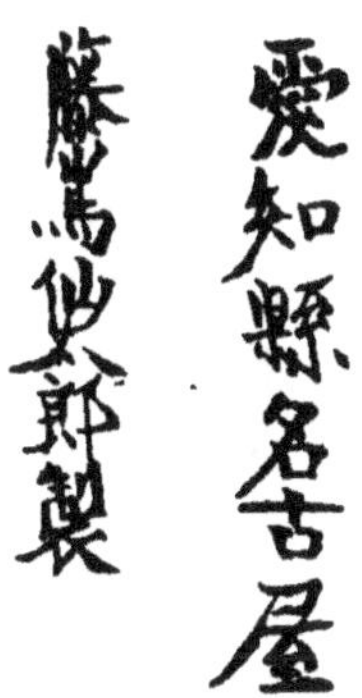

No. 376.

Painted in red upon a Flower Pot of porcelain, decorated in gold, red and other colours. AI-CHI KEN, NA-GO-YA, FUJI-SIMA SEN-TA-RO SEISU. *Made by Fujisima Sentaro, Nagoya, in the division of Aichi.*

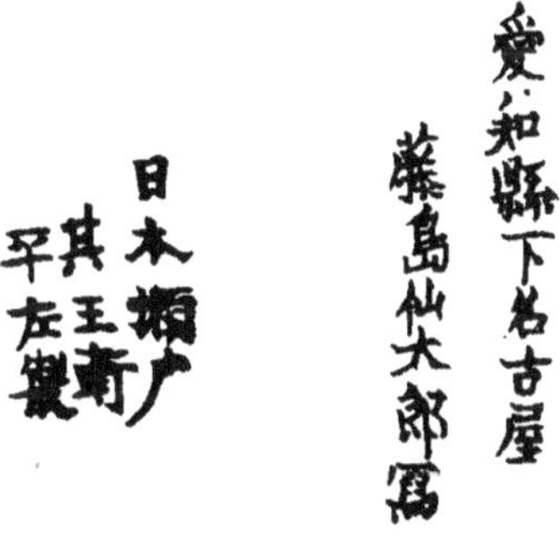

No 377.

Painted upon a Covered Bowl of porcelain, decorated in various colours; the inscription to the right is painted in red, and that to the left in blue. AI-CHI KEN KA, NA-GO-YA. FUJI-SIMA SEN-TA-RO UTSUSU. NIP-PON, SE-TO, KI-O-KEN HEY-ZA SEISU. *Made by Kioken Heyza, Seto, Japan. Copied* (or painted) *by Fujisima Sentaro, Nagoya, in the division of Aichi.*

No. 378.

Painted in blue upon a Bottle of porcelain, decorated in the *sometsuke* style. SHIGE-JIU SEISU. *Made by Shigejiu.*

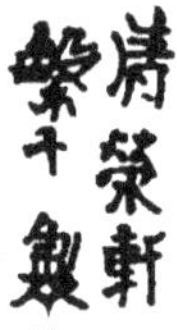

No. 379.

Painted in blue upon a Bottle of porcelain, decorated as above. SEI-YEN-KEN SHIGE-JIU SEISU. *Made by Seiyenken Shigejiu.*

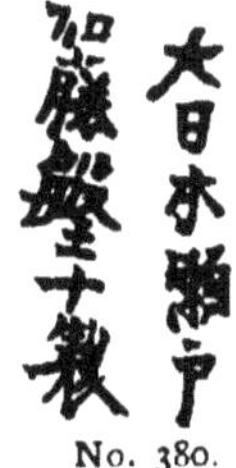

No. 380.

No. 381.

Painted in blue.—No. 380 upon a Vase of porcelain covered with brown glaze, and No. 381 upon a Cup of porcelain, with *sometsuke* decoration. DAI NIP-PON, SE-TO, KA-TO SHIGE-JIU SEISU. *Made by Kato Shigejiu, Seto, Great Japan.*

No. 382.

Painted in blue upon a Plate, with *sometsuke* decoration. NIP-PON, SE-TO, KA-TO SHIGE-JIU TSUKURU. *Made by Kato Shigejiu, Seto, Japan.* Note: The name of this maker is frequently read as HANJIU.

No. 383.

Painted in red upon a Vase. HACHIJU HICHI-GO. *No.* 87.

No. 384.

Painted in blue upon a Cup of ordinary *sometsuke* porcelain. KI-JU SEISU. *Made by Kiju.*

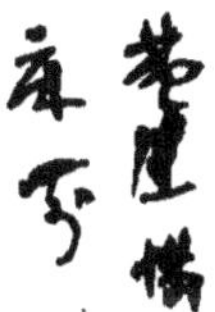

No. 385.

Painted in blue upon a Cup of similar ware to the foregoing example. RO-REN SHO-ZEN NI MITSU. A phrase signifying *The reed and the lotus flower fill the garden under the veranda.*

No. 386.

Painted in blue upon a Cup of *sometsuke* ware. SHIN-TO-KEN FUDE-SUKE SEISU. *Made by Shintoken Fudesuke.*

No. 387.

Painted upon a Figure of faience. TOYO-SUKE. *Toyosuke,* the name of the maker, who resides at Nagoya.

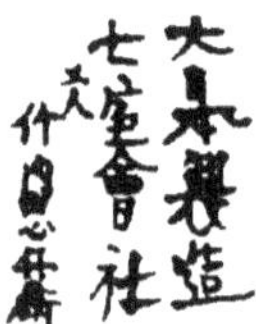

No. 388.

Painted in gold upon a Cup of porcelain, decorated with gold designs in imitation of inlaid metal. DAI NIP-PON, SEI-ZO, SHIP-PO KUWAI-SHA, KO-ZIN, TAKE-UCHI CHIU-BE-YE. *Takeuchi Chiubeye, artist, of the Shippo Company, Great Japan, made* this Cup.

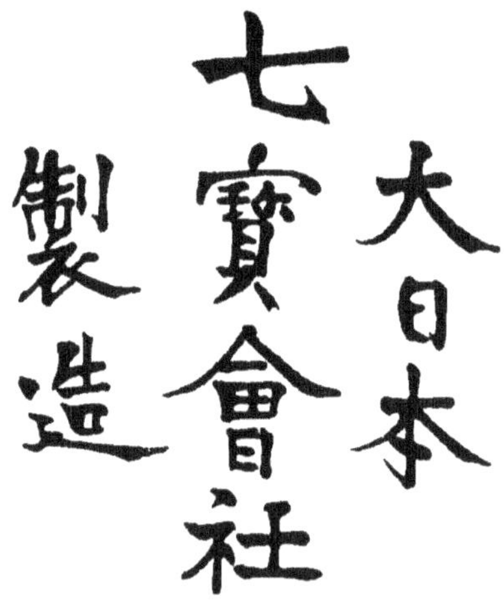

No. 389.

Painted in blue upon a Vase of porcelain covered with *cloisonné* decoration. DAI NIP-PON, SHIP-PO KUWAI-SHA, SEI-ZO. *The Shippo Company of Great Japan made* this Vase.

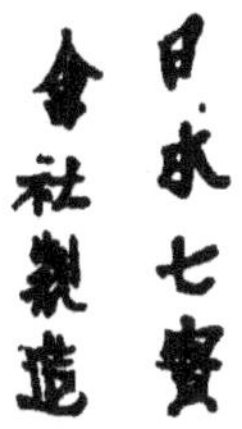

No. 390.

Painted in blue upon a Jar of porcelain covered with *cloisonné* decoration. NIP-PON, SHIP-PO KUWAI-SHA SEI-ZO. *The Shippo Company of Japan made* this Jar.

No. 391

Painted in black upon a Plate of pottery made at the Inuyama factory. GEN-ZAN. *Genzan*, the maker's name.

No. 392.

Painted in black upon a Plate similar to the preceding specimen. KEN-ZAN. *Kenzan*, the maker's name.

No. 393.

Painted in blue upon a Teapot of porcelain. KA-ZAN U-GO. *Kazan ugo*, a phrase signifying *A mountain after the summer rain.*

No. 387.

Painted upon a Figure of faience. Toyo-suke. *Toyosuke*, the name of the maker, who resides at Nagoya.

No. 388.

Painted in gold upon a Cup of porcelain, decorated with gold designs in imitation of inlaid metal. Dai Nip-pon, sei-zo, Shit-po Kuwai-sha, ko-zin, Take-uchi Chiu-be-ye. *Takeuchi Chiubeye, artist, of the Shippo Company, Great Japan, made this Cup.*

No. 389.

Painted in blue upon a Vase of porcelain covered with cloisonné decoration. Dai Nip-pon, Ship-po Kuwai-sha, sei-zo. *The Shippo Company of Great Japan made this Vase.*

Painted in blue [illegible] decoration. [illegible] The [illegible] Company [illegible]

Painted in blue [illegible] Inuyama [illegible]

Painte[illegible] specimen [illegible]

Painte[illegible] [illegible]

No. 394

Painted upon a Vase of porcelain decorated, in various colours, with a portrait of ONONO KOMACHI, a lady of great beauty who lived in ancient days. NIP-PON, SE-TO, KA-TO KISHI-TA-RO KORE O SEISU. *Kato Kishitaro, Seto, Japan, makes this.* The inscription at the side reads: O-NONO KO-MACHI NO DZU. *A portrait of Onono Komachi.*

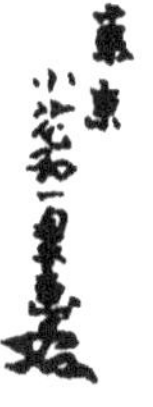

No. 395.

Painted upon the above example. TO-KIO, O-KA-WA ICHI-RAKU YEGAKU. *Painted by Okawa Ichiraku, Tokio.* The lower character is the mark of the painter.

No. 396.

Impressed upon a Tea Bowl of porcelain, made at Seto by a member of the family of YEIRAKU, of Kioto, who has recently settled in Owari. YEI-RAKU, the seal of the maker.

No. 397

Painted in blue upon a *sake* Bottle of porcelain. Hoku Han seisu. *Made by Hoku Han.*

No. 398.

Painted in blue upon a Bottle of porcelain, decorated in various colours. Ru-sai Yei-zan. *Rusai Yeizan*, the maker's name. The lower mark is his seal.

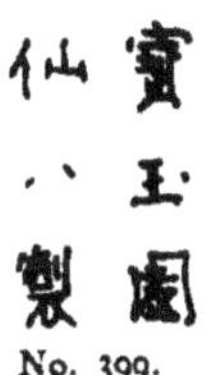

No. 399.

Painted in blue upon a Saucer of porcelain of ordinary *sometsuke* decoration. Ho-gioku-yen Sen-pachi seisu. *Made by Hogiokuyen Senpachi.*

No. 400.

The Kutani mark, occasionally forged upon porcelain made in Owari and decorated in Kaga style.

ISE POTTERY.

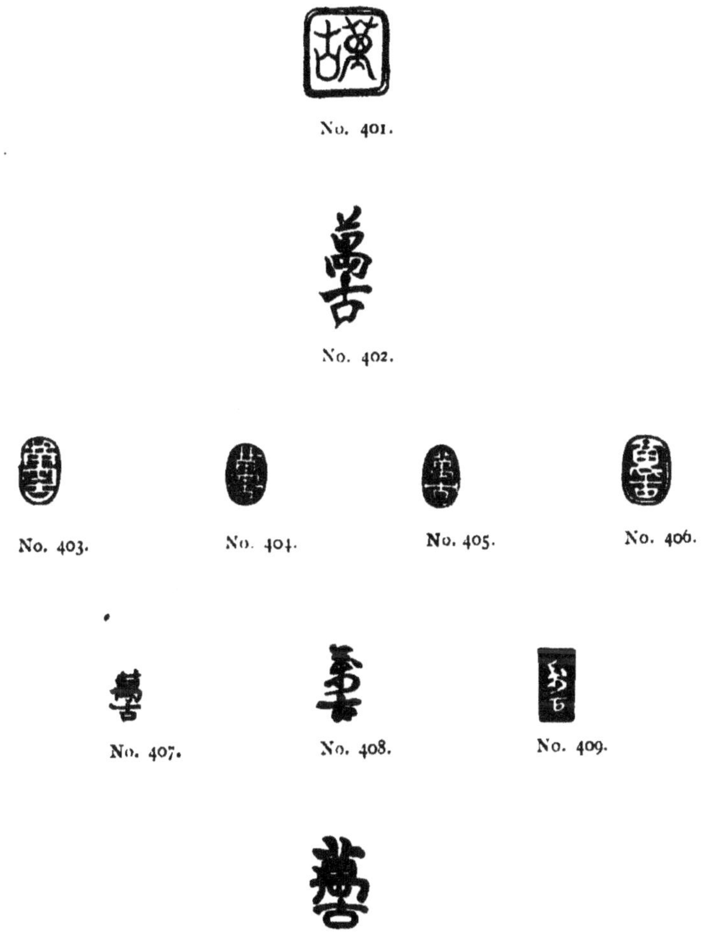

No. 401. No. 402. No. 403. No. 404. No. 405. No. 406. No. 407. No. 408. No. 409. No. 410.

Various forms of the word BANKO, copied from pottery made at Kuwana, Yokkaichi, and other places in the province of Ise. The mark, which signifies *For ever*, or literally, *Ancient ten thousand* (*ban*, ten thousand, *ko*, old or ancient), is generally stamped upon the wares, but sometimes it is painted as shown in example No. 402. Upon the older specimens the form given in No. 401 is used, whilst the other marks are found upon more modern examples.

No. 411.

Impressed upon a Teapot of Ise ware. SAI-YAKU FU-YEKI. The expression, Saiyaku Fuyeki, refers to the unvarying character of the material used in the manufacture of Banko ware.

No. 412

Impressed upon a Teapot of Ise ware. NIP-PON, BAN-KO. *Banko ware, Japan.*

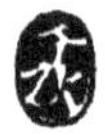

No. 413.

No. 414.

Impressed upon a Teapot of Ise ware. Examples of the word SEN-SHU. *A thousand autumns.*

No. 415.

Impressed upon a Teapot of Ise ware. BANKO, FUYEKI. *Banko ware. Unchanging.*

No. 416.

No. 417.

No. 418.

Impressed upon a Teapot of Ise ware. SENSHU. FUYEKI. *A thousand autumns. Unchanging.*

No. 419.

Impressed upon a Teapot of Ise ware. MORI UJI. The *Mori family*, of Yokkaichi, the most noted makers of Ise ware.

No. 420.

Impressed upon a Teapot of Ise ware. The upper seal is the Banko stamp, old style. The lower seal reads: NIPPON, YU-SETSU. *Banko ware, Yusetsu* (the maker), *Japan.*

No. 421.

Impressed upon a Koro of earthenware. The inscription is the same as the preceding one.

No. 422.

Impressed upon a Teapot of Ise ware. The upper mark is the Banko seal, and the lower one reads, NIPPON, YUSETSU.

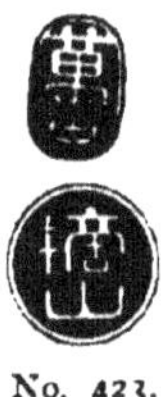

No. 423.

Impressed upon a Saucer of common pottery. The upper mark is the Banko seal. The lower one reads TEKI-ZAN. *Tekizan*, the name of the maker.

No. 424.

Impressed upon a Teapot of Ise ware. GAN-TO SAN-ZIN. *Ganto Sanzin*, the name of the maker.

No. 425.

Impressed upon a Teapot of Ise ware. BANKO. GANTO SANZIN.

No. 426.

Incised upon a Teapot of choice Ise ware. GAN-TO SAN-ZIN TSUKURU. *Made by Ganto Sanzin.* The two small marks are BAN-KO, and the large one is Ganto Sanzin's seal.

No. 427.

Impressed upon a Teapot of Ise ware. Yo-fu-ken Shiu-jin tsukuru. *Made by the Master of the Yofu factory.*

No. 428.

Impressed upon a Teapot of Ise ware. Ban-ko. Yo-fu-ken. Sen-shu. *Banko ware. Yofu factory. A thousand autumns.*

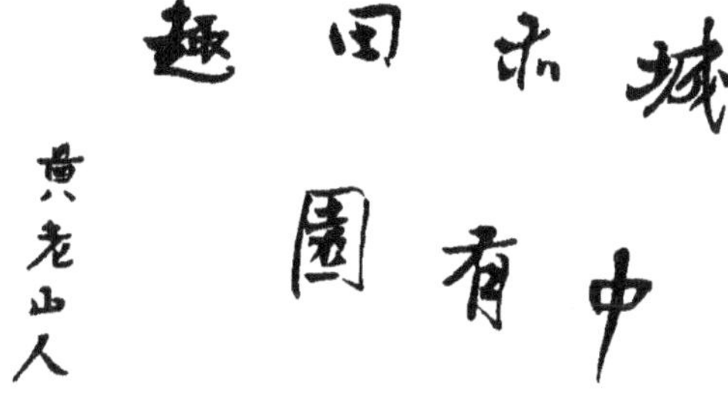

No. 429.

Painted in black upon a Cup of common Ise pottery. The characters to the left are Ko-ro San-zin. *Koro Sanzin,* the maker's name. The others read: Jo chiu mata ari den yen no omomuki *Even in the city there is some aspect of the country.*

AA

No. 430.

Painted in red upon a Vase of pottery. HIAKU SAN-JIU NI BAN. *Hiaku sanjiu ni ban*, meaning Number 132.

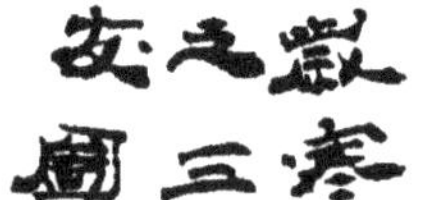

No. 431.

Painted in brown upon a Teapot of choice Ise ware. SAI KAN NO SAN U NO DZU. *A sketch of the three friends of winter*, referring to the trees with which the article is decorated —the *oumai*, the *matsu*, and the *take*, the plum, the pine and the bamboo.

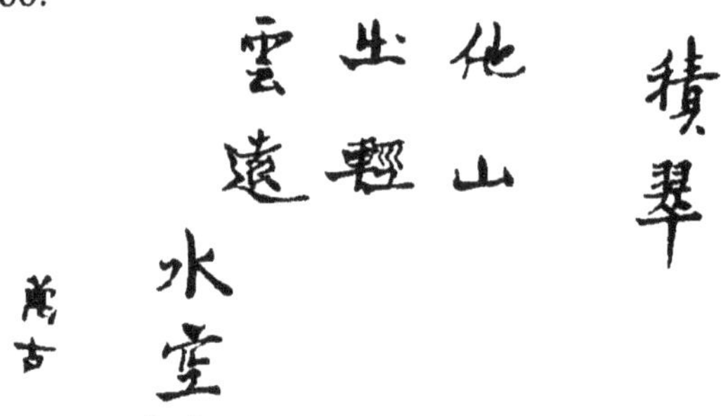

No 432.

Painted in brown upon a Saucer Dish of pottery. SEKI SUI TA SAN IZU KEI UN YEN SUI MUNASHI. *By the increase of the verdure another mountain comes out. The clouds being distant, the water is clear.* The characters to the left are BANKO.

No. 433.

Incised upon a *sake* Bottle of pottery. DAI FU-SO-KOKU. SI-SUI, TO-SI, YEN-SO-SHA SEISU. *Made by Yensosha, potter, of Sisui, Great Japan.* FUSOKOKU is the scholastic name of Japan.

No. 434.

Painted in blue upon a Water Vessel of faience. JIU, meaning *Longevity.*

No. 435.

No. 436.

No. 437.

Painted in blue upon a Vase of faience. No. 435.—FUKU, meaning *Happiness, luck,* and so forth. No. 436.—ROKU, *Wealth and prosperity.* No. 437.—JIU, *Longevity.* The three words together are read FUKU-ROKU-JIU, and signify *Good fortune.*

No. 438. No. 439. No. 440. No. 441. No. 442.

Painted in blue upon a Water Vessel of faience. No. 438.—TAMOTS, *To enjoy*. No. 439.—SHIO, *Pine tree*. No. 440.—JIU, *Longevity*. No. 441.—KAKU, *Stork*. No. 442.—REI, *Age*. SHIO JIU KAKU REI O TAMOTS. A phrase, *To enjoy the longevity of the pine tree and the age of the stork*.

No. 443. No. 444. No. 445. No. 446.

No. 447. No. 448. No. 449. No. 450.

Painted in blue upon a Water Vessel of faience. No. 443.—FU. No. 444.—KI. No. 445.—CHO. No. 446.—SEI. No. 447.—FUKU. No. 448.—TOKU. No. 449.—ZI. No. 450.—ZAI. FU-KI CHOSEI FUKU-TOKU ZIZAI. A phrase, *Prosperity, longevity, fortune, and freedom*.

No. 451.

Painted in blue upon a Water Vessel of faience. FUKU. *Prosperity, happiness, and luck*.

TOKIO

PAINTING AND POTTERY.

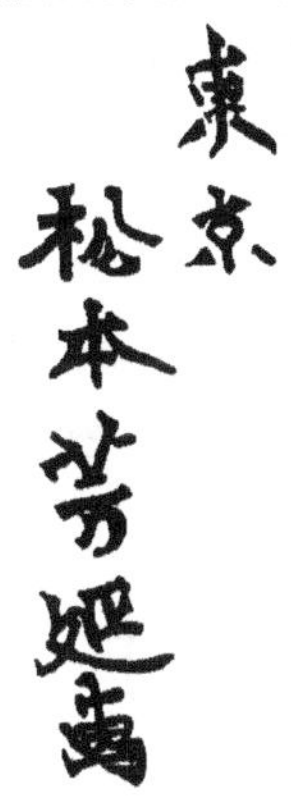

No. 452.

Painted in red upon a Bowl of Kioto faience, decorated with great skill. To-kio, Matsu-moto Ho-yen yegaku. *Painted by Matsumoto Hoyen, Tokio.*

No. 453.

Painted in red upon a Covered Bowl of porcelain, probably Hizen ware. Dai Nip-pon, To-kio, Kin-ko-sha, ni oite, Atago Ko-sai kore o saigasu. *Painted in colours, by Atago Kosai, at the Kinko factory, Tokio, Great Japan.*

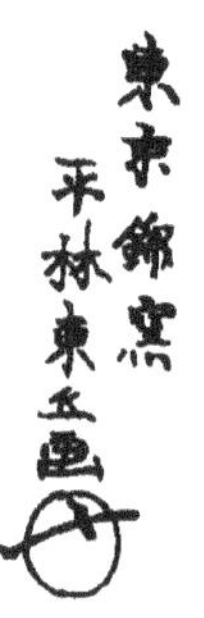

No. 454.

Painted in gold upon a Vase of Owari porcelain. To-kio, Kin-ko, Hira-bayashi To-kiu yegaku. *Painted by Hirabayashi Tokiu, Kinko* (factory) *Tokio.*

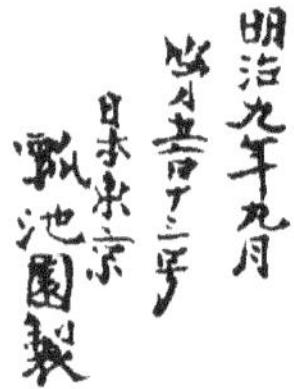

No. 455.

Painted in red upon a Vase of porcelain. Mei-ji, Ku-nen, Ku-gatsu Dai-go-hiyaku-jiusan-go Nip-pon, To-kio, Hio-chi-yen seisu. *Made by Hiochiyen, Tokio, Japan. No. 513. Ninth month, ninth year, of the period of Meiji.* 1876 A.D.

No. 456.

Painted in red upon a Tea Jar of Kioto faience. To-kio, Cho-getsu yegaku. *Painted by Chogetsu, Tokio.*

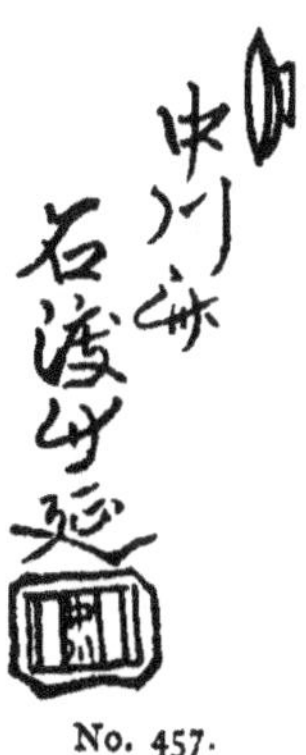

No. 457.

Painted in red upon a Vase of semi-porcelain, made in Satsuma. CHIU-SEN-SAI ISI-WATARI TIKU-YEN. *Isiwatari Tikuyen*, the name of the painter; *Chiusensai*, probably the name of the workshop. The marks at the beginning and end of the inscription are the seals of the painter.

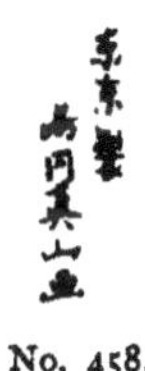

No. 458.

Painted in red upon a Vase of faience. TO-KIO SEI. SIMA-UCHI SHIN-ZAN YEGAKU. *Painted by Simauchi Shinzan. Tokio manufacture.*

No. 459.

Impressed upon a Figure of pottery, made in 1875 A.D. NIP-PON, TO-KIO, TO-KO, RAKU-HO. *Rakuho, potter, Tokio, Japan.*

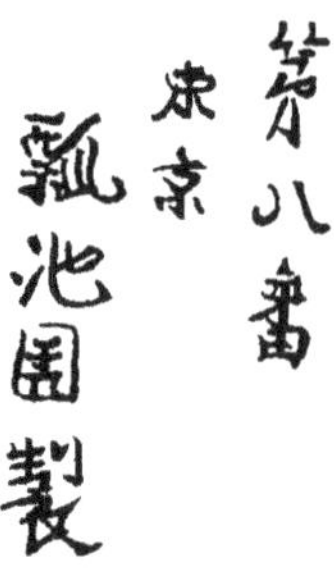

No. 460.

Painted in red upon a Vase of faience. DAI-HACHI-BAN. TO-KIO, HIO-CHI-YEN SEISU. *Made by Hiochiyen, Tokio.* No. 8.

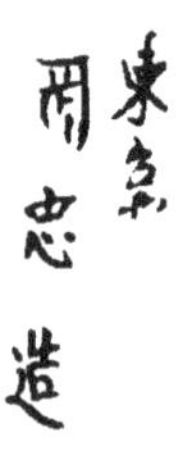

No. 461.

Painted, upon a Plate of Kioto faience, in red and black, the latter upon a splash of white enamel. TO-KIO, OKA CHIU TSUKURU. *Made by Oka Chiu, Tokio.* The name of the maker or painter is OKAMURA, but he has omitted the latter part of it in this inscription, and added his second name of CHIU.

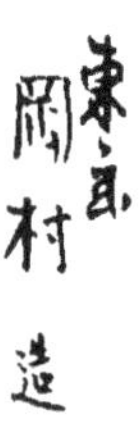

No. 462.

Painted, as above, upon a Plate. TO-KIO, OKA-MURA TSUKURU. *Made by Okamura, Tokio.* Probably this, and the preceding specimen, were painted, not made, by the artist, or artists, named.

No. 463.

Painted in red upon a Cup of fine egg-shell porcelain, made at Arita, in Hizen. TO-KIO, YAMA-MOTO SHU-GETSU YEGAKU. *Painted by Yamamoto Shugetsu, Tokio.*

No. 464.

Painted in red upon a Cup of porcelain, probably Hizen ware. KIN-KO-SHA. *The Kinko factory.*

No. 465.

Painted in red upon a Vase of imitation Satsūma ware. DAI NIP-PON. SHIGE-TAKE, GETSU-ZAN UTUSHU. *Copied by Getsuzan Shigetake, Great Japan.*

No. 466.

Impressed upon a Brazier of pottery, made in the district of Imado, Tokio. GOSABURO, the name of the maker.

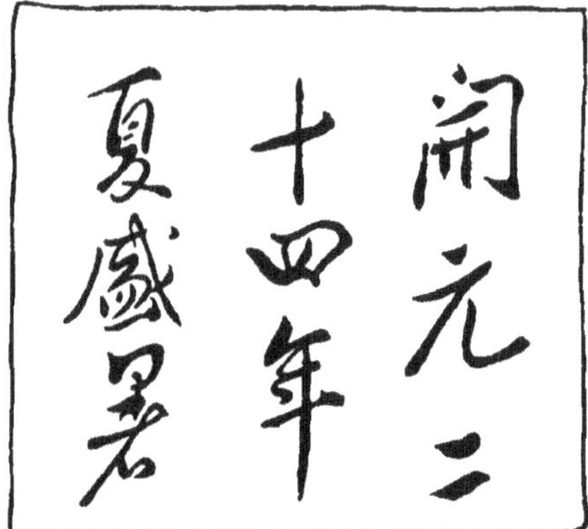

No. 467.

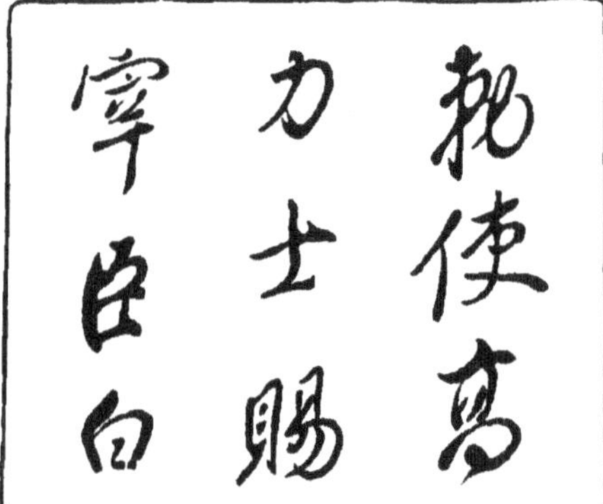

No. 468.

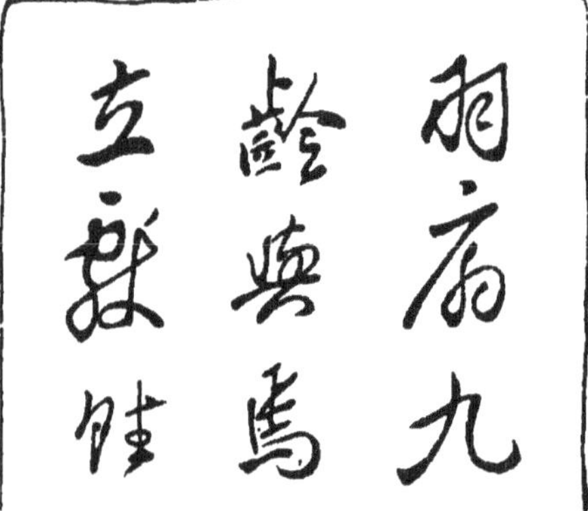

No. 469.

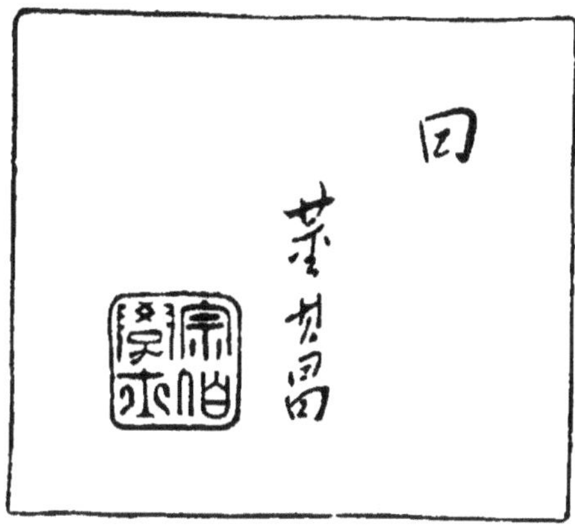

No. 470.

The inscriptions numbered 467 to 470 appear in relief upon the sides of a Flower Basket of faience, made at Imado, a district of Tokio, in the latter part of the 18th century; they are one-fourth of the original size. The inscriptions, read from the upper characters of each column commencing with those to the right, and concluding with the single character in the upper part of the mark given above, run as follows: KAI-GEN NI-JIU-YO NEN NATSU SEI-SHO CHIOKU-SHI KO-RIOKU-SHI TAMOO SAI-SHIN HAKU-U-SEN KIU-REI AZUKARU YEN TATTSUTE KEN-JIN IWAKU. It is a portion of a description of a scene at the Chinese Court: *In June, the summer of the 24th year of Kaigen, the imperial messenger, Koriokushi, brings the fans of white feathers to the ministers, among whom was Kiurei, and standing before them he presents the imperial gifts, and says ——.* The centre inscription of No. 470 is TOKISHIO, the name of the Chinese scholar who wrote the phrase; the right-hand characters in the seal-mark are SOHAKU, his professional name, and the left-hand characters are GAKUSHI, a title given to learned men.

No. 471.

Impressed upon a Bowl of earthenware. Si-sei. *Sisei*, the name of the maker.

No. 472.

Impressed upon a Cup of faience. Sei-si. *Seisi*, the name of the maker.

No. 473.

Impressed upon a Cup of pottery. Sei-si. *Seisi*, the name of the maker.

No. 474.

Painted in black upon a Bowl of pottery, said to have been made by Miura Kenya, about 1850 A.D., at Asakusa, a district of Tokio. Ken-ya. *Kenya*, the name of the maker. The style of this mark appears to be an imitation of that of Shisui Kenzan, of Kioto, of which Numbers 237 and 238 are examples.

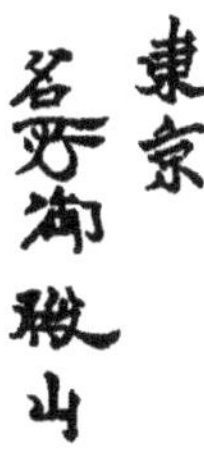

No. 475.

Painted in blue upon a *sake* Cup of porcelain, made in Mino, and painted in Tokio. TO-KIO, MEI-SHO GOTEN-YAMA. *The famous place of Gotenyama, Tokio*, the scene with which the Cup is decorated.

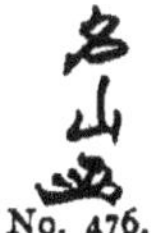

No. 476.

Painted in blue upon a *sake* Cup of porcelain, made in Mino, and painted in Tokio. MEI-ZAN. *Meizan* being the name of the painter; the lower mark is his seal.

No. 477.

Painted in blue upon a *sake* Cup of porcelain, made in Mino, and painted in Tokio. TO-KIO MEI-SHO, SHIBA ZO-JIO-ZI SAUMON. *The temple Zojiozi of Shiba, the famous place of Tokio*, a view of which appears upon the Cup.

No. 478. No. 479.

Painted in blue upon Cups of porcelain, made in Mino, and decorated in Tokio. CHO-SO-SAI SAI-KO KO. *Made by Chososai Saiko.* Both inscriptions are the same.

No 480.

Painted in red upon a Cup and Saucer of egg-shell porcelain, made in Hizen, and decorated in Tokio. SAN-GO-KU ICHI MEI-ZAN. *Meizan, the first* (maker) *of the three countries,* Japan, India, and China, signifying the whole world. The lower character is the maker's seal.

No. 481.

Painted in red and black upon a Cup of porcelain, made in Mino, and decorated in Tokio. SHUN-ZAN HITSUSU. *Painted by Shunzan.* The lower character is the painter's seal.

No. 482.

Painted in blue and red upon a *sake* Bottle of porcelain, made in Mino, and decorated in Tokio. SHIN-ZAN. *Shinzan,* the name of the maker. The lower character is his seal or that of the workshop.

No. 483.

Painted in red and black upon a *sake* Bottle of porcelain, made in Mino, and decorated in Tokio. Go-zan. *Gozan*, the name of the painter; the lower mark is his seal or that of the workshop.

No. 484.

Painted in blue upon the interior of a *sake* Cup of porcelain, made in Mino, and decorated in Tokio. Ureshike taku hio. A Japanese phrase which cannot be translated into English.

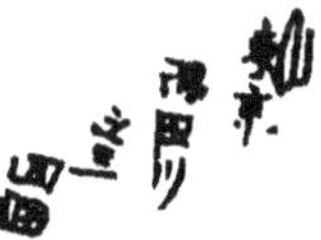

No. 485.

Painted in red and brown upon a *sake* Cup of porcelain, made in Mino, and decorated in Tokio. *View of the Sumida River, Tokio*, the scene depicted upon the Cup. The seals on this and the succeeding examples are the marks of the painter.

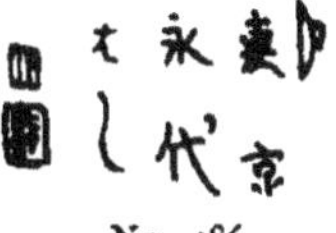

No. 486.

Painted in red and black upon a similar Cup. *View of the Yeidai Bridge, Tokio.*

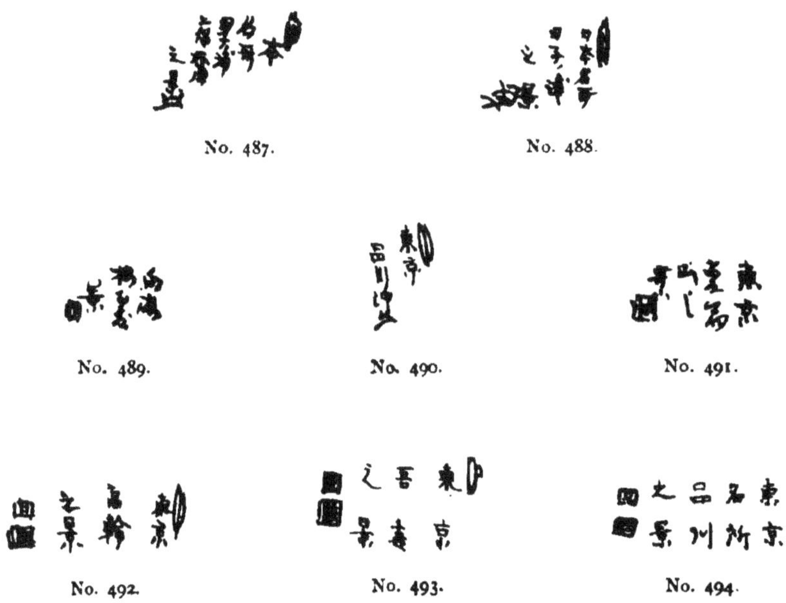

No. 487. No. 488.

No. 489. No. 490. No. 491.

No. 492. No. 493. No. 494.

Inscriptions painted in red and black in the interiors of *sake* Cups of porcelain, made in Mino and decorated in Tokio, descriptive of the scenes depicted upon them.

No. 487.—*View of Miho no Matsuwara, Tagonoura, the famous place of Japan.*

No. 488.—*View of Tagonoura, the famous place of Japan.*

No. 489.—*View of the Plum Garden in Mukozima, Tokio.*

No. 490.—*View of Shinagawa Bay, Tokio.*

No. 491.—*View of Atagoyama, Tokio.*

No. 492.—*View of Takanawa, Tokio.*

No. 493.—*View of Azuma Bridge, Tokio.*

No. 494.—*View of Shinagawa, the famous place of Tokio.*

THE MINOR KILNS.

No. 495.

Impressed upon a Vase of faience made by MIYAKAWA KOZAN, of Ota, a suburb of Yokohama; this factory was established in 1860 A.D., by a Tokio merchant, named Suzuki Yasubeye, who brought Kozan from Kioto to manage it. It is here that most of the imitations of Satsuma faience have been made. KO-ZAN, the name of the maker.

No. 496.

Impressed upon a Vase of faience. MA-KUZU KO-ZAN TSUKURU. *Made by Makuzu Kozan.* Kozan came from the district of Makuzu, in Kioto, and often uses the word as part of his mark.

No. 497.

Inlaid in white clay upon a Flower Pot of brown pottery. MIYA-KAWA KO-ZAN TSUKURU. *Made by Miyakawa Kozan.*

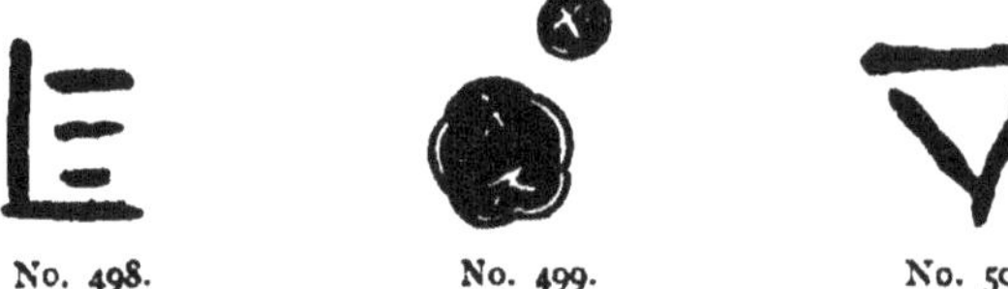

No. 498. No. 499. No. 500.

Impressed upon faience and stoneware made at Ota. The marks of the makers.

No. 501.

Painted in gold upon a Vase of Ota faience. KATSU O TOKI SEI-YO NO SAKE. *The sake which is taken the morning after intoxication quenches the thirst;* descriptive of the scene depicted upon the vase.

No. 502.

Impressed upon a Bottle of Ota faience. DEN-KO. *Denko,* the name of the maker.

No 503.

Inlaid in white clay upon a Flower Pot of brown pottery. MA-KUZU KO-ZAN. *Makuzu Kozan,* the name of the maker.

No. 504.

Incised upon a Figure of Bizen stoneware, said to have been made in the 13th century. SAN, the mark of the maker.

No. 505.

Incised upon the Figure of a Horse of ancient Bizen ware. The mark of the maker.

No. 506.

Stamped upon a Fruit Basket of ancient Bizen ware. The mark of the maker.

No. 507.

Incised upon an Eagle of ancient Bizen ware. The mark of the maker.

No. 508.

Incised upon a Bird of ancient Bizen ware. CHO, the name of the maker.

No. 509.

Incised upon a Figure of ancient Bizen ware. KICHI, the name of the maker.

No. 510.

Stamped upon an Eagle of ancient Bizen ware. YEI-ZAN. *Yeizan*, the name of the maker.

No. 511.

Stamped and incised upon a Lion of ancient Bizen ware. The lower characters are TEI-ICHI. *Teïichi*, the name of the maker. The upper character reads Ko, and is probably his mark.

No. 512.

Stamped upon an Ash Bowl of Bizen *Hitasuke* ware, said to have been made about 1579 A.D. The mark of the maker.

No. 513.

Stamped upon a Water Jar of Bizen *Migakite* ware, said to have been made about 1760 A.D. The mark of the maker.

No. 514.

Scratched upon a Cake Box of Bizen ware made about 1840 A.D. YOSHI-KAGE SEISU. *Made by Yoshikage.*

No. 515.

A Japanese ode, scratched upon a *sake* Bottle of modern Bizen stoneware; the characters are *Hira-kana* and Chinese. TAKE SUKOSHI ARITE TORI NAKU KOHAN KANA, which Mr. Kawakami has rendered into English as follows: *It is in the month of mild October that the birds, with their gentle, yet sweet song, visit the few bamboos that remain sadly here and there.*

No. 516.

Painted in blue .upon a Cup of Aidz porcelain, with *sometsuke* decoration, made in the province of Mutsu. RAKU-SEI, KU-KO. The name of the maker, *Kuko*, and of the place where he resided, *Rakusei*.

No. 517.

Painted in blue upon a Teapot of Aidz porcelain, decorated in blue and brown. HOSEI-KEN TSUKURU. *Made by Hoseiken.*

No. 518.

Painted in blue upon a Teapot of modern Aidz porcelain. KA-ZAN UGO. A phrase: *The mountain after the Summer rain.*

No. 519.

Stamped upon a Vase of the choicest Celadon ware. NAN-KI, ZUI-SI-DO SEISU. *Made by Zuisido, Nanki.* The latter is another name for the province of Kii.

No. 520.

Stamped upon a Group of Tortoises of Celadon ware. ZUI-SI. *Zuisi*, the maker's name.

No. 521.

Stamped upon a Vase of Kii porcelain, made about 1800 A.D. KAI-RAKU-YEN SEISU. *Made by Kairakuyen.*

No. 522.

Stamped upon a Dish of Kii pottery. SAN-RAKU-YEN SEISU. *Made by Sanrakuyen.*

No. 523.

Impressed upon a Water Vessel of faience, made at Koriyama, in the province of Yamato. AKA-HADA-YAMA. *Akahadayama*, the name of the factory. The seal is the mark of KISHIRO, the maker.

No. 524.

Painted upon a Water Vessel of faience, similar to the above example; the inscription in black, the seal in red. KI-SHIRO UTSUSU. *Kishiro copies.* The seal is his mark.

No. 525.

Painted upon the preceding example. KI-YEN, SHIU-JIN. *The Master of the Kiyen factory.* The seals are probably his marks or those of the painter.

No. 526.

Stamped upon a Brazier of Yamato pottery. AKAHADA, the name of the ware.

大和宝奇玉造

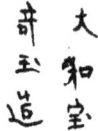

No. 527.

Painted in red upon a Cup of egg-shell porcelain made in Yamato. YA-MATO, HOKIGIOKU TSUKURU. *Made by Hokigioku, Yamato.*

No. 528.

Stamped upon a figure of an Okame Woman of Awaji faience. MIN-PEI. *Minpei*, the name of the maker.

No. 529.

Painted in gold upon a Flower Vase of faience. NIP-PON, AWAJI, GA-SHU SAN-PEI. *Sanpei Gashu* (the maker), *Awaji, Japan.*

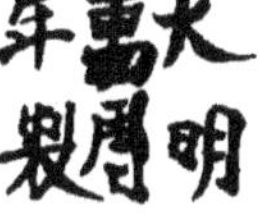

No. 530.

Painted in black upon a Cup of porcelain, made in Awaji about 1830 A.D. DAI-MING, MAN-REKI NEN SEI. *Made in the year of Manreki, during the dynasty of Dai Ming*, 1573-1620 A.D. A forgery of the Chinese mark of the Wan-li period.

No. 531.

Stamped upon a Dish of pottery. So-MA. *Soma*, the name of the ware.

No. 532.

Stamped upon a Cup of Soma pottery. KANE-SIGE. *Kanesige*, the name of the maker.

No. 533.

Stamped upon a Cup of Soma pottery covered with Celadon glaze. The mark of the maker.

No. 534.

Partly in relief, and partly painted in black, upon a Tea Bowl of Soma pottery. *The crests of the Prince of Soma.* Bowls of this ware are prized in Japan owing to their supposed virtue of warding off attacks of paralysis.

No. 535.

Painted in red upon a large *sake* Cup of Mino porcelain. GETS-SHO. *Getsho*, the name of the maker or painter.

No. 536.

Painted in blue, under the glaze, upon a *sake* Cup of Mino porcelain. The mark of the maker. It is very seldom that any mark, except that of the painter, is placed upon Mino porcelain. Numerous examples of the latter are given in the division of Tokio painting.

No. 537.

Incised upon a Vase of Takatori stoneware, made at Sobara, in the province of Chikuzen. *Ki*, the name of the maker.

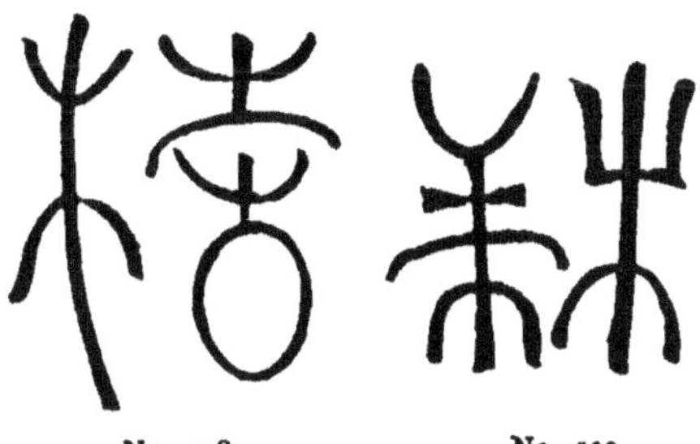

No. 538. No. 539.

In relief upon a Vase of Takatori stoneware. Ornaments, or the marks of the maker.

No. 540.

Impressed upon a Box of Fujina faience, made in the province of Idzumo. WUN-SUI. *Wunsui*, the name of the maker.

No. 541.

Impressed upon a Teapot of similar ware. *Wunsui*, the name of the maker.

No. 542.

Impressed upon a Water Pot of similar ware. *Wunsui*, the name of the maker.

No. 543.

Impressed upon a Saucer of similar ware. UN-KI. *Unki*, the name of the maker.

No. 544.

Stamped upon an Ash Bowl of Minato pottery, made at Sakai, in the province of Idzumi. MINATO YAKI. *Minato ware.*

No. 545.

Stamped upon a Dish of Minato pottery. SEN-SHU, SAKAI, HONG MINATO YAKI, KICHI-YEMON. *Genuine Minato ware*, made by *Kichiyemon*, *Sakai*, *Senshu*.

No. 546.

Stamped upon a Flower Pot of Yatsushiro pottery, made in the province of Higo. GEN, the name, or mark, of the maker.

No. 547.

Stamped upon a Hanging Flower Vase of Yatsushiro pottery, said to have been made about 1800 A.D. SAI, the name, or mark, of the maker.

No. 548.

Stamped upon a Teapot of modern Yatsushiro pottery. JI, the name of the maker.

No. 549.

Stamped upon a Jar of pottery made at the Shigaraki kiln, at Nagano, in the province of Omi. The mark of the maker.

No. 550.

Stamped upon a Figure of faience of considerable age. KO-TO, HIO-NEN-SAI. *Hionensai* being the maker, who lived at *Koto*, the East side of the Lake Biwa, in the province of Omi.

No. 551.

Stamped upon a *sake* Bottle of pottery, made at Uji, in the province of Yamashiro. ASA-HI. *Asahi*, the name of the ware, which is so called from its resemblance to a renowned tea bowl of Corean manufacture known by the same name, which signifies "morning light."

No. 552.

In relief upon a Bottle of pottery, made in the province of Yamashiro. The mark of the maker.

No. 553.

Stamped upon an Ash Bowl of pottery, made at Toyourayama, in the province of Nagato. TOYOU-RA-YAMA, the name of the ware.

PART II.

ILLUMINATED MSS.

AND

PRINTED BOOKS.

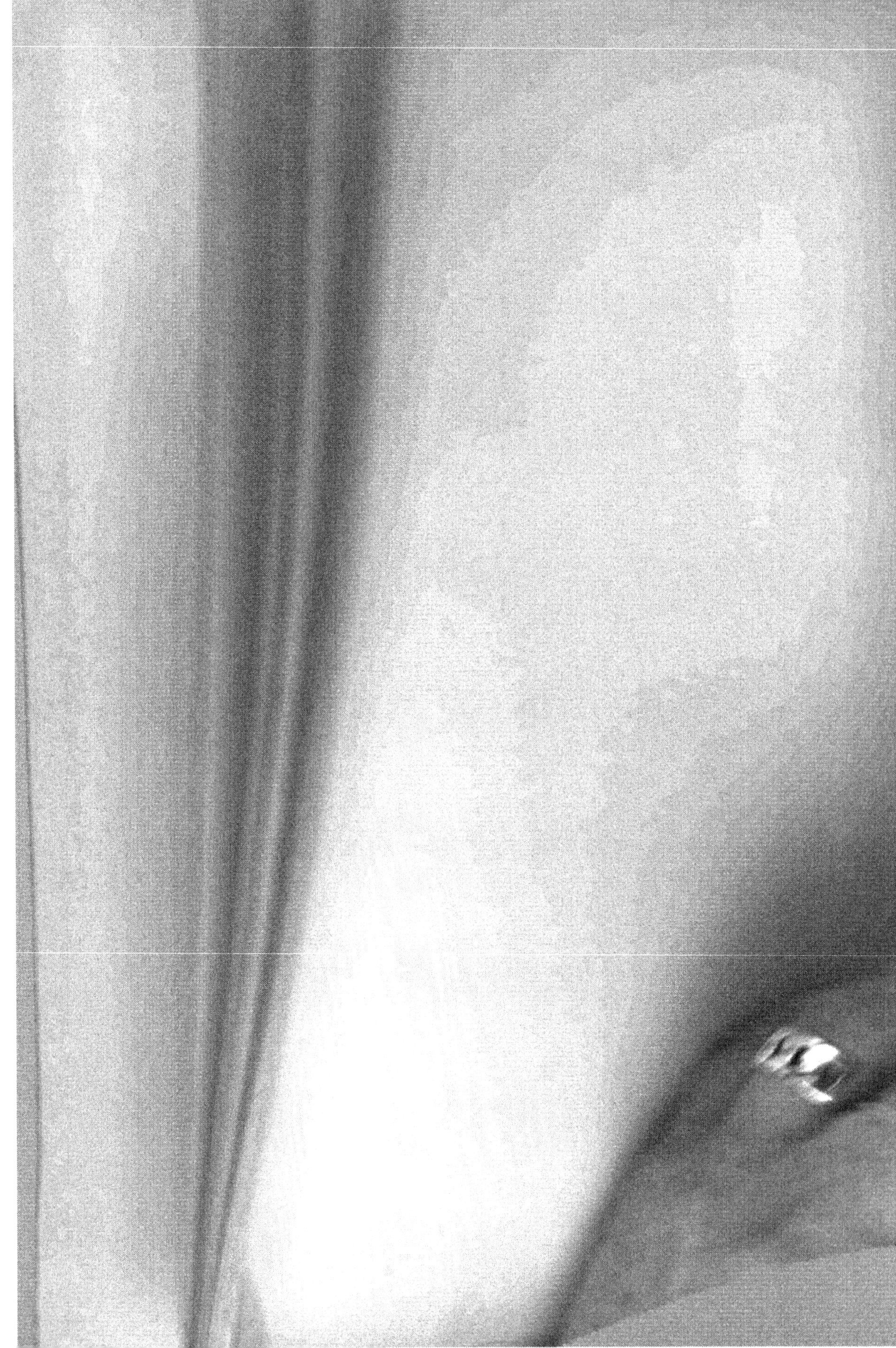

ILLUMINATED MANUSCRIPTS AND PRINTED BOOKS.

THE records of Japan state that the art of painting was introduced into the country from the Corea in the year 463 A.D., but the works of that period no longer exist, nor have we any information as to their character; the earliest known example of the art is a portrait of the prince Shotoku, said to date from the seventh century, which is preserved in the temple of Horiuji in the province of Yamato. About that time an official department for the encouragement of the art was established under the name of Guwa-koshi, which was afterwards changed to Edokoro, but it is probable that the works of this period did not extend beyond the decoration of the Imperial palaces, and little progress was made until the fourteenth century, when the great school of Tosa was established by Tsunetaka.

This celebrated artist, who was then the director of the Edokoro, having been rewarded with the appointment of vice-governor of the province of Tosa, assumed that name, and gave it to the school of painting of which he was the founder; the family name was changed to Sumiyoshi by his descendant Hiromichi, in the period of Kwambun, 1661 to 1673 A.D., but the name of the school remained unaltered, and the descendants of Tsunetaka hold a distinguished place amongst the artists of the present day.

The second great school is that of Kano, which was founded by Kano Masanobu, who lived between the periods of Chokio and Tembun, 1487 to 1555 A.D., and his descendants also still worthily uphold the fame of their ancestor. The most celebrated representatives of this family, belonging to the Tsukiji, Kajibashi and Nakabashi branches, have resided in Tokio during the last two centuries under the patronage of the Tokugawa Shôgunate, the members of which have not only supported them by liberal grants of money but availed themselves of their instruction.

The paintings of the Tosa school are remarkable as specimens of minute and delicate manipulation, and resemble in many respects the fine miniature painting found in the illuminated missals of the middle ages; they are executed in full-toned colours, often with a lavish use of gold, and represent scenes of court life, with the figures of nobles and ladies clad in robes of ceremony, or depict the warriors of ancient days engaged in the warfare with which the history of Japan is associated. The artists of the Kano family, on the other hand, have always loved to depict the natural beauties of their country or to illustrate the mythological legends of China, and their drawings of scenery, and studies of men, animals, birds and foliage, are executed with freedom and truthfulness, and are singularly beautiful.

Another school, of a kindred character to that of Tosa, was founded by Iwasa Matabei in the period of Tensho, 1573 to 1592 A.D., and out of this grew, a century later, that of Utagawa; the works of these schools are known as the Ukiyo, or popular, style. The most celebrated master of this school was Hokusai, who lived between the periods of Bunsei and Tempo, 1818 to 1844 A.D. He illustrated the manners and customs of his own times, as well as the warlike scenes of the middle ages, and his works, which are exceedingly graphic, and often most humorous, are still very popular, and are reproduced in the ordinary block-printed books of the country for the amusement of the people, and as text books for educational use.

The fourth, and last, of the leading schools of painting, the Sumie style, is of Chinese origin, and has always been held in high esteem by the cultured class of Japan. The works of this style are executed in Chinese ink, and the artists, by a few strokes of the brush, produce with great skill and dexterity most artistic and faithful representations of their subjects. In a modification of this style, known as the Bunjinga school, colours are introduced, but only sparingly.

Block printing was practised in Japan at a very early period, and it is said that a book was printed for distribution amongst the Buddhist temples in this manner in 770 A.D., but the art does not appear to have become general until the early part of the fourteenth century; only modern examples have reached Europe. Printing with types is stated to have been introduced during the sixteenth century, doubtless from China, but it was not largely used until recent times.

The most ancient form of book is the roll, or *Makimono;* the examples which have reached this country vary in length from eleven to forty-five feet, and in breadth from ten to eighteen inches; they commence at the right hand side and read towards the left, like all Japanese books and inscriptions, and are generally of paper, but occasionally the painting is upon silk mounted upon paper. Folding books, named *Oribon*, and books which are sewn, known as *Shomotsu*, are also of considerable antiquity, and the latter form is in general use at the present time, but the name is most correctly applied to works which are partially or entirely written, whilst picture-books which are sewn are called *Yebon*. The general term for books of all descriptions is *Hong*. Hanging paintings, or written inscriptions in the same form, are known as *Kakimono*. In nearly all cases the title of the work is written upon a label affixed to the exterior of the book, but the name of the artist is seldom given except upon the paintings themselves, which occasionally bear his signature or seal.

In analysing the various characters found in the list of marks, those which express the word Volume may be taken first. The word *Maki* is most frequently used, but upon the older works *Satsu* is occasionally found ; the literal meaning of the latter word is a slip of bamboo, and its application in the sense named arises from the fact that in China, in very ancient times before paper was in general use, thin slips of wood took its place.

SATSU. *Volume.* MAKI. *Volume.*

When the work consists of a single volume, the word *Zen* is used, and when there are a number of volumes, each of them is marked with the character *Maki* and the appropriate number, as shown by the examples given :

ZEN. *Single volume.*

MAKI NO ICHI. *1st volume.* MAKI NO NI. *2nd volume.* MAKI NO SAN. *3rd volume.* MAKI NO SHI. *4th volume.*

MAKI NO GO. *5th volume.* MAKI NO ROKU. *6th volume.* MAKI NO HICHI. *7th volume.* MAKI NO HACHI. *8th volume.*

The foregoing characters are those most frequently used upon modern books, a different system being followed in marking the old works, such as many of the fine examples from which the majority of the inscriptions are taken; the volumes of these are seldom more than three in number, and the words *Jo*, *Chiu* and *Ge*, meaning, literally, top, middle and bottom, are used to designate the first, second and third volumes respectively; when there are only two volumes, the words *Jo* and *Ge* are used. The characters *Teng*, *Chi* and *Zing*, meaning heaven, earth and man, are occasionally used in the same sense.

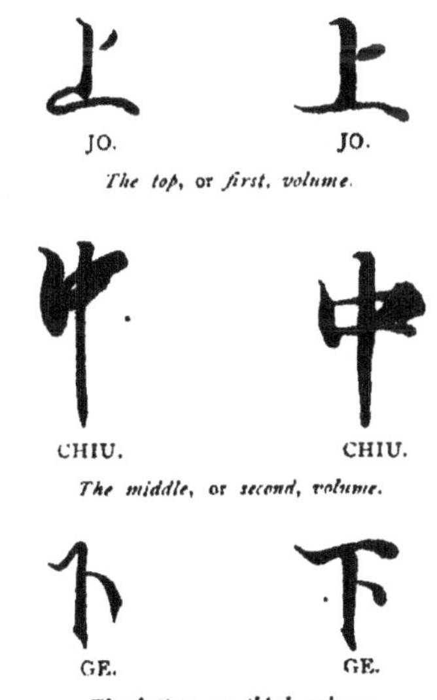

JO. JO.
The top, or *first, volume.*

CHIU. CHIU.
The middle, or *second, volume.*

GE. GE.
The bottom, or *third, volume.*

To designate the last volume, the word *Owari*, shown on the following page, is sometimes used.

FF

OWARI.

End volume.

When the books which are referred to form part of a set, this is expressed after the following manner:

HICHI NO JO

The first volume of seven

Works are frequently divided into two or more parts, and when this is the case it is stated in the inscription upon each of the volumes.

HEN.

Part.

SHOHEN.

First part.

KUHEN.

Ninth part.

SHOHEN.

First part.

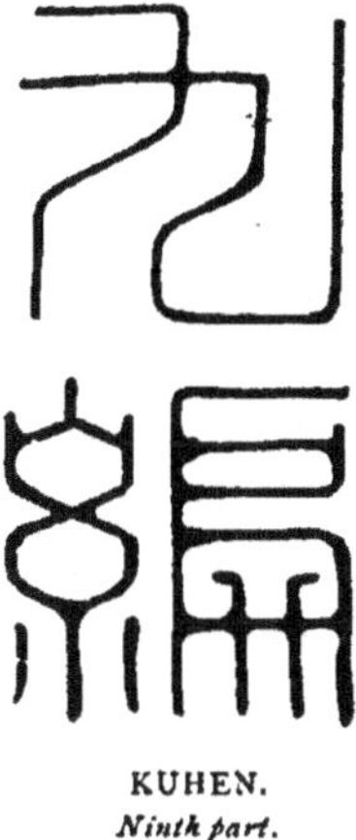

KUHEN.
Ninth part.

When several volumes of the same work are placed in portfolios or separate wrappers, the word *Chitsu* is used in the following manner:

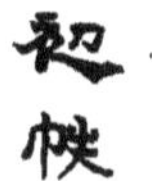

SHO CHITSU.
First case, or portfolio.

In connection with the foregoing marks, *Dai*, number, sometimes occurs.

DAI.
Number.

When the information contained in a work has been collected or arranged by the writer, the word *Hensu* appears as part of the title.

HENSU.
Collected or Arranged.

Ichiran is found upon books containing panoramic views of any part of the country.

ICHIRAN.
Synopsis.

Paintings are occasionally mounted and surrounded by borders of paper and silk, when the word *Hioho* follows the name of the workman.

HIOHO.
Mounted.

The characters *Yegaku* and *Hitsu*, the latter being read as *Hitsusu* when used with the name of a painter, do not appear so frequently upon books as upon pottery; the word *Dzusu*, having the same meaning, is sometimes used. The examples given below are copied from works of the Kano and Tosa families.

YEGAKU. HITSUSU. HITSUSU. HITSUSU. DZUSU.
Painted by.

The former of the two characters given below is copied from an ancient *kakimono*, and the latter from a modern *yebon*.

YEGAKU.

YEGAKU.

When a painter copies the works of another artist he uses the character *Bosu* in connection with his name, but when he paints from nature or imagination the word *Utsusu*, having a similar signification, is more correct.

BOSU. *Copied.* UTSUSU. *Copied.* UTSUSU. *Copied.*

Occasionally the artist couples the word respectfully with his name, as a sign of deference to his patron.

TSUTSUSHINDE. *Respectfully.* TSUTSUSHINDE YEGAKU. *Respectfully paints.* TSUTSUSHINDE. *Respectfully.*

Should a writer desire to show that the work is entirely his own, he joins the words *Zi roku* with his name.

ZI ROKU. *Written by himself.*

Characters signifying views, pictures, sketches and so forth, are frequently found on the labels upon books of paintings or drawings of scenery. The following character appears upon an *oribon* containing a series of views of the scenery of Lake Biwa:

KEI.
Views.

The word *Dzu* is used to signify a picture, view or map; examples of this character are given below.

DZU. DZU. DZU.
Picture, View or Map.

The latter mark is taken from a *yebon* of Hokusai's sketches, and the small characters to the right give the word in *Hira-kana* letters for the information of those who are unacquainted with Chinese words.

When a written description accompanies the paintings or drawings, the words *Kaishi* or *Dzuye* are used to express this; the latter word is written in various styles, of which two examples are given below.

DZUYE. DZUYE. KAISHI.
Paintings or Drawings with description.

When the pictures are unaccompanied by any description another form of the word *Dzuye* is used, as shown by the following character:

DZUYE.
Paintings or Drawings without description.

Many other characters having a similar or kindred significance appear in the list of marks, of which the following are examples:

GAFU. *Picture Book.*
MANGA. *Rough Sketches.*
DZUFU. *Picture Book.*
GATSU-U. *Collection of Pictures.*
SHINKEI. *Faithful Views.*
ZO. *Portraits.*
MEISHO. *Famous Places.*
MANGA. *Rough Sketches.*
YEZO. *Portraits.*

A favourite subject of Japanese painters is the illustration of the historical tales of their country, and the characters *Mono-gatari*, having this meaning, frequently occur in the titles of the works of this nature; the following examples are copied from ancient works:

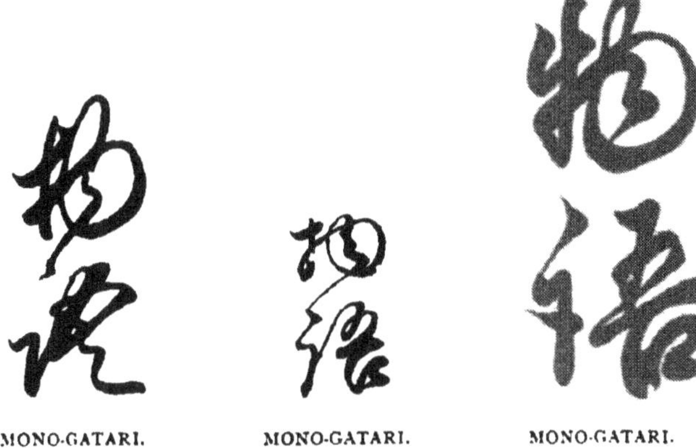

MONO-GATARI. MONO-GATARI. *Historical Tales.* MONO-GATARI.

The marks given above are Chinese, but the words are frequently found written in a combination of Chinese words and *Hira-kana* letters; the inscriptions which follow illustrate this, and afford an indication of the difficulties which beset the correct interpretation of ancient Japanese inscriptions.

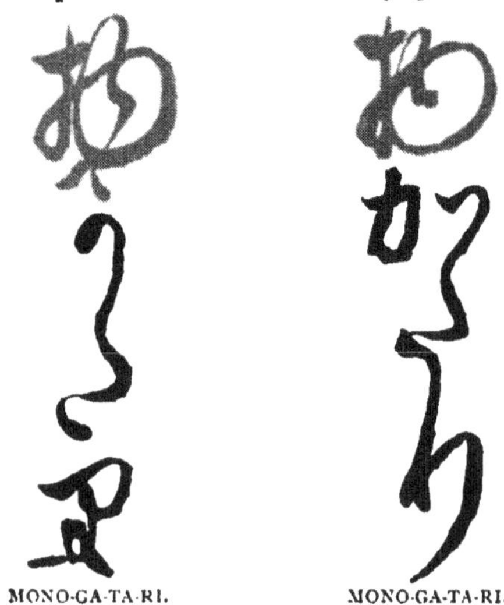

MONO-GA-TA-RI. MONO-GA-TA-RI.

Historical Tales.

The upper character in each of the foregoing inscriptions is the Chinese word *mono*, and the lower ones form the word *gatari*, written in *Hira-kana* letters; the letters of this alphabet are in many cases derived from different Chinese words, and are written in various forms and styles, which renders their translation a task of extreme difficulty.

The characters *Riu*, a school, and *Sotei*, the disciple of a school, are seldom found in the marks upon books, but they are occasionally used in the following manner:

RIU. *A School.*	YENSHIU RIU. *The School of Yenshiu.*	SOTEI. *Disciple of a School.*	KANDA SOTEI. *Disciple of the School of Kanda*

The list of marks furnishes three instances of the titles which were conferred upon painters, or were assumed by them. Two of them are of considerable interest, from the fact that they are found in connection with the names of distinguished members of the families of Tosa and Kano. The title of *Sakon no Shogen* was one which proceeded directly from the Court of the Mikado, and was of the highest honour, being reserved for men distinguished in the arts of war and peace. It was of a purely honorary character, being that of the chief inspector of the palace, a nominal office of the Court. The instance given upon the next page is taken from an *oribon*, in the Bowes Collection, entitled Sanju Roku Kasen, containing the portraits of thirty-six poets and poetesses of ancient times, painted by Mitsuoki Tosa, about the period of Manji, 1658 to 1661 A.D. The first inscription, which gives the title in full, is found at the close of the work in connection with the name of the artist, whilst the second, an abbreviation of the title, is used by the painter as his seal, and is stamped upon each painting.

SAKON NO SHOGEN.

SHOGEN.

The title of *Hogan*, which probably emanated from a government department or from the Shôgun, and not from the Mikado, is one which is conferred only upon painters; the example which is here given is taken from a *makimono*, in the Bowes Collection, painted by Tosan Kanrakusai, a member of the Kano family, who resided in Tokio under the patronage of the Shôgun.

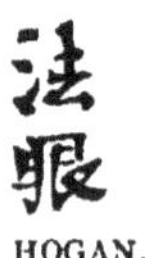

HOGAN.

The third illustration is that of *Koji*, a title which is assumed by painters and scholars; the example given is found in the *makimono* referred to above, in connection with the name of Hichisho, the most accomplished master of writing in modern times, who wrote the text of the work referred to; he died in 1858.

KOJI.

The only other character connected with the marks upon books to which it is necessary to draw attention is that of *Shinsu*, a modern word coined since the country was opened to European influences, and the publication of books became a business; it is derived from *shin*, the term used for the wood employed in the manufacture of the blocks for printing.

SHINSU
Publishers.

No. 554.

Painted in black upon one of the pages of an *oribon*, entitled *Sanju Roku Kasen*, containing thirty-six leaves, upon each of which is painted in gold and colours the portrait of a poet or poetess of ancient times; the grounds of the portraits are clouded with gold, and opposite each is written an ode composed by the poet depicted. To-SA, SA-KON NO SHO-GEN, MITSU-OKI HITSUSU. *Painted by Mitsuoki Tosa, Sakon no Shogen.* Mitsuoki was a distinguished member of the Tosa family, who lived during the period of Manji, 1658 to 1661 A.D., and was honoured by the Mikado with the title of Sakon no Shogen. This work, which is a perfect example of the Tosa school of painting, is preserved in the Bowes Collection.

No. 555.

An abbreviation of the title of Sakon no Shogen. SHOGEN, the seal of Mitsuoki Tosa, stamped in red upon each of the paintings referred to above.

No. 556.

Painted in black upon a page of an *oribon*. TSUNE-NOBU HITSUSU. *Painted by Tsunenobu*. This artist, a distinguished member of the Tsukiji branch of the Kano family, died in the third year of the period of Shotoku, 1712 A.D.

No. 557.

Painted in black upon a page of an *oribon*. MINE-NOBU HITSUSU. *Painted by Minenobu*, a member of the Tsukiji branch of the Kano family, who lived during the period of Shotoku, 1711 to 1716 A.D.

No. 558.

Painted in black upon a page of an *oribon*. CHIKA-NOBU HITSUSU. *Painted by Chikanobu*. It is not clear whether this artist was one of the Kano family, but he was a well-known disciple of that school; he lived during the period of Shotoku.

No. 559.

Painted in black upon a page of an *oribon*. Probably NORI-NOBU HITSUSU. *Painted by Norinobu*, an artist of the Kano school, who died 1724 A.D.

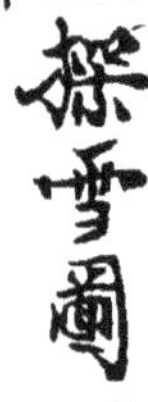

No. 560.

Painted in black upon a page of an *oribon*. TAN-SETSU DZUSU. *Painted by Tansetsu*, an artist of the Kano school, who died 1713 A.D.

No. 561.

Painted in black upon a page of an *oribon*. DO-SHUN HITSUSU. *Painted by Doshun*, an artist of the Kano school, who died in 1723 A.D.

No. 562.

Painted in black upon a page of an *oribon*. TAN-SHIN HITSUSU. *Painted by Tanshin*. This artist, a member of the Kajibashi branch of the Kano family, died in the third year of the period of Kioho, 1718 A.D.

No. 563.

Painted in black upon a *makimono*. SHI-JO DO-JO KAI-SHI. HICHI NO JO. *Shijo Dojo kaishi*, the title of the book, meaning *Pictures, with descriptions, of the Shijo Dojo*, one of the seven bridges of Kioto. HICHI NO JO means *The first volume of seven*.

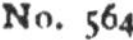

No. 564. No. 565.

Copied from an *oribon* containing six paintings upon silk, illustrating the seasons or festivals of Japan, of which an account is given in *Keramic Art of Japan*.

No. 564 is the title of the book; it is painted in black upon a paper label, clouded with gold, which appears upon the outside of the *oribon:* SHIN ROK-KA-SEN. *Shin Rokkasen. New six seasons.*

No. 565 appears upon one of the paintings. GIOKU-DO GEN-BOKU YEGAKU. *Painted by Genboku Giokudo*, an artist of the Kano school. The seal is the mark of Giokudo.

No. 566.

Painted in black on a white silk label, clouded with gold, upon an *oribon* containing eight views of scenery painted by a Kano artist, and accompanied by MS. descriptions in Chinese and *Hira-kana* characters. SHO-SHO HACHI KEI. *Eight views of Shosho*, the title of the work.

No. 567. No. 568.

Painted in black upon the labels attached to two *makimono* containing a panoramic view of the battle of Yashima, magnificently illuminated in the Tosa style; probably seventeenth century. This battle is the most notable event in the history of Japan, and was fought in 1185 A.D., near Hiogo; it was the concluding event of the war waged between the great houses of Taira and Minamoto. The defeat of the house of Taira on this occasion led to the foundation of the Shôgunate of the Minamoto family. No. 567. YA-SHIMA KATTSU-SEN DZU. JO. *Picture of the battle of Yashima. First volume.* No. 568. GE. *Last volume.*

No. 569. No. 570.

These inscriptions are taken from a large *oribon* containing eighteen paintings, upon silk, of flowering shrubs, executed in the most perfect style of the Kano school. They were painted in the period of Bunkwa, 1804 to 1818 A.D. No. 569. Engraved upon the wooden cover of the book: KU-BETSU-JO. ICHI. *Kubetsu-jo*, the name of the work; *First volume*. No. 570. Painted within the book. KI MASA-TAMI ZI-ROKU. *Ki no Masatami*, the name of the artist; *zi-roku, written by himself*. The upper of the two seals is NO IN MASA-TAMI, *The seal of Masatami*, and the lower one is SHI TO, his second name.

題言

蓋畫花木芳草者莫妙得造化發生之勢也夫枝之偃仰葉之疏密花之向背色之濃淡不能與形求之則焉能極精妙乎哉雖然畫于艸卉之花瓣凝蟬光彩奪目有生意之美色則非丹粉之所能及其堆以盡其姿態性情為專一也余見一花得一草不顧拙劣輒必寫之以備後之摸本焉世之稱本艸家之徒動挖艸卉花實根莖詳圖其花遺雖如畫子遺果之少損畫樣且失風致是非余之所好也蓄之我跡吾癖以為帳中之秘爾

紀正氏自錄

The inscription upon the opposite page is copied from the *oribon* painted by Masatami, from which the marks given on the preceding page are taken, and of which it forms the Preface. It is written upon yellow silk, and is a superb example of caligraphy; the original page measures 11⅝ inches by 15¼ inches, and the copy here given has been reduced in size by Mr. Kawakami, who has also rendered it into English as follows:—

Those who paint flowering shrubs and rare grasses cannot do better than conceive the spirit of their natural power of growth. As to whether the branches should be bending downward or looking upward—whether the leaves should be thick or thin—whether the flowers should show their faces or backs—whether the colours should be deep or light—how can we attain perfection unless we study from the very objects? But we always find our power unequal to the task when we come to the flowers of some humble plants, whose daintiness and brilliancy dazzle our vision, and in which there is the sweet colour of life and growth. Indeed, they are beyond the sphere of the art, because there is no surrounding object by means of which we can impart life to the bare flowers. Therefore in this pursuit it is only necessary that we should do our best in preserving the shapes, the aspects, and peculiarities of the flowers which we intend to produce. Whenever I see a flower or a grass, I never fail, in spite of my meagre ability in painting, to copy it out, so that it may serve the purpose of a model in the future. Indeed, those who are called Botanists do not fail to paint plants and their flowers and fruits, and their roots and stems, in the most minute way; and though they seem never to leave one single point untouched, yet they too often spoil the style of painting, and, besides, lose the fine spirit. Such is far from what I desire. In short, I know only to satisfy the extreme disposition of my own mind, and make this work the treasure of my study.

Ki no Masatami. Written by himself.

No. 572.

Painted in black, on a gold label, upon a *makimono* containing a panoramic view of the garden of Uyeno, at Tokio, painted in colours and gold. Ukiyo school. Late 18th century. UYE-NO DZU. *Views of Uyeno.*

No. 573.

Painted in black, on a gold label, upon a companion *makimono* to that named above. It contains a panoramic view of the garden of ASAKUSA, at Tokio. ASA-KUSA DZU. *Views of Asakusa.*

No. 574.

No. 575.

Painted in black on paper labels, clouded with gold, upon two *makimono*, beautifully painted with a panoramic view of the Tokaido, the highway from Tokio to Kioto. Tosa school. No. 574. TO-KAI DO-CHIU. JO. *Dochiu Tokai, The journey of the Tokaido* [the final syllable of the latter word being omitted]. *First volume.* No. 575. GE. *Last volume.*

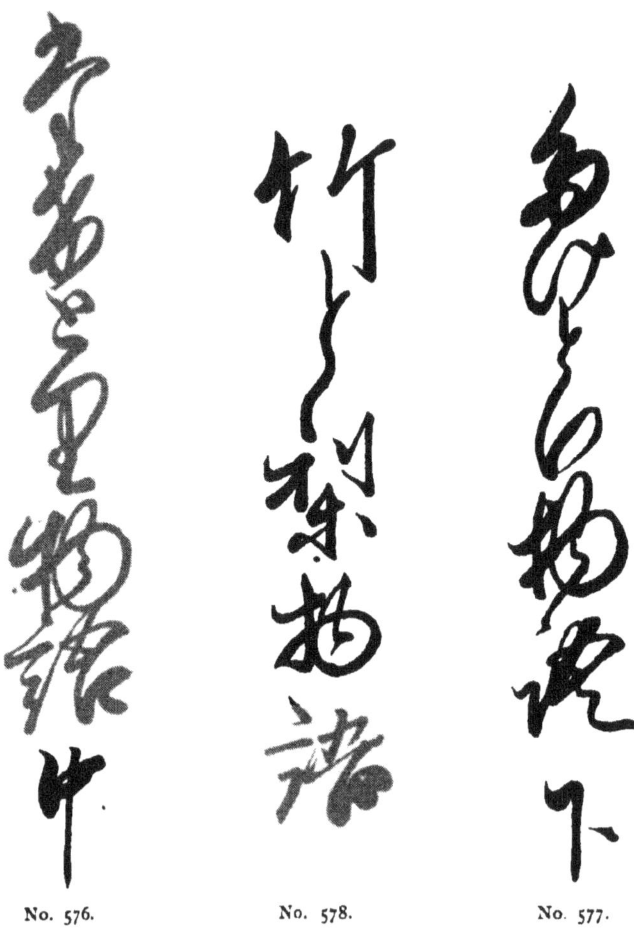

No. 576. No. 578. No. 577.

The inscriptions given above are copied from two *makimono*, and the lacquered case which contains them. They all have the same meaning: TA-KE TO-RI MONO-GATARI. *Take-tori monogatari*, the title of the work, which illustrates the manners and customs of the Japanese nobility. It contains numerous paintings executed in the highest style of the Ukiyo branch of the Tosa school, and they are accompanied by descriptive MSS. in Chinese and *Hira-kana* characters. Early works. The characters at the foot of Nos. 576 and 577 are CHIU and GE respectively, meaning the middle and last volume.

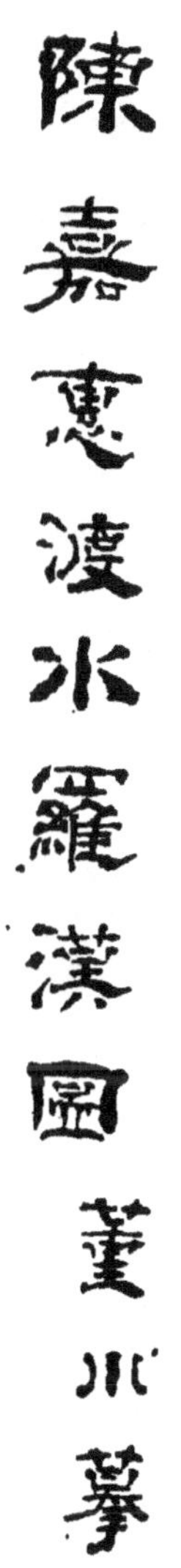

No. 579.

Painted in black upon a paper label; the title of a *makimono* containing a series of paintings executed in the Kano and Sumie styles. CHIN-KA-KEI, TO-SUI RA-KAN DZU. TO-SEN BOSU. *The picture of Tosui Rakan*, a Buddhist priest crossing a river, painted by *Chinkakei*, a Chinese artist, and *copied by Tosen*.

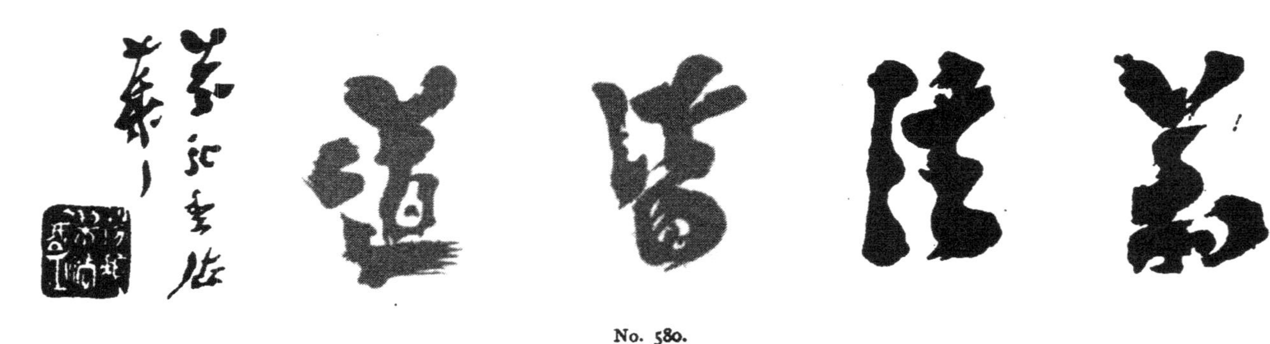

No. 580.

This inscription is taken from the *makimono* copied by Tosen, No 579, and is reduced in size from the original, which measures 34 inches in length. It is a splendid specimen of the writing of FUNDA RIHO-AN, a celebrated master of the art. Commencing at the right hand the four larger characters read: BAN-PO MINA MICHI—a Chinese phrase signifying *All rules are in conformity with natural laws.* The smaller characters are FUN-DA RI-HO-AN. The seal is referred to upon the next page.

No. 581.

This seal is stamped in red upon the *makimono* No. 579. Jo-ZE. *Like this*—. The commencement of a well-known phrase in a Buddhist book.

No. 582.

The seal of Funda Riho, stamped in red in the *makimono* referred to above. FUN-DA RI-HO. SHU-SHI. The term *Shushi* is applied to one who indulges in *sake*, with the view of inducing a dreamy state of thought.

No. 583.

From the *makimono* referred to on the previous page; the inscription painted in black, the seals stamped in red. To-SEN, Ho-GAN, YEGAKU. *Painted by Tosen, Hogan;* the latter being his title. The upper seal reads KA-NO, *Kano* being the family name of the painter; and the lower one reads KAN-RAKU-SAI, *Kanrakusai*, his professional name.

No. 584.

Stamped in red upon the same *makimono*. AN-SEI OTSU-BO SHI-JIU-KU O HICHI-SHO, KO-JI. *Hichi-sho, Koji, an old man of forty-nine, in the Zodiac year of the Hare, of the period of Ansei,* 1854 to 1860 A.D. Hichi-sho, who died about 1858, was the greatest master, in modern times, of the art of writing; the title of Koji is one which is assumed by scholars.

No. 585.

The inscription painted in black, and the seal stamped in red, in an *oribon* containing a series of paintings in lacquer. This style was invented by Zeshin Shibata, a celebrated artist of the present day; his works are highly esteemed in Japan. ZE-SHIN. The seal is his mark.

No. 586.

Painted in black on a paper label upon a *makimono* containing illustrations of the greatest beauty, executed in the Tosa and Kano styles, and an account of the Chinese fairy tale Kosuiden, written in Chinese and *Hira-kana* characters. KO-SU-I-DEN, the title of the work. The date is probably the first half of the 17th century.

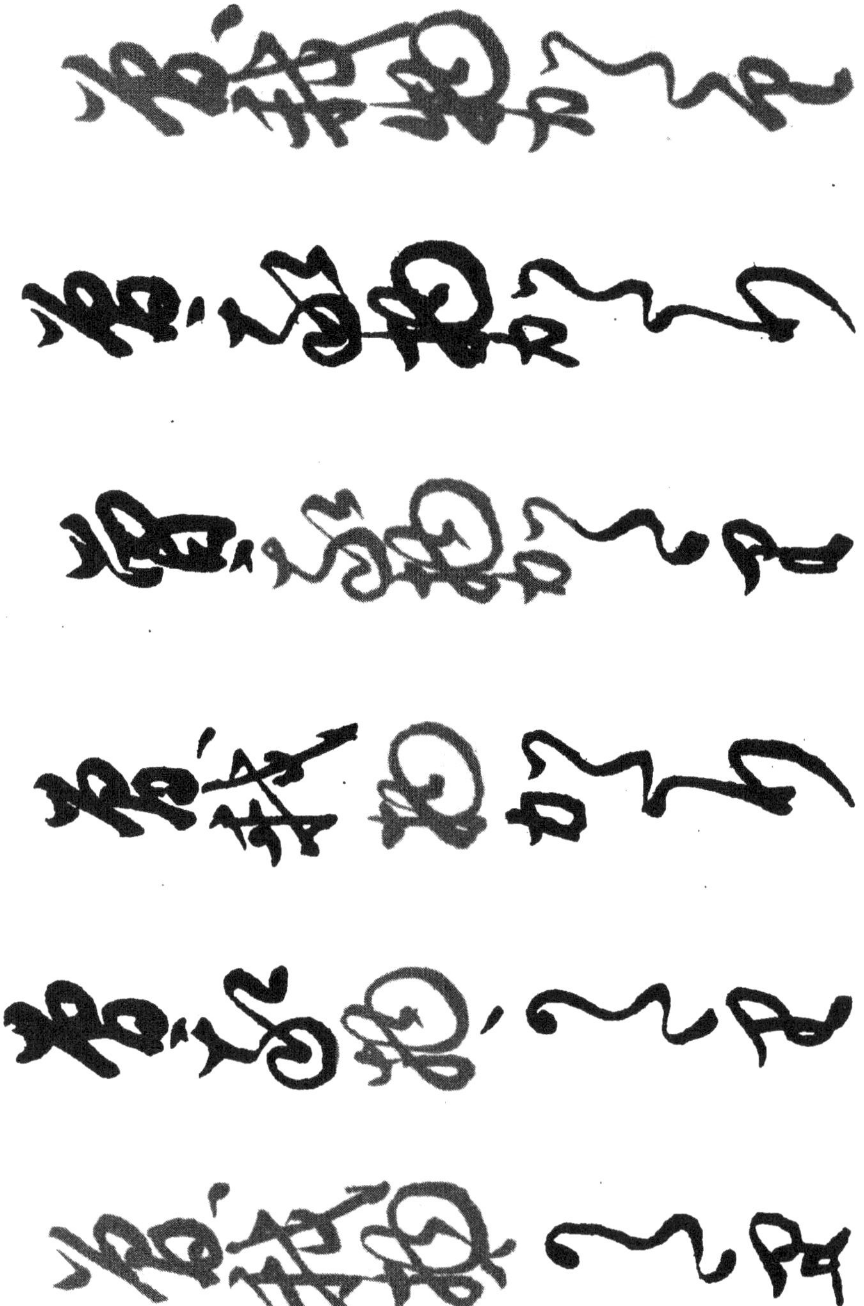

No. 593.

Painted in black on a green paper label, decorated with gold, upon a *shomotsu*, the last volume of a set of twelve. The work illustrates the historical tale of the Soga family, and comprises 128 pages of illuminated paintings, accompanied by manuscripts relating the complete story of the sons of Soga, one of Yoritomo's generals, who was murdered by another general; they were infants at the time of the murder of their father, and were trained to avenge his death, and on reaching manhood fulfilled their mission. The paintings are executed in the highest style of the Tosa school, and the date of the work is probably the middle of the 17th century. The inscriptions on the opposite page are copied from different volumes, and have all precisely the same meaning: SO-GA MONO-GA-TA-RI. *The tales of the Soga family.* The above mark is copied from the last volume, and reads : SOGA MONOGATARI. MAKI NO DAI JUNI. OWARI. *The tales of the Soga family. Volume Number 12. Last volume.*

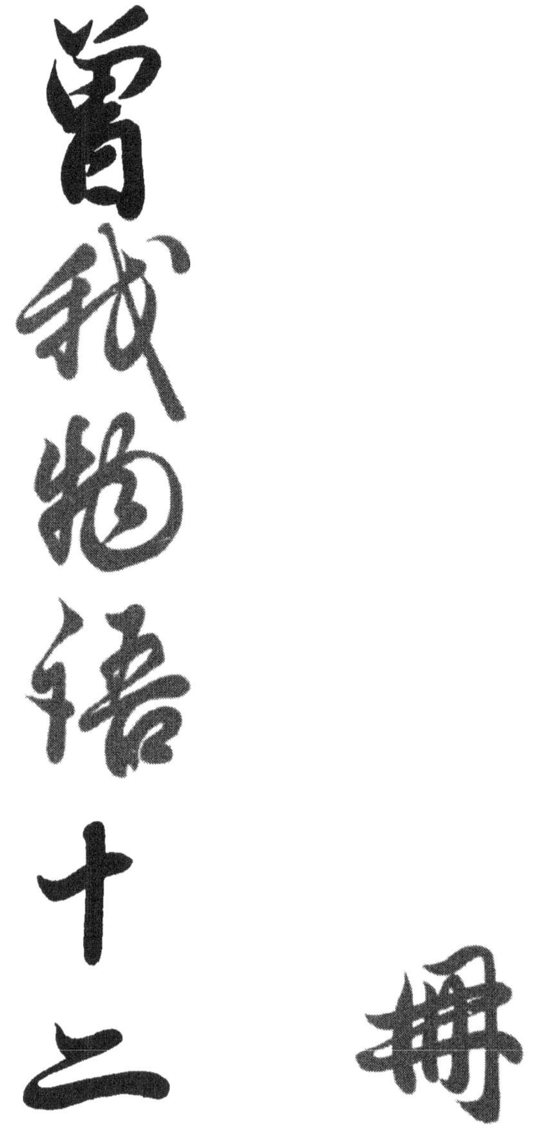

No. 594.

Painted in gold upon the lacquered case containing the tales of the Soga family. SO-GA MONO-GATARI; JU-NI SATSU. *Soga monogatari; twelve volumes.*

No. 505.

From a *kakimono* of silk upon which a representation of Buddha is painted in colours and gold. The inscription is written in black, the seal stamped in red. ON E-DOKORO. KAN-DA SO-TEI, FUJI-WARA MOCHI-NOBU TSUTSUSHINDE YEGAKU. *Respectfully painted by Mochinobu Fujiwara, a disciple of the school of Kanda. On Edokoro;* the name of the official department of painting. The right-hand characters in the seal are FUJI-WARA, and those to the left are MOCHI-NOBU.

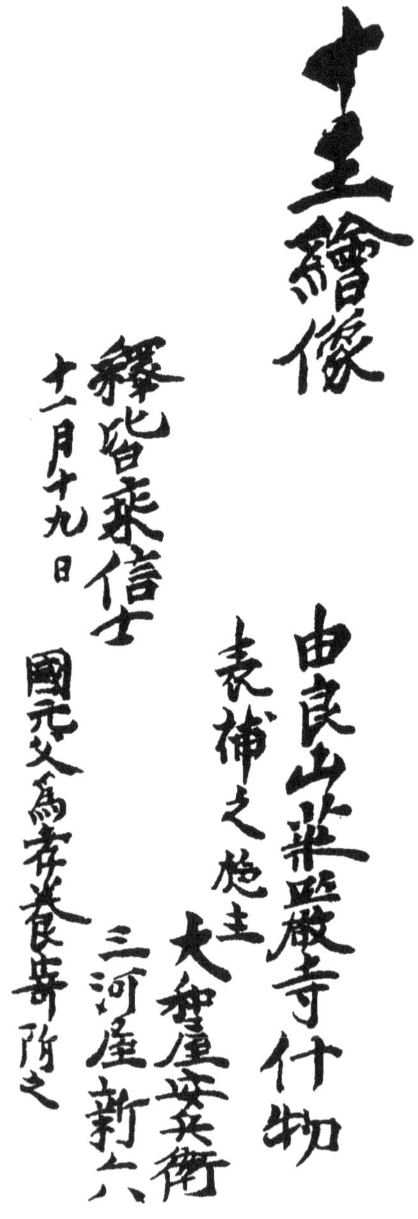

No. 596.

No. 596.

The inscription given on the opposite page is a copy, on a reduced scale, from one written in black upon the back of an ancient *kakimono*, one of a set of eight in the Bowes Collection illustrating the Buddhist Inferno, a full description of which appears in *Keramic Art of Japan.*

Commencing with the upper character of the right-hand column, and taking the inscription throughout in this manner, it reads as follows:—

JIU-O YE-ZO.
YU-RA-SAN, SO-GEN-JI JIU-MOTSU.
HIO-HO NO SHI-SHU,
YAMATOYA YASUBIOYE,
MIKAWAYA SHINROKU,
SHAKU KAI-JO SHIN-SHI.
JIU ICHI GATSU JIU KUN-CHI.
KUNI-MOTO, CHICHI TAME KO-YO KI-FUSU KORE O.

The portrait of Jiuo—the property of the temple of Sogenji Yurasan.

This is mounted and given by Yamatoya Yasubioye and Mikawaya Shinroku as a mark of filial duty to their father (who is now dead, and to whom the posthumous name Shaku Kaijo Shinshi is given), in their native land.

The 19th day of the 11th month.

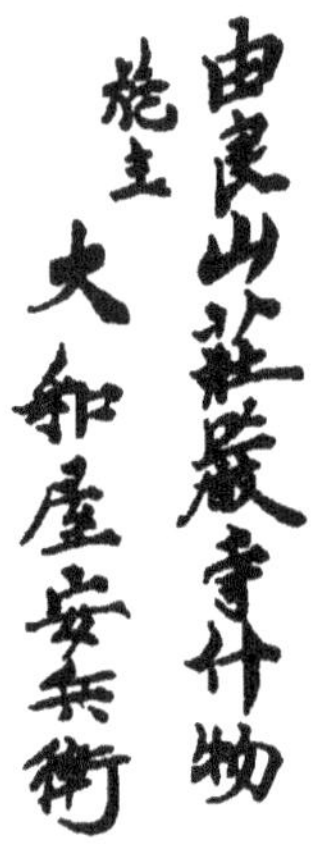

No. 597.

From another *kakimono* of the set mentioned on the previous page. YU-RA-SAN, SO-GEN-JI JIU-MOTSU. SHI-SHU YAMATOYA YASUBIOYE. *The property of* the temple of *Sogenji, Yurasan; given by Yamatoya Yasubioye.*

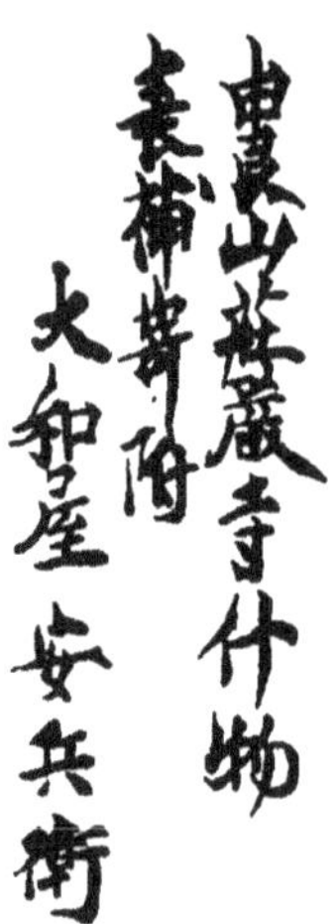

No. 598.

From another of the set of *kakimono* named above. YU-RA-SAN, SO-GEN-JI JIU-MOTSU. HIO-HO KI-FUSU YAMATOYA YASUBIOYE. *The property of* the temple of *Sogenji, Yurasan. Mounted and given by Yamatoya Yasubioye.*

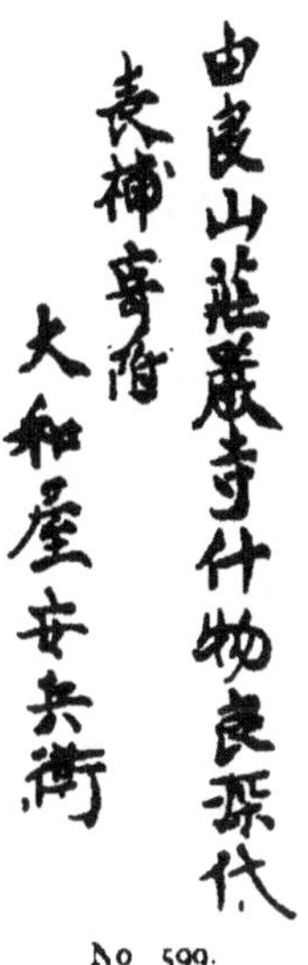

No 599.

From another *kakimono* of the set already referred to. YU-RA-SAN SO-GEN-JI JIU-MOTSU. RIO-SHIN DAI, HIO-HO KI-FUSU YAMATOYA YASUBIOYE. *The property of* the temple of *Sogenji, Yurasan. Mounted and given by Yamatoya Yasubioye* when *Rioshin* was the chief priest.

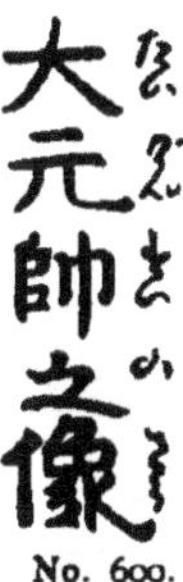

No. 600.

From a block-printed *yebon* of Hokusai's sketches. TAI-GEN-SUI NO ZO. *Portrait of the Field Marshal.* The characters to the right give the inscription in *Hira-kana* letters for the benefit of the illiterate Japanese who do not understand the Chinese language.

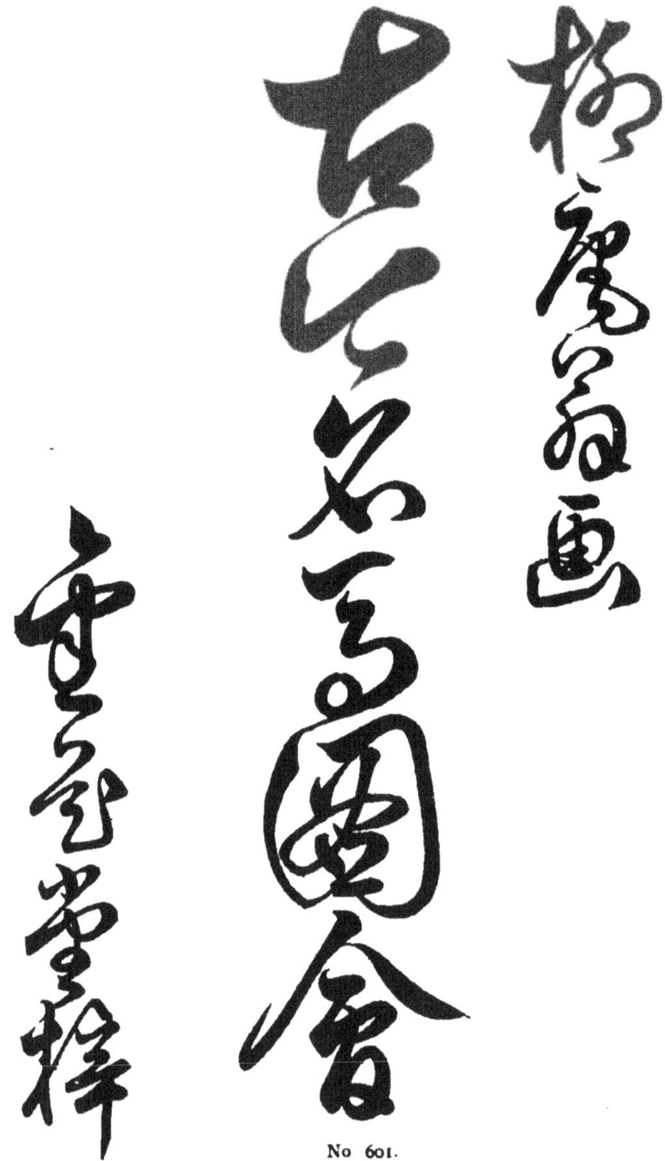

No 601.

From a modern block-printed *yebon*. RIU-AN O YEGAKU. KO KON MEI BA DZUYE. KINKWADO SHINSU. *The pictures of ancient and modern fine horses. Painted by the old man Riuan. Published by Kinkwado.*

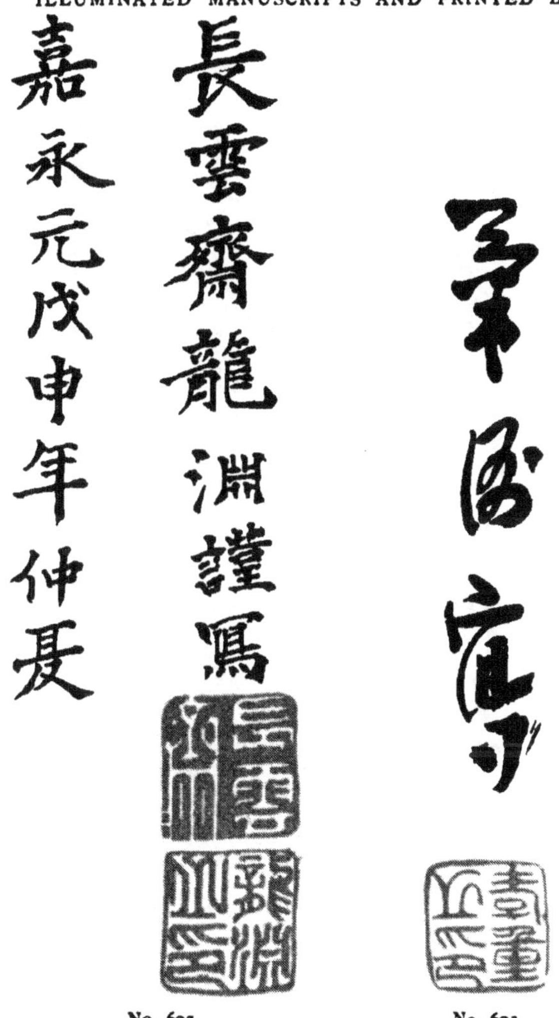

No. 602. No. 603.

Painted upon *kakimono;* the inscriptions in black, the seals in red. No. 602. CHIO-UN-SAI RIO-YEN TSUTSUSHINDE UTSUSU. KA-YEI GAN BO-SHIN TOSHI CHIU-KA. *Respectfully copied by Rioyen Chiounsai in the midsummer of the Zodiac year of the Monkey, in the first year of the period of Kayei,* 1848 A.D. The upper seal reads: CHIOUNSAI; the lower one: NO IN RIOYEN. *The seal of Rioyen.* No. 603. KIKU-SHIU UTSUSU. *Copied by Kikushiu.* The seal reads: NO IN SHI-JIU. *The seal of Shijiu.*

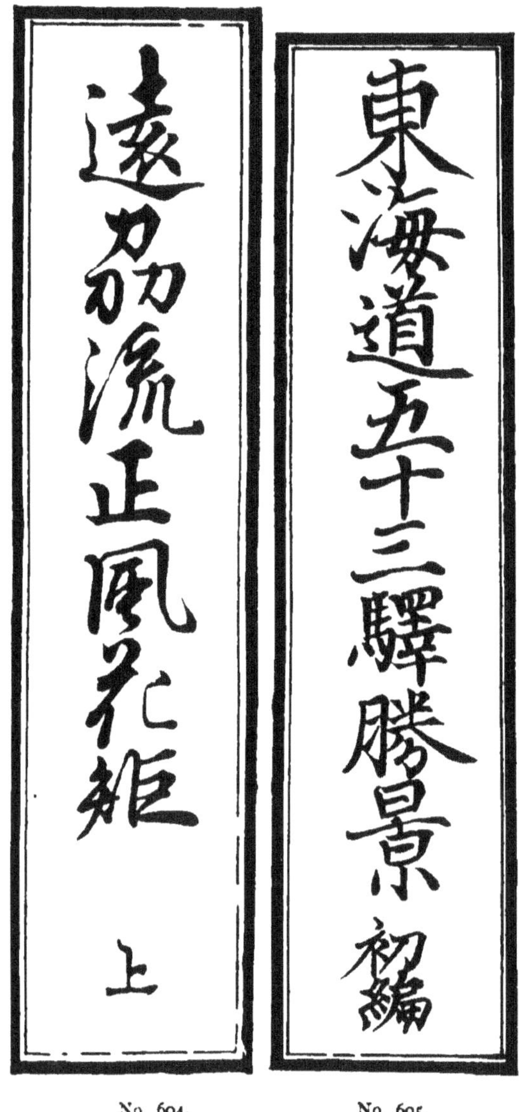

遠州流正風花矩 上
東海道五十三驛勝景 初編

No. 604. No. 605.

Printed in black upon modern block-printed *yebon*. No. 604. YEN-SHIU RIU SEI-FU KWAKI. JO. *The rules for arranging flowers in the true style of the Yenshiu school. Volume first.* No. 605. TO-KAI-DO GO-JIU-SAN YEKI SHO-KEI. SHO-HEN. *The beautiful views of the fifty-three stations of the Tokaido. The first part.*

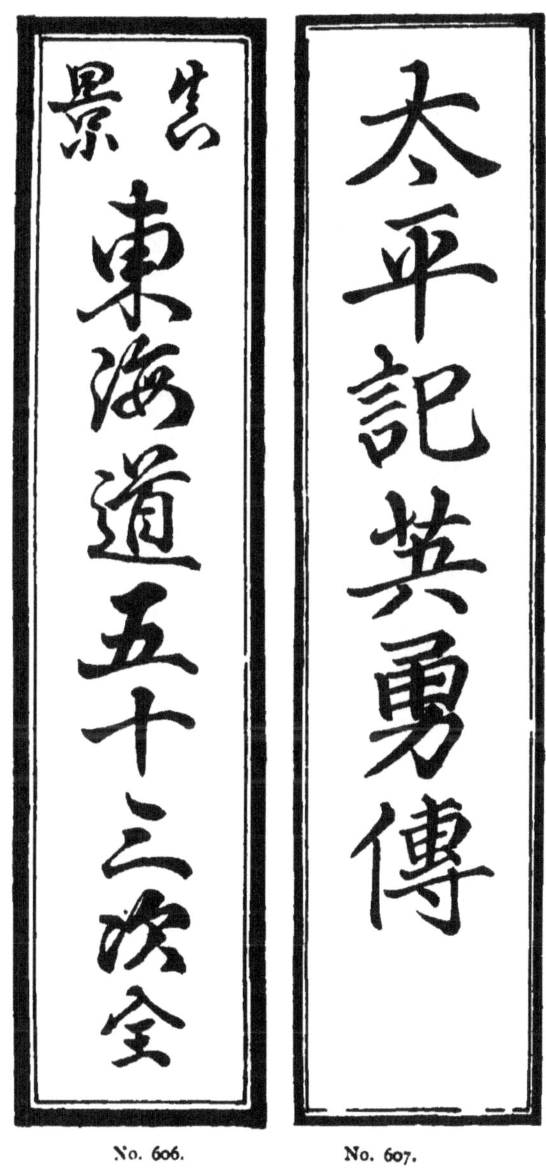

No. 606. No. 607.

Printed in black upon modern block-printed *yebon*. No. 606. SHIN-KEI TO-KAI-DO GO-JIU-SAN TSUGI. ZEN. *The faithful views of the fifty-three stations of the Tokaido. Single volume.* No. 607. TAI-HEI-KI. YEI-YU DEN. *The record of the Great Peace. The lives of wise and brave men.*

No. 608. No. 609.

Printed in black upon modern block-printed *yehon*. No. 608. TO-KAI-DO GO-JIU-SAN YEKI. HON-ZAN DZUYE. JO. *Fifty-three stations of the Tokaido. The paintings by Honzan. The first volume.* No. 609. BAN-BUTSU DZUYE. I-SAI GA SHIKI. SHO-CHITSU. ZEN. *Pictures and descriptions of ten thousand objects. Isai's rules of painting. First portfolio. Single volume.*

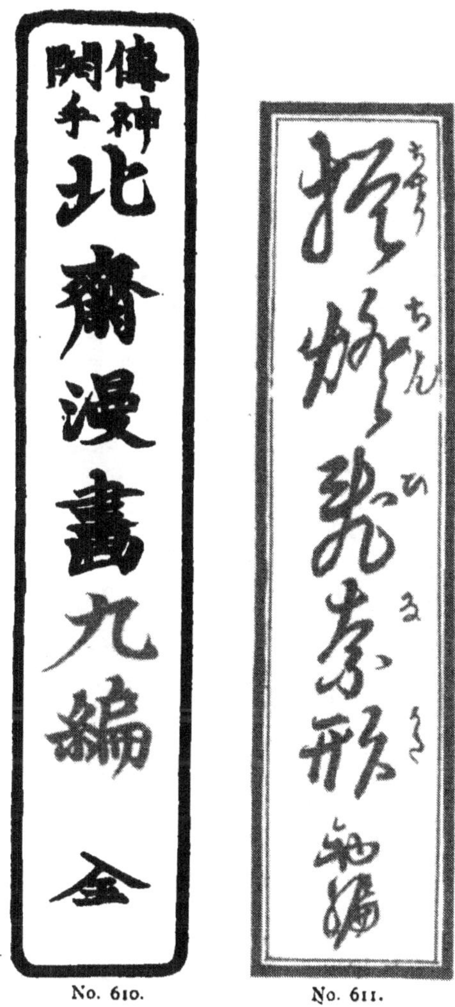

No. 610. No. 611.

Printed in black upon block-printed *yebon*. No. 610. DEN-SHIN KAI-SHU. HOKU-SAI MAN-GA. KU-HEN. ZEN. *Rough sketches by Hokusai. Ninth part. Single volume.* The upper characters, *Denshin kaishu*, meaning *Facile hand by Divine inspiration*, are added by the publisher, in admiration of the genius of Hokusai. No. 611. CHIO-CHIN HI-NA-GATA. SHO-HEN. *Designs for lanterns. First part.* The small characters give the inscription in *Hira-kana* letters for the benefit of those unacquainted with the Chinese language.

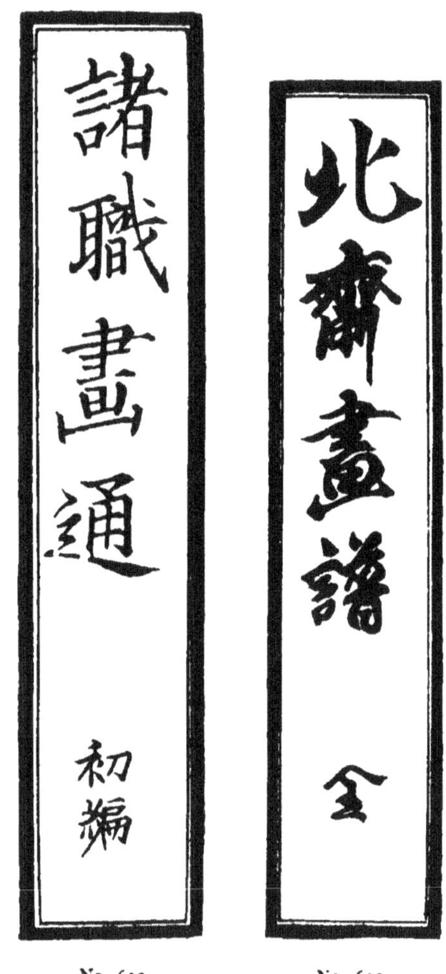

No. 612. No. 613.

Printed in black upon block-printed *yebon*. No. 612. SHO-SHOKU GA-TSU-U. SHO-HEN. *Pictures representing various professions. First part.* No. 613. HOKU-SAI GAFU. ZEN. *The picture-book of Hokusai. Single volume.*

No. 614.

No. 615.

Printed in black, No. 614 upon a type-printed *shomotsu*, No. 615 upon a block-printed *yebon*. No. 614. BUN-GEI RUI-SAN, JI-SHI. JO. SAKAKI-BARA YOSHI-NO, HENSU. MAKI ICHI. *The epitome of Literary Arts. The first volume of the history of characters. Collected by Sakakibara Yoshino. Volume 1st.* No. 615. BAN-SHO SHA-SHIN DZUFU. NI-HEN. ZEN. *The faithful pictures of various objects. Second part. Single volume.*

No. 617. No. 618.

No. 619. No. 616. No. 620.

Printed in black on modern block-printed *yebon*. No. 616. DAI NIP-PON MEI-SHO ICHI-RAN. *A synopsis of the famous places in Great Japan.* No. 617 is a description of one of Hokusai's sketches. OSA-KO-BE SU-GARU TOYO-RA NO SATO NI RAI O TORO. *Osakobe no Sugaru captures the thunder in the village of Toyora.* No. 618 is also descriptive of a sketch by Hokusai. O-RAN-DA JIN YORU TEN-MON O KANGAYERU DZU. *The picture of a Dutchman studying astronomy in the night-time.* The small characters are *Hira-kana*. Nos. 619 and 620 are also from a book illustrated by Hokusai; the first is MAN-GA. *Rough sketches;* the second is KU-HEN. *Ninth part.*

PART III.

LACQUER, ENAMELS, METAL, WOOD, IVORY, &c.

LACQUER, ENAMELS, METAL, WOOD, IVORY, &c.

ONE of the most characteristic, and probably the most ancient and extensive, of the Art industries of Japan, is that of Lacquer working. For more than a thousand years the sap drawn from the *Rhus vernicifera*, a tree which is cultivated in nearly every part of the country, has been in general use for purposes of utility or ornament. The varnish made from it was used in the embellishment of the tombs of the Mikados of ancient days, of the palaces of the princes, their armour, and in the decoration of almost every article of furniture and every object which entered into the daily use of rich and poor alike.

As early as the fourth century a Government department was established for the encouragement of the art, which, however, does not appear to have made much progress until the seventh century, when it was generally applied to the purposes which have been named.

The leading kinds of lacquer are—the *Hira-makiye*, or flat gold; the *Togi-dashi*, or black and gold; the *Taki-makiye*, or raised gold; the *Nashiji*, or lacquer sprinkled with gold, in imitation of the skin of a pear, which is known in Europe as aventurine from its resemblance to the Venetian glass so called; the *Ro-iro*, or pure black; and the *Shu-nuri*, or pure red lacquer.

Five examples of ancient work, said to have been made between the sixth and the thirteenth centuries, are preserved in the temples and museums of Japan, and native records give the names of successive noted artists who have lived from the twelfth century to the present day; but the choice works which are now so highly prized date only from the seventeenth century, when the age of luxury and refinement which has since continued, commenced, and the exquisite examples of flat and raised gold lacquer were produced by artists who worked under the patronage of the feudal nobles. These rare specimens do not bear the signatures of the makers, for it was not the custom to sign, or indeed mark in any way whatever, such objects of art. when they were produced for the special use of the patron prince of the artist. The list of marks given in this volume is, therefore, a meagre one, and contains no inscription of an earlier date than the period of Anyei, 1772 to 1781 A.D. This appears upon a luncheon-box, in red and gold lacquer of exquisite quality, in the Bowes Collection; but not a single example of the older work in *hira* or *taki-makiye* in this, or indeed in any other collection so far as the author is aware, is marked, and the remainder of the inscriptions are copied from specimens of comparatively recent manufacture, and none of them present any points of interest which call for special remark.

Perhaps even more remarkable than the beautiful lacquer wares are the ancient works of *cloisonné* enamelling upon copper. Singularly little is known of the origin of this art, of its development, or of the use to which the examples were put. It is indeed stated that the process was introduced from China towards the end of the sixteenth century, and this is confirmed by the colouring of what are supposed to be the earlier efforts of the Japanese artists, which, in this respect, bear a strong resemblance to the Chinese enamels of the fifteenth and sixteenth centuries, whilst still showing evidence of the greater delicacy of manipulation, beauty and grace of design, and refinement of colouring characteristic of the nobler works of a later period, which appear to have been unknown to Japanese writers, whose remarks refer only to the work upon porcelain, and the coarse imitations upon copper, which have been extensively produced during the past ten years.

The ancient works are very seldom marked, indeed two examples only have come under our notice upon which the names of the makers appear, and four others upon which there are inscriptions of a different nature, none of which afford any information as to the date of the ware. It does not come within the scope of this brief notice of the art to speculate upon the uses to which these productions may have been put, but the presence of the imperial insignia upon many of the choicest pieces, and the character of the designs and ornamentation of most of them, confirm the opinion which has been expressed by the ablest Japanese authorities, that they were made for the use of the Mikados, or formed part of the treasures of the chief temples, which were presided over by members of the imperial family; and this supposition receives support from the fact that nearly all the finest examples were sent to this country shortly after the revolution in 1868, when many of the temples were dismantled.

The efforts of the Japanese workers in bronze, iron, and other Metals, whether of the present day, or of ancient times, are of great beauty and of endless variety. The art appears to have originated in the eighth century, when colossal figures of Buddha, and bells of great size and rare workmanship, are said to have been cast, and erected in the gardens surrounding the temples. But these ancient works have disappeared, having been destroyed by the earthquakes, which have always been of frequent occurrence in Japan, or during the civil wars which raged in that country during the earlier years of its history.

The oldest example of bronze casting now existing in Japan is probably that of the gigantic statue of Buddha, which stands at Kama Koura, where it was erected in the thirteenth century. Temple bells of great antiquity may also still be found in Japan, notwithstanding the immense number which were shipped to this country during the revolutionary period, to meet with no better fate than to be melted down as old metal. Few of these ancient works bear the marks of the founders, nor do the makers of the exquisite modern bronze flower-vases, and other objects, follow the example of the potters of their country, in signing or otherwise marking their productions.

It was different with the workers in iron, who engraved their names upon the sword-blades and sword-guards which were made for the warriors of Old Japan, and it was a general custom, also, with the manufacturers of the mirrors, which are so common in that country for personal use or for presentation to the temples, to cast their names upon the objects they made.

The list of marks and seals concludes with those found upon Wood and Ivory carvings, which, almost alone amongst the branches of Japanese art, appear to have withstood the blighting effect of European influence, and in which works are still produced equalling, if not surpassing, in beauty of workmanship and in artistic merit, the best efforts of former days.

The characters used by workers in metal and wood differ in many respects from those employed by potters. *Saku* is commonly used in place of *Zo*, to express the words *made by* or *the make of*; both words have precisely the same meaning, and are read as *tsukuru* when found in combination with the names of makers.

Iron Sword Guard.

TSUKURU (ZO).

Made by or *the make of.*

Bronze Mirror. *Bronze Dragon.* *Wood Carving.*

TSUKURU (SAKU).

Made by or *the make of.*

Another word, having the same meaning, is frequently found upon ancient iron sword-guards, from which the following examples are taken:

SEISU.

Made by.

Occasionally the characters *Kore o tsukuru* appear upon metal and wood, as shown below, but the seal-form, as illustrated in the second example, is very seldom used.

Bronze. KORE O TSUKURU. *Makes this.*

Wood. KORE O TSUKURU. *Makes this.*

When a workman is about to cast an important bronze, he appears to select a lucky day for the operation, and, when the object is finished, he engraves upon it the words signifying this, together with the month and the year in which it occurred.

KICHI NICHI. *Lucky Day.*

KICHI SHO NICHI. *Day of Lucky Omen.*

[illegible]

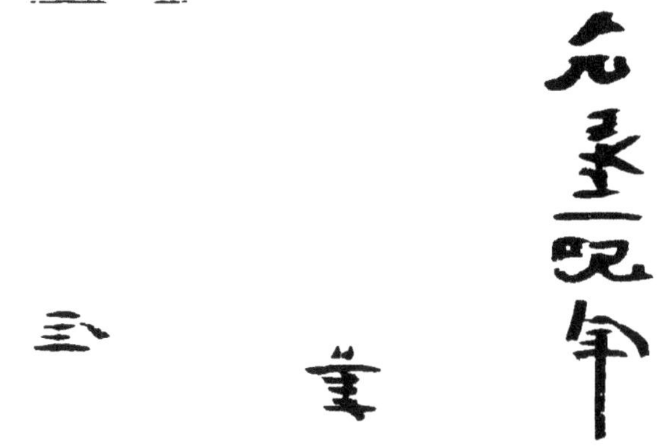

[illegible]

[illegible] not uncommon amongst [illegible] one amongst the makers [illegible] been that of *N[illegible]*, which [illegible] shaven his head after the fashion [illegible]

It was very customary for the makers of mirrors in olden times to assume the family name of one of the distinguished families of the nobility of Japan, which they used in conjunction with their own name in the inscriptions which are generally cast upon mirrors. The two upper characters in the example given below are Fujiwara, and the two lower ones are Mitsushige, the former being the assumed, and the latter the real, name of the maker.

The conceit of mirror makers carried them even further than this, for the characters *Tenka ichi*, meaning the first man in the world, frequently form part of their inscriptions, and carvers in wood occasionally use the same expression.

Mirror. *Wood Carving.* *Mirror.*

TENKA ICHI.

The first man in the world.

Mirror.

TENKA ICHI NO SAKU.

The manufacture of the first man in the world

The character *On*, a word signifying respect or honour, is applied in various ways; an artist may use it as a prefix to show that he is in the service of a prince, or when an object is intended for presentation to a noble, or for use in a temple, the word is coupled with its name. Its use is not determined by any fixed rules, but the examples given below will serve to indicate the manner in which it is sometimes applied. The upper character in each case is the word *On*, and in the first instance it is used upon a wooden case containing a valuable tea-jar of ancient Bizen stoneware, which was probably the prized possession of some daimio; the second is engraved upon a noble casting of a dragon, dating from the period of Genroku; and the third forms part of the inscription engraved upon an incense burner, dedicated to some honourable purpose by the ruler of the province of Bishiu.

ONCHAIRE. *On Tea-case.* — ONDAIKUSHI. *Artist to the Prince.* — ONKORO. *On Incense Burner.*

The words *Jiu*, or *Jiunin*, meaning a resident, or resident in, are frequently found upon metal work, especially upon sword-guards, in connection with the names of the town and province in which the maker resided.

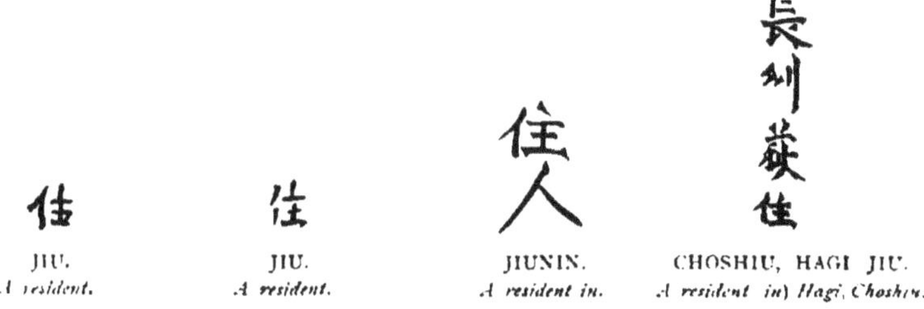

JIU. *A resident.* — JIU. *A resident.* — JIUNIN. *A resident in.* — CHOSHIU, HAGI JIU. *A resident in) Hagi, Choshiu.*

In concluding this analysis of the marks given in the following pages, it is only necessary to draw attention to the characters shown below.

LACQUER WARE.

No. 621.

Painted in gold, upon a white metal label, on a Luncheon Case of *shu-nuri* lacquer decorated with gold. AN-YEI, NEN SEI. *The manufacture of the period of Anyei*, 1772 to 1781 A.D.

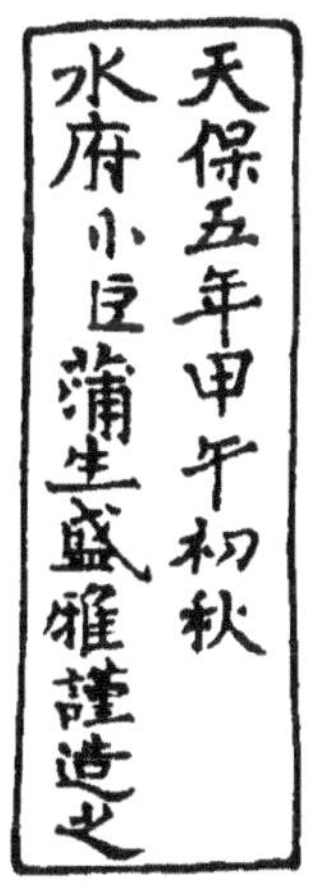

No. 622.

Engraved upon a Table of carved lacquer. TEM-PO, GO-NEN, KO-GO, SHO-SHIU, SUI-FU, SHO-SHIN, GAMO-O, MORI-TSUNE, TSUTSUSHINDE TSUKURU KORE O. *Moritsune Gamo-o, a humble subject of Suifu, respectfully made this in the first autumn [or seventh month] of the fifth year, the Zodiac year of the Horse, of the period of Tempo*, 1834 A.D. Suifu is another name for the province of Mito.

No. 623.

Painted in gold upon a Paper Box of rustic wood-work decorated with gold lacquer. FU-SO, MI. KOKU JIU. These are the right-hand characters: they mean, *Resident of the province of Mimasaka*, the character *Mi* being an abbreviation of the name of this province. *Fuso* is one of the names by which Japan is known. The three characters on the left cannot be literally rendered into English, but they mean that the maker was a native of Kazusa, and that his professional name was Usuke. The seal is that of YOSHIKAWA, the maker.

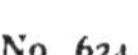

No. 624.

No. 625.

Painted in black, the lower character stamped in red, upon slate-coloured lacquer; No. 624, upon a Writing Table, and No. 625 upon a Writing Case. HARU-MASA SEI-HO. *Harumasa Seiho*, the name of the maker.

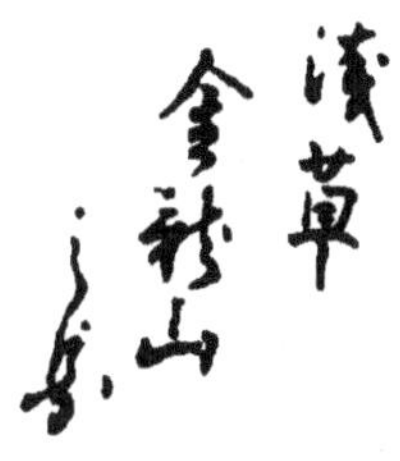

No. 626.

Painted in gold upon a Writing Case of choice carved lacquer. ASA-KUSA, KIN-RIU-ZAN NO DZU. *View of* the temple of *Kinriuzan*, in the garden of *Asakusa*, the scene with which the case is decorated.

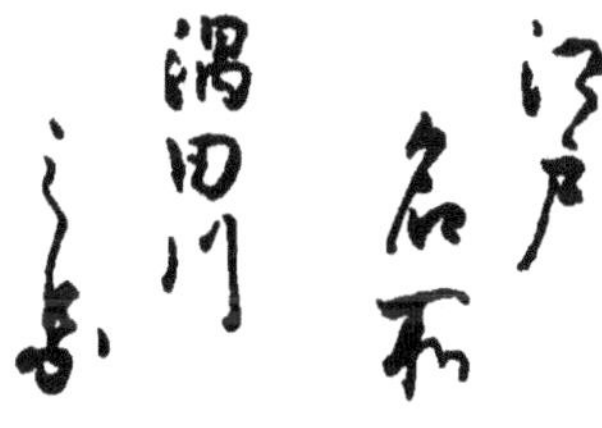

No. 627.

Painted in gold upon the Writing Case referred to above. YE-DO MEI-SHO; SUMI-TA-GAWA NO DZU. *The famous place of Yedo; the view of Sumitagawa;* a representation which appears upon the specimen.

No. 628.

Painted in gold upon a panel of pearl on an ancient wooden Medicine Box decorated with lacquer. YAMA-KAWA. *Yamakawa*, the name of the maker.

No. 629

Engraved upon a Box of *shu-nuri* lacquer. DAI MING KA-SEI NEN SEI. *Made in the year of Kasei, during the dynasty of Dai Ming*, 1522 to 1566 A.D. A forgery of the Chinese mark of the Kia-tsing period.

No 630.

Painted in gold upon a *sake* Cup of *shu-nuri* lacquer. SEI-KUA-SAI. *Seikuasai*, the name of the maker.

No. 631.

Painted in gold upon a *sake* Cup of *shu-nuri* lacquer. TO-SEN. *Tosen*, the name of the maker.

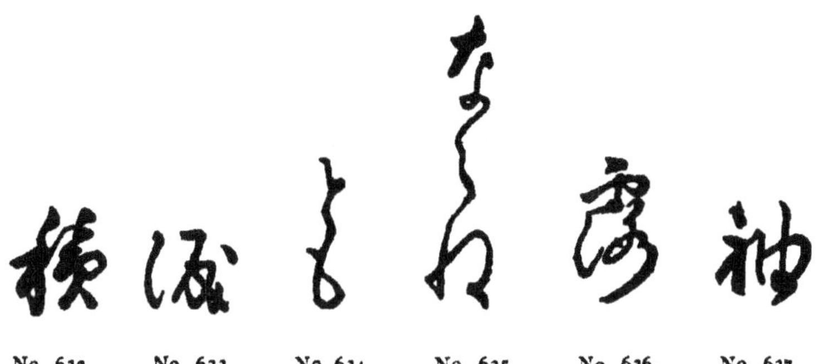

No. 632. No. 633. No. 634. No. 635. No. 636. No. 637.

The inscriptions given above are inlaid in gold and silver on a Writing Case of lacquer decorated with flowers of engraved gold and silver, in relief. No. 632. TSUMU. No. 633. NAMIDA. No. 634. TOMO. No. 635. NARANU. No. 636. TSUYU. No. 637. SODE. Probably these words are part of a Japanese ode, but the meaning is not clear.

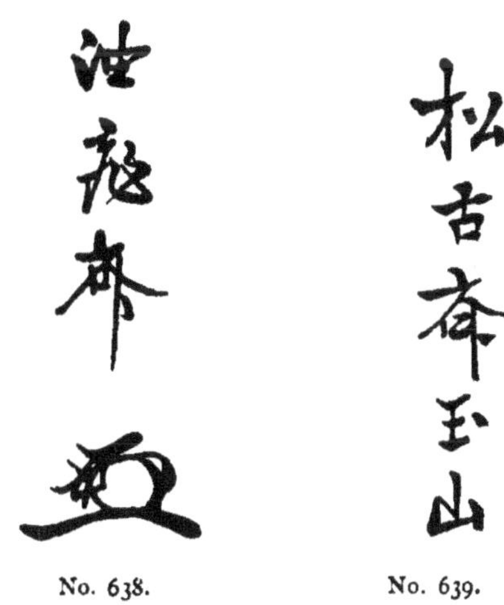

No. 638. No. 639.

Painted in gold upon modern lacquer; No. 638 upon a Tray; No. 639 upon a Plaque. The first inscription reads: YU-HI-SAI. *Yuhisai*, the name of the maker; the lower mark is his seal. The second reads: SHO-KO-SAI GIOKU-ZAN. *Shokosai Giokuzan*, the name of the maker.

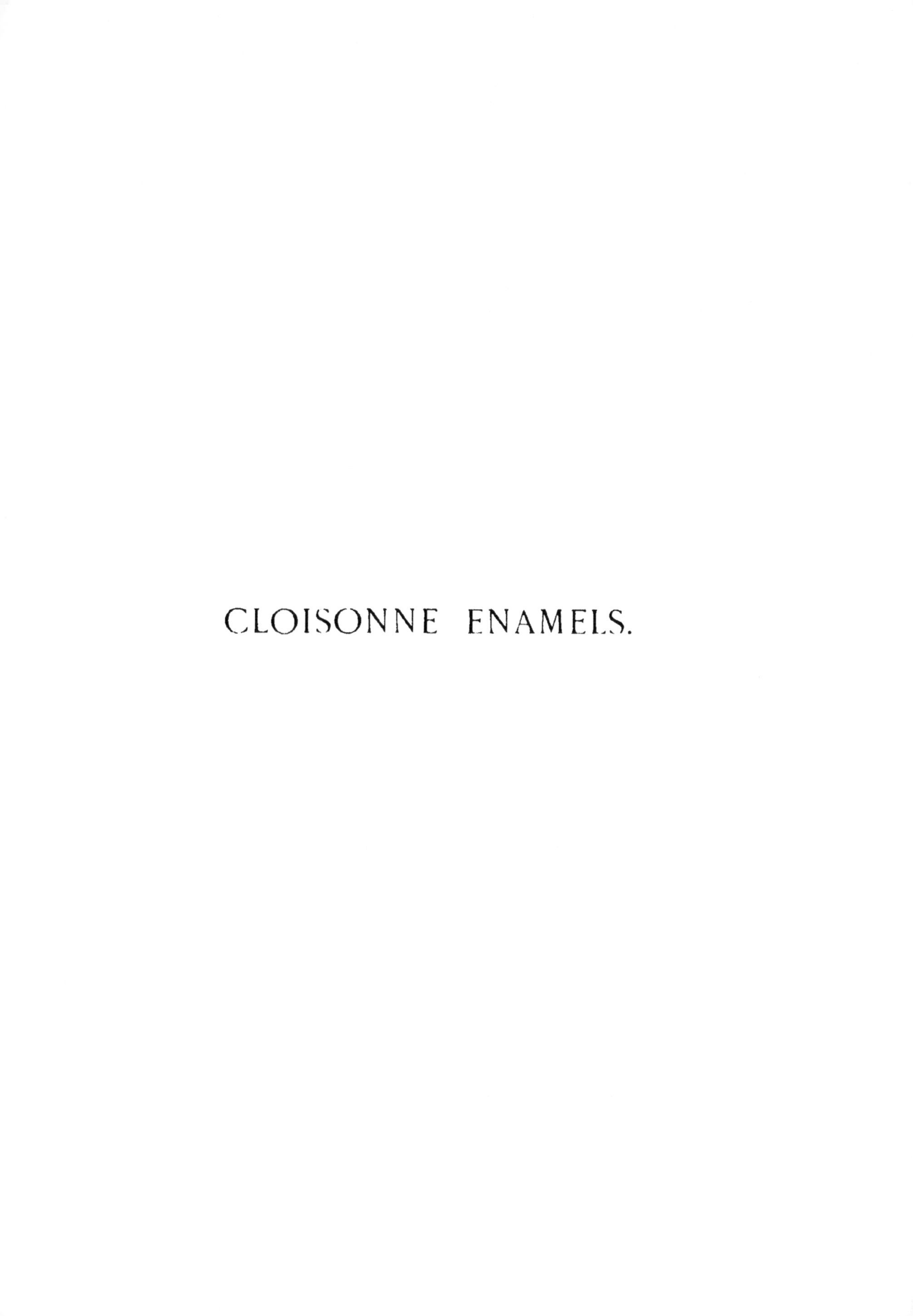

CLOISONNE ENAMELS.

No. 640.

Rendered in enamel, in relief, upon a Dish of old ware. The old style of the character MAN, meaning *Ten thousand*, *A myriad*, *All*, and so forth; this form of the mark is now obsolete in Japan. The character is common to many countries, and is known as the Swastika, amongst other names.

No. 641.

The mark given above is a copy of the top of a Table in the Bowes Collection, reduced in size, of middle period ware. It is rendered in *cloisonné* enamel, and forms part of the decoration of the work. The inscription to the left is GIOKU-SHO-DO. *Giokushodo* being the name of the maker. The other inscriptions are a medley of Dutch and Japanese, written in English, the meaning of which is not clear.

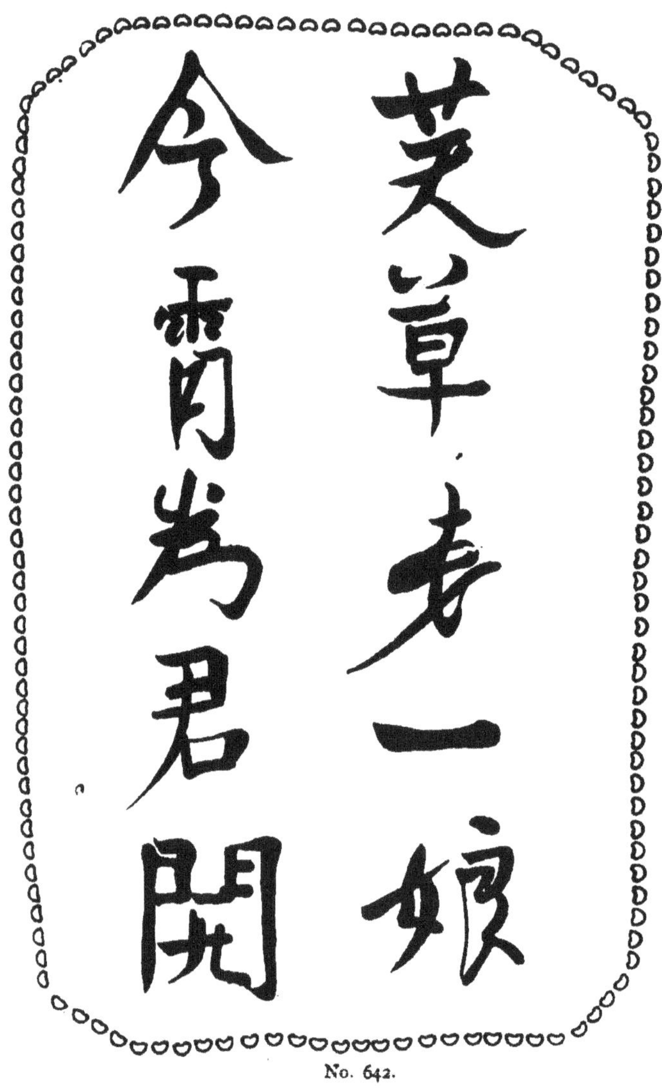

No. 642.

The inscription given above, and that upon the next page, are rendered in *cloisonné* enamel upon a pair of Vases, forming part of the decoration. No. 642. FU-SO DAI-ICHI MUSUME KON-SHO TAMENI KIMI HIRAKU. No. 643. HANA HOTTSU SHIRU SHIN-I SAN-KO FUMU TSUKI KITARE. The inscriptions, taken together, are a burlesque of a well-known Japanese poem which is said to have been composed by a

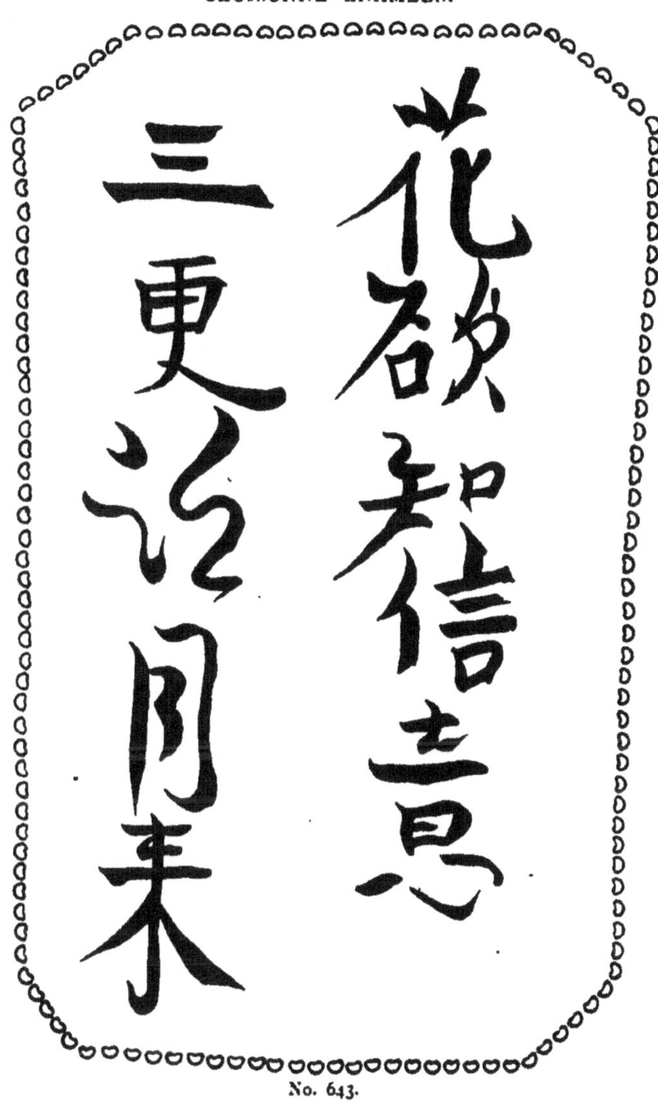

No. 643.

lady named Kamei Shokin as a reply to the solicitations of her lover:

> *'Tis the first plum in Japan,*
> *It will bloom to-night for your sake.*
> *If you wish to know the true will,*
> *Come at twelve o'clock when the moon is bright.*

No. 644.

Rendered in *cloisonné* enamel underneath a Bowl of old ware in the South Kensington Museum; the dark spaces are enamel, and the *cloisons* are shown by the white lines. JIU. *Longevity.*

No. 645.

Rendered in *cloisonné* enamel upon the back of a Dish of middle period ware in the Bowes Collection; the characters are worked in metal *cloisons* upon a panel of lilac enamel ground, which is surrounded by a border of red enamel. BI-SHIU, YASU-MATSU, CHIO-ZO. *Chiozo*, the name of the maker; *Yasumatsu*, the town where he resided; *Bishiu*, the name of the province in which it is situated, commonly known as Owari. The characters are Chinese, and are not of modern style.

METAL WORK.

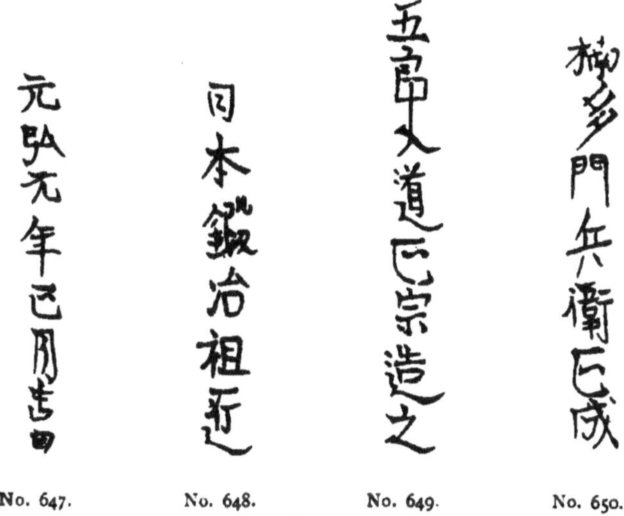

No. 647. No. 648. No. 649. No. 650.

Engraved upon a Sword in the possession of Frederick Holder, Esq., of Liverpool. No. 647. GEN-KO, GAN-NEN, SHO-GATSU, KICHI-NICHI. *The lucky day of the first month of the first year of the period of Genko*, 1331 A.D. No. 648. NIP-PON, KA-JI SO-SHO. *The master of smithing in Japan.* No. 649. GO-RO, NIU-DO, MASA-MUNE TSUKURU KORE O. *Goro, Niudo, Masamune, made this;* Niudo is a title assumed by a layman who shaves his head in imitation of the Buddhist priests. No. 650. KUSUNOKI TA-MON-HIO-YE MASA-SHIGE. *Kusunoki Tamonhioye Masashige.* The whole of the inscriptions may be read as follows: — *In the lucky day of the first month of the first year of the period Genko, Goro Niudo Masamune, the master of smithing in Japan, made this for Kusunoki Tamonhioye Masashige*, a great patriot, who lived in the period of Genko, and faithfully served his master, the emperor Godaigo, during that turbulent period.

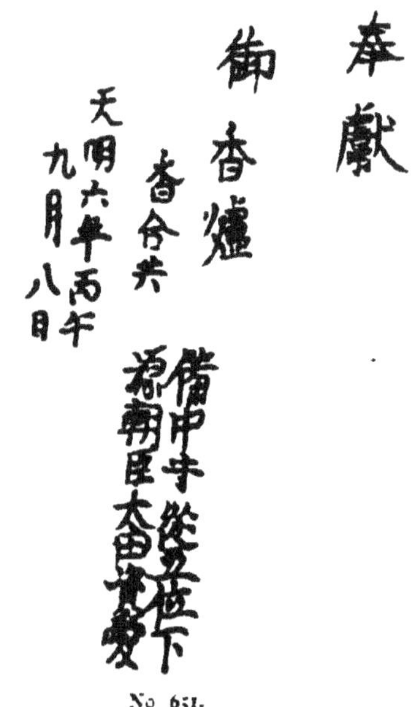

奉獻
御香爐
香合共
天明六年丙午
九月八日
備中守從五位下
源朝臣太田資敬

No 651.

Engraved upon a Koro of metal gilt, ornamented with repoussé work of the highest beauty. In the Bowes Collection. Commencing, as customary, with the characters to the right, the inscription reads as follows: — HO-KEN ON KO-RO KO-GO TOMO BI-SHIU KAMI JU-GO-I-GE MINAMOTO A-SON O-TA SUKE-HISA TEM-MEI ROKU-NEN HEI-GO KU-GATSU HACHI-CHI. *Hoken*, dedicated; *Onkoro*, an incense burner, the prefix *on* signifying that it was dedicated with respect; *Kogo*, an incense box; *tomo*, together with; *Bishiu kami*, a title, meaning the ruler of the province of Bishiu; *Jugoige*, a grade or order in rank; *Minamoto*, the name of the family from which the donor was descended; *Ason*, subject of the Court; *Ota Sukehisa*, the name of the donor; *Temmei*, the year-period: *Rokunen*, the sixth year; *Hei-go*, the Zodiac year of the Horse: *Kugatsu*, the ninth month; *Hachichi*, the eighth day. *An incense burner, together with an incense box, humbly dedicated by Bishiu no kami jugoige Minamoto no Ason Ota Sukehisa, on the 8th day of the 9th month of the 6th year, Hei go, of the period of Temmei,* 1786 A.D.

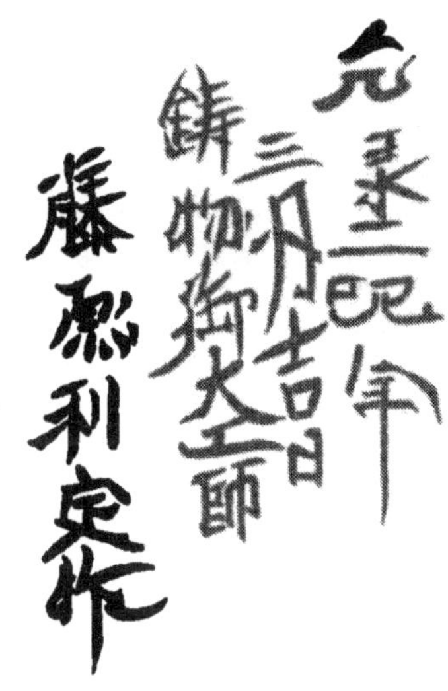

No. 652.

Engraved upon a bronze Dragon of important size; in the Bowes Collection. GEN-ROKU NI KI-SHI TOSHI SAN-GATSU KICHI-NICHI I-MONO ON-DAI-KU-SHI FUJI-WARA TOSHI-SADA TSUKURU (SAKU). *Made by Toshisada Fujiwara, artist to the prince; a casting on the lucky day of the third month of the Zodiac year of the Snake, the second year of the period of Genroku,* 1689 A.D. The prefix *On*, before daikushi (artist), may be taken as signifying that the artist was in the service of a prince.

No. 653. No. 654.

In relief upon a pair of bronze Mirrors, one of which bears the crest of the prince of Owadsima. No. 653. TEN-KA ICHI. *Tenka ichi. The first under the heaven*, or *in the world.* No. 654. TEN-KA ICHI SAKU. *Tenka ichi no saku*, meaning *The manufacture of the first man in the world.*

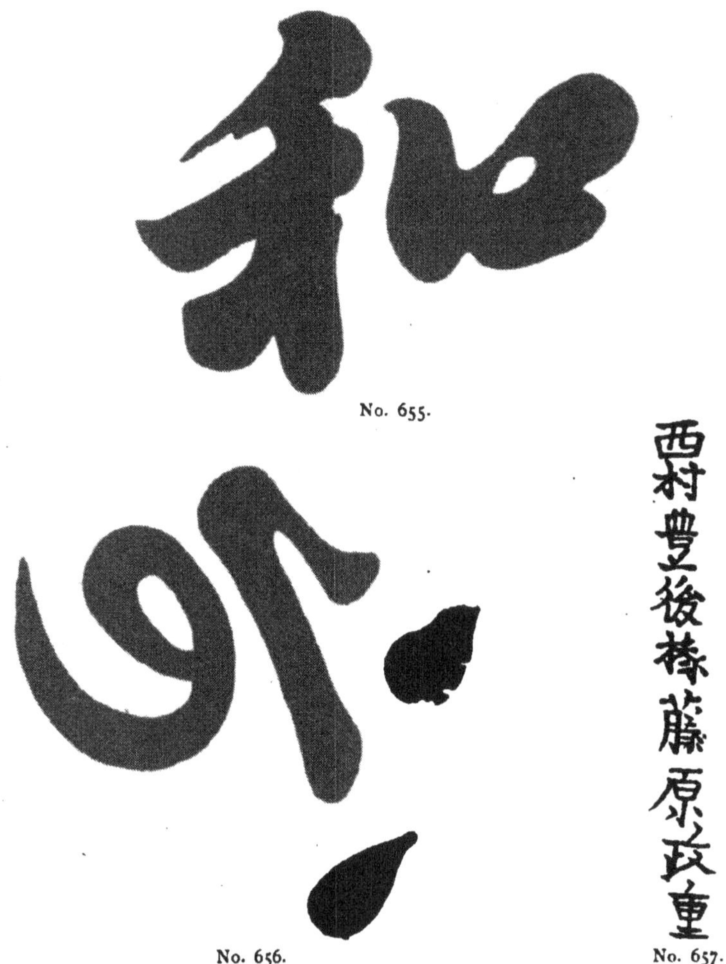

No. 655.

No. 656.

No. 657.

All the above marks appear upon a single Mirror; the larger ones are rendered in relief, in white metal, upon the bronze back of the mirror, and the inscription to the right is cast in relief in the bronze. No. 655. Wa. No. 656. Ka. *Wa-ka, Japanese Poem*, referring probably to the subject with which the mirror is decorated. No. 657. Nishi-mura, Bun-go-jo, Fuji-wara, Masa-shige. *Masashige Nishimura*, the name of the maker; the name of *Fujiwara* and the title of *Bungo no jo*, Governor of the province of Bungo, are both assumed.

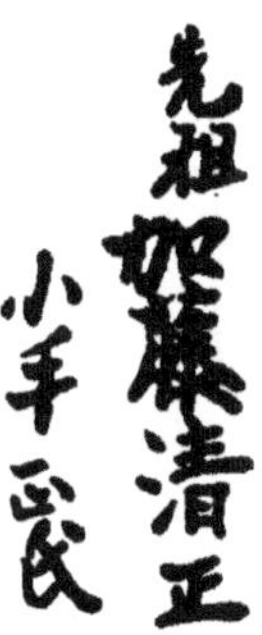

No. 658.

Painted in gold upon the under part of an ancient Tobacco-box of iron, damascened with silver. SEN-ZO KA-TO KIYO-MASA KO-HEI MASA-UZI. *Kato Kiyomasa, the ancestor of Kohei Masauzi.* Kiyomasa was a noted warrior, a favorite of Taico Sama, and the ancestor of the original possessor of the box.

No. 659.

Engraved upon an iron Sword-guard, beautifully decorated with flowers in relief. The upper group of characters on the left read: OTSUBANI KAYESU AKARIYA YUBOTAN, a Japanese ode. The three lower characters are illegible. The seal, which is of gold, is that of the maker, MATSUSHITA O.

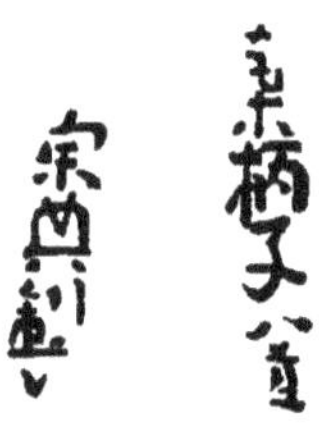

No. 660.

Engraved upon an ancient iron Sword-guard, which bears a representation of the well-known story of the men of Heike searching for Yoritomo, who was concealed in a tree; the figures and accessories are beautifully rendered in the engraved metal, which is inlaid with gold, silver, and copper. MO-GARA-SHI, NIUDO, SO-TENG SEISU. *Made by Soteng Mogarashi, Niudo.*

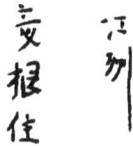

No. 661. No. 662.

Engraved upon an ancient Sword-guard, which bears a representation of the battle of Shizugadake. No. 661. KO-SHIU, HIKO-NE JIU. No. 662. MO-GARA-SHI, SO-TENG SEISU. *Made by Soteng Mogarashi, a resident of Hikone, in Koshiu,* the province of Omi.

No. 663.

Engraved upon a brass Sword-guard. NAGA-HARU. *Nagaharu,* the name of the maker.

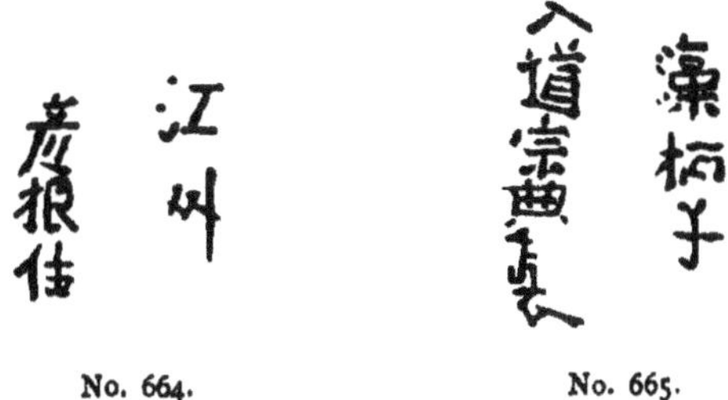

No. 664. No. 665.

Engraved upon an ancient Sword-guard, which bears a representation of the story of Benkei, the faithful servant of Yoshitsune, capturing Shojun, who was sent by Yoritomo to kill his master. No. 664. KO-SHIU, HIKO-NE JIU. No. 665. MO-GARA-SHI, NIU-DO, SO-TENG SEISU. *Made by Soteng Mogarashi, Niudo, a resident of Hikone, in Koshiu,* the province of Omi.

No. 666.

Engraved upon an ancient iron Sword-guard, enriched with the figures of three sages, executed in inlaid metals. JO-GETSU-SAI HIRO-YOSHI. *Jogetsusai Hiroyoshi,* the maker. The small mark at the foot is his seal.

No. 667.

Engraved upon an ancient iron Sword-guard. JU-ZAN TSUKURU (ZO). *Made by Juzan.*

No. 668.

Engraved upon a brass Sword-guard. HIRO-NOBU. *Hironobu*, the maker.

No. 669.

Engraved upon a copper Sword-guard, inlaid with gold and silver. HAMA-NO KI-ZUI. *Hamano Kizui*, the name of the maker.

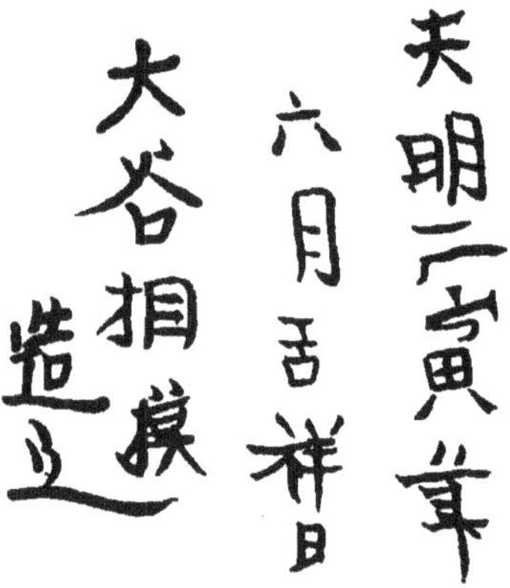

No. 670.

Engraved upon a bronze figure of Quanon. TEM-MEI NI TORA TOSHI ROKU-GATSU KICHI SHO NICHI O-YA SA-GAMI TSUKURU KORE O. *Oya Sagami made this on the day of lucky omen, in the sixth month of the Zodiac year of the Tiger, the second year of the period of Temmei*, 1782 A.D.

No. 671.

Engraved upon an ancient iron Sword-guard. O-MORI, HIDE-MASA. *Omori Hidemasa*, the name of the maker; the lower mark is his seal.

No. 672.

Inlaid in silver upon an iron Stirrup, decorated with the crest of the prince of Kaga, and with flowers and designs executed in the same metal. KA-SHU JIU SHIGE-HISA TSUKURU (SAKU). *Made by Shigehisa, a resident of Kashu*, the province of Kaga.

No. 673.

Engraved upon a brass Sword-guard, bearing a representation of Yamatodake no mikoto crossing the bay of Awa. NAGA-HARU. *Nagaharu*, the name of the maker; the lower character is his seal.

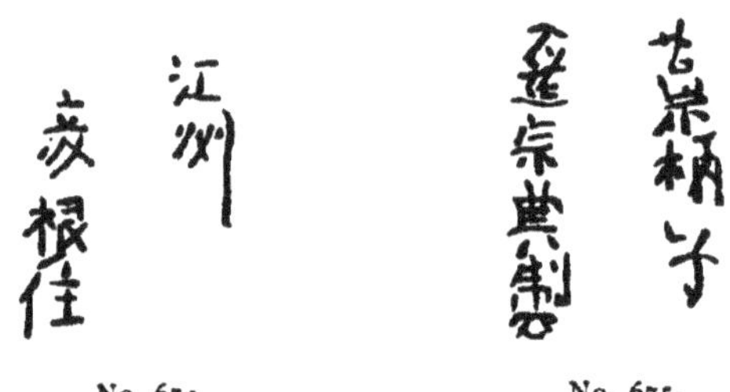

No. 674. No. 675.

Engraved upon an ancient iron Sword-guard, inlaid with various metals, and bearing a representation of the battle of Ichinotani, showing Naozane challenging Atsumori to combat. No. 674, KO-SHIU, HIKO-NE JIU. No. 675, MO-GARA-SHI, NIU-DO, SO-TENG SEISU. *Made by Soteng Mogarashi, Niudo, a resident of Hikone, in Koshiu,* the province of Omi.

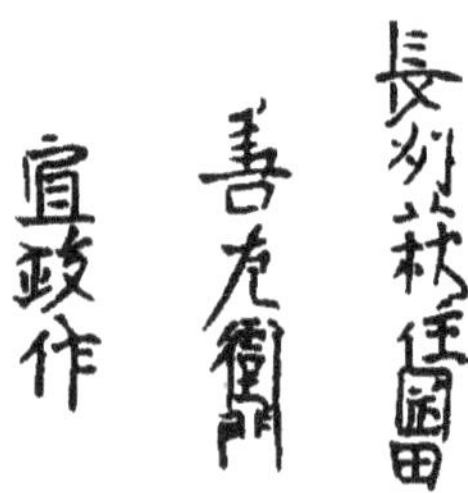

No. 676.

Engraved upon an ancient iron Sword-guard, enriched with gold. CHO-SHIU, HAGI JIU, OKA-DA ZEN-ZA-YE-MON NOBU-MASA TSUKURU (SAKU). *The make of Okada Zenzayemon Nobumasa, a resident of Hagi, in Choshiu,* the province of Nagato.

No. 677.

Engraved upon a brass Sword-guard. HIDE-HISA. *Hide-hisa,* the name of the maker.

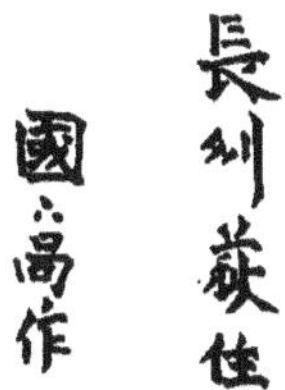

No. 678.

Engraved upon an iron Sword-guard. CHO-SHIU, HAGI JIU, KUNI-TAKA TSUKURU (SAKU). *Made by Kunitaka, a resident of Hagi, in Choshiu,* the province of Nagato.

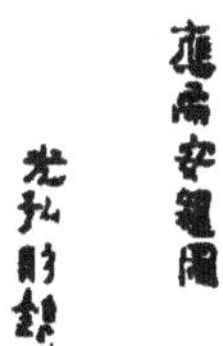

No. 679.

Engraved upon a brass Sword-guard, ornamented with medallions filled in with coiled dragons. OZITE MOTOME YASU-CHIKA DZUSU. MITSU-HIRO CHIO-SHIU. *Designed by Yasuchika* (a painter), *in answer to a demand. Engraved by Mitsuhiro.*

No. 680.

Inlaid on an iron Dish, with figures in relief, and enriched with gold, silver and coloured alloys; of superb workmanship; the inscription is in gold and the border in silver wire. Modern work. KIO-TO JIU, KOMA-I SEISU. *Made by Komai, a resident of Kioto.*

No. 681.

Engraved upon a brass Sword-guard. JI-SEI-TEI SHO-SHIN. *Jiseitei Shoshin*, the name of the maker.

No. 682.

Cast in relief upon a bronze Mirror, bearing the crest of the Prince of Sendai, in a lacquered case. JI-MURA, TO-SA KAMI, FUJI-WARA, MITSU-SHIGE. *Mitsushige Jimura*, the maker, who assumes the name of Fujiwara and also the title of the governor of the province of Tosa.

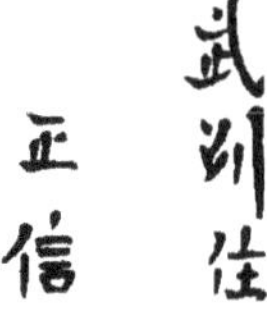

No. 683.

Engraved upon an ancient iron Sword-guard of beautiful workmanship. BU-SHIU JIU MASA-NOBU. *Masanobu*, the maker, *a resident of Bushiu*, the province of Musashi.

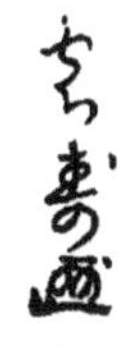

No. 684.

Engraved upon an ancient iron Sword-guard, ornamented with the figures, rendered in various coloured metals, of Bisjamon, Girogin, and Daikoku, the gods of Glory, Long Life, and Wealth, these being the three of the seven household gods to which the warriors of Japan make their supplications. UNJIU. *Unjiu*, the name of the maker; the lower character is his mark.

No. 685.

Engraved upon an ancient iron Sword-guard, upon which is a representation of Rihaku, the greatest of Chinese poets, resting by the waterfall. SO-TEN TSUKURU (SAKU). *Made by Soten.*

No. 686.

Engraved upon an ancient iron Sword-guard. NAO-MASA. *Naomasa*, the name of the maker.

No. 687.

Engraved upon an ancient iron Sword-guard, ornamented with the figure of Kan-wu, a Chinese warrior, executed in gold, silver, and coloured metals. YASU-NORI. *Yasunori*, the name of the maker.

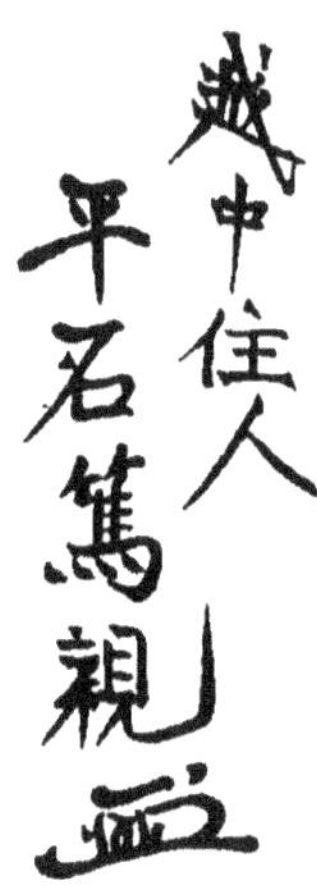

No. 688.

Engraved on a Flower Stand of bronze, one of a pair upon which appear the incident of the Japanese hero, Yoshitsune, fencing with the Tengu; this scene is beautifully rendered in carved and damascened work. YE-CHIU JIU-NIN, HIRA-ISHI ATSU-CHIKA. *Hiraishi Atsuchika*, the name of the maker, *a resident of Yechiu*. The lower mark is the seal of the maker.

No. 689.

In relief upon a bronze Mirror, decorated with the matsu and the oumai, the pine and plum trees, emblems of longevity. FUJI-WARA, YOSHI-NAO TSUKURU (SAKU). *Made by Yoshinao Fujiwara.*

No. 690.

In relief upon a bronze Mirror. FUJI-WARA MASA-YASU TSUKURU (SAKU). *Made by Masayasu Fujiwara.*

No. 691.

In relief upon a bronze Mirror, bearing the crest of the prince of Hikone, the family which gave hereditary regents to Japan. FUJI-WARA TSUKURU (SAKU). *Made by Fujiwara.*

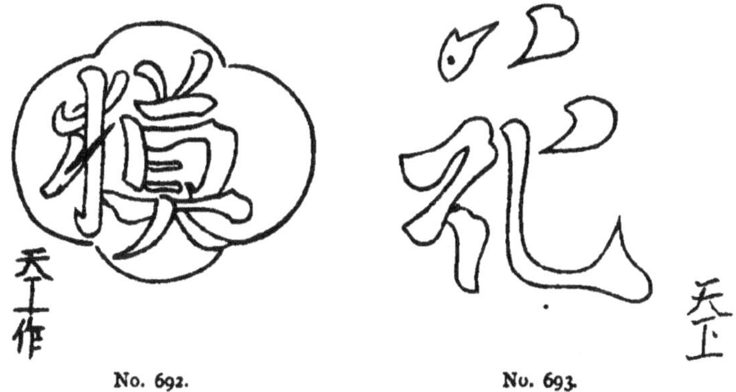

No. 692. No. 693.

In relief upon a pair of bronze Mirrors. The two large inscriptions, taken together, read KWA-BO, meaning *A design for a flower.* The small characters on No. 692, read TENKA ICHI NO SAKU or *The manufacture of the first man in the world.* Those on No. 693 are TENKA ICHI, *The first man in the world.*

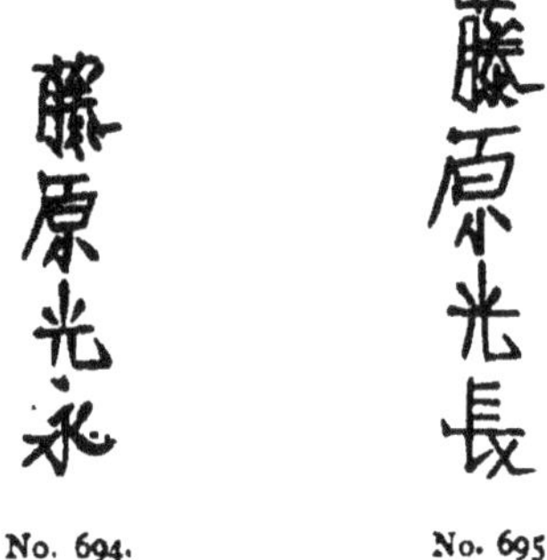

No. 694. No. 695.

In relief upon a pair of bronze Mirrors, bearing the crests of the princes of Aki and Hikone. FUJI-WARA MITSU-NAGA. *Fujiwara Mitsunaga*, the name of the maker. The lower character in each of the inscriptions has the same meaning.

No. 696.

In relief upon a bronze Mirror. TEN-KA ICHI, NISHI-MURA FUJI-WARA. YOSHI-KATSU. *Yoshikatsu Nishimura*, *Fuji-wara*, *the first man in the world*, the name of the maker.

No. 697.

Engraved on a panel of gold inserted in a Netsuke of repoussé bronze inlaid with gold. CHIO-MIN. *Chiomin*, the name of the maker; the lower character is his mark.

No. 698.

In relief upon a bronze Mirror, bearing the crest of the prince of Kokura. TEN-KA ICHI, UWA-JIMA, IDZU-MI KAMI. *Uwajima, the first man in the world, the ruler of Idzumi.* The name of the maker, and the titles which he assumes.

No. 699.

In relief upon a bronze Mirror, bearing the crest of the prince of Nanbu. TEN-KA ICHI, FUJI-WARA TSUKURU (SAKU). *Made by Fujiwara, the first man in the world.*

No. 700.

In relief upon a bronze Mirror. TEN-KA ICHI SAKU. *The manufacture of the first man in the world.*

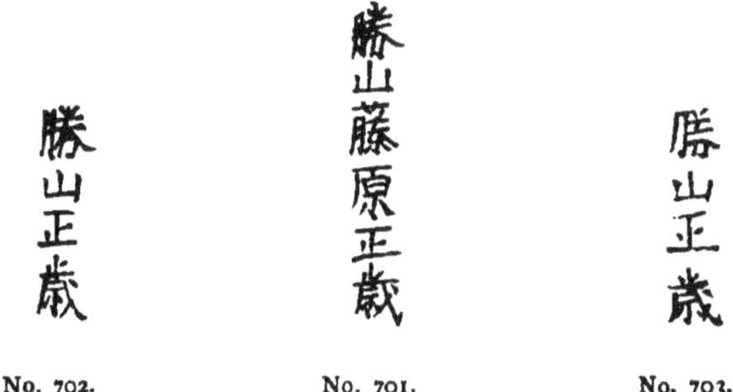

No. 702. No. 701. No. 703.

In relief upon bronze Mirrors. No. 701. A mirror decorated with the *matsu* (pine tree) and *take* (bamboo), and with the *Tsuru-kame* (the crane and the tortoise), all of them emblems of longevity. KATSU-YAMA, FUJI-WARA, MASA-TOSHI. *Masatoshi Katsuyama, Fujiwara.* The name of the maker. Nos. 702 and 703 appear upon a pair of mirrors decorated with the *kiri;* the inscriptions are the same: KATSU-YAMA MASA-TOSHI; the name of the maker, who, in these instances, has omitted his assumed name of Fujiwara.

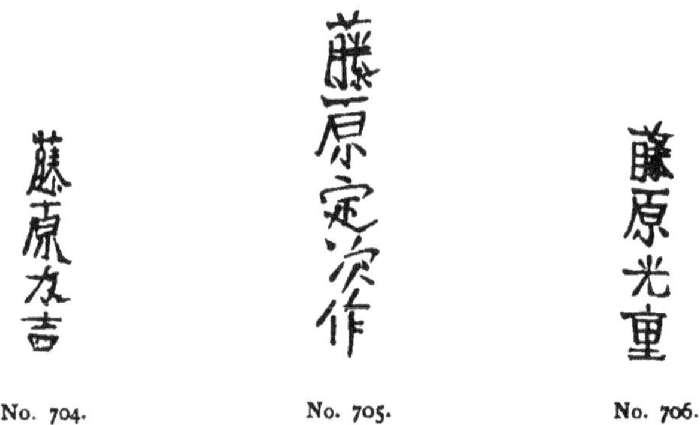

No. 704. No. 705. No. 706.

In relief upon bronze Mirrors. No. 704. FUJIWARA TOMOYOSHI; the name of the maker. No. 705. FUJI-WARA SADA-TSUGU TSUKURU (SAKU). *Made by Sadatsugu Fujiwara.* No. 706. FUJIWARA MITSUSHIGE; the name of the maker.

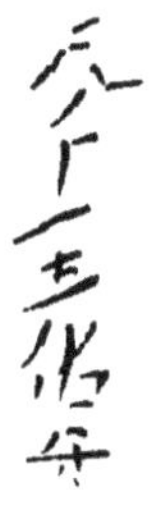

No. 707.

In relief upon a bronze Mirror. TEN-KA ICHI. TO-SA KAMI. *The first man in the world. The Governor* of the province of *Tosa.*

No. 708.

Engraved on a gold ground upon an iron Tray of modern workmanship. HO-GIOKU. *Hogioku,* signifying Jewelry.

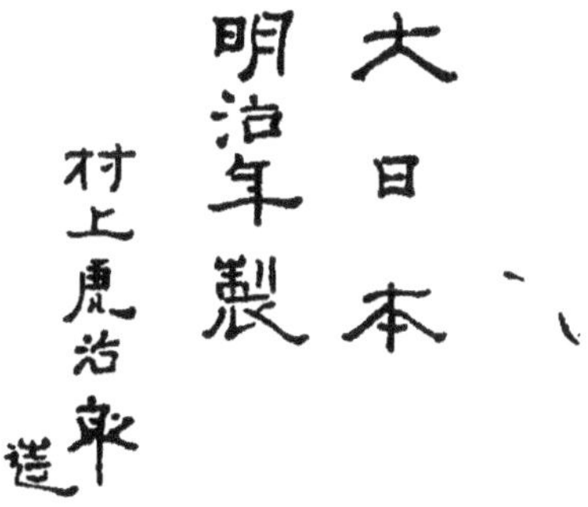

No. 709.

Upon a Tray of white metal of modern workmanship. DAI NIP-PON, MEI-JI NEN SEI, MURA-KAMI TORA-JI-RO TSUKURU (ZO). *Made by Torajiro Murakami. The manufacture of the period of Meiji. Great Japan.*

WOOD AND IVORY
CARVINGS, &c.

No. 710.

Painted in gold upon a Mask of carved and gilded wood. Masks of this kind were used, in the feudal days, by the actors who were retained at the Court of the Shôgun and by the princes. IDE-ME TO-HAKU UTSUSU. MITSU-NAO. *Mitsunao*, the maker, who *copies* the work of *Tohaku Ideme*. The lower character of the left-hand inscription is the mark of the maker.

No. 711.

Painted in red and gold upon a Mask similar to that named above. KO-AKU KAMI, SHIGE-YASU. *Shigeyasu*, the name of the maker. *Koaku no kami*, probably the name of the historic character represented by the mask. The small figure to the right is a mere mark; the large one on the left is the mark of the maker.

No. 712.

Burnt in upon a Mask of carved wood. IDE-ME MITSU-HISA. *Mitsuhisa Ideme*, the name of the maker.

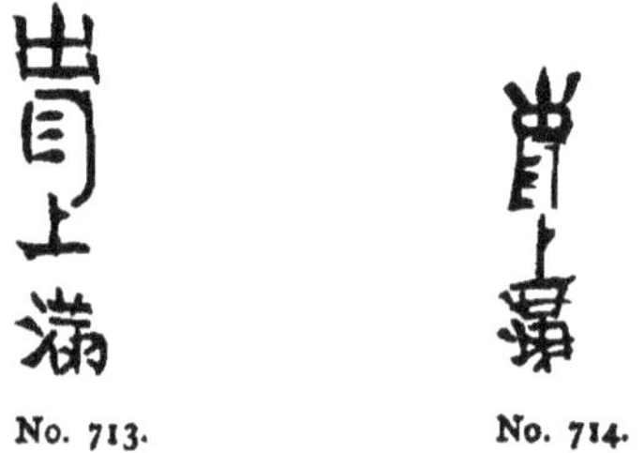

No. 713. No. 714.

Carved upon small Masks of wood used as *Netsuke*. IDE-ME UYE-MITSU. *Uyemitsu Ideme*, the name of the maker.

No. 715.

Carved upon a wooden *Netsuke*. The mark of the maker.

No. 716.

Carved upon a wooden Mask used as a *Netsuke*. TEN-KA ICHI, IDE-ME MIGI-MITSU. *Migimitsu Ideme, the first man in the world;* the name of the maker.

No. 717.

Carved upon a wooden *Netsuke*. IDE-ME MIGI-MITSU. *Migimitsu Ideme*, the name of the maker.

No. 718.

Burnt in upon a Mask of carved and gilded wood. IDE-ME. *Ideme*, the family name of the maker.

No. 719.

Carved upon a wooden Mask used as a *Netsuke*. IDE-ME. *Ideme*, the family name of the maker.

No. 720.

Carved upon a wooden Mask used as a *Netsuke*. JO-BUN. *Jobun*, the name of the maker.

No. 721.

Carved upon a wooden Tray of modern workmanship. Do, the name of the maker.

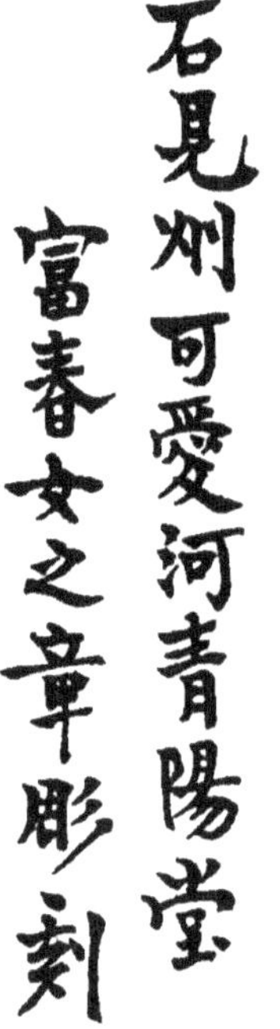

石見州可愛河青陽堂
富春女之章彫刻

No. 722.

Engraved upon an ivory *Netsuke* of exquisite workmanship; the inscription is enlarged, the original being exceedingly minute, as the facsimile to the right shows. IWAMI SHIU, KA-AI GAWA, SEI-YO-DO, TOMI-HARU JO NO SHO CHIO-KOKU. *Chiokoku sho no jo Tomi-haru Seiyodo Ka-ai gawa shiu Iwami.* Meaning:—*Engraved—the mark of the lady Tomi-haru in the house of Seiyo by the river Ka-ai, in the province of Iwami.*

No. 723.

Engraved on a panel of soapstone upon a Plaque of wood, decorated with flowers rendered in relief in pearl, ivory and soapstone. Ko-u in. *Mark* or *Seal of Kou,* the maker. In this instance the character no (of), which is generally found in combination with in (mark or seal), is omitted.

No. 724.

Carved upon a Plaque of wood, ornamented with flowers executed in pearl, ivory and various coloured stones, in relief. Shima-mura Toshi-taka tsukuru kore. *Kore o tsukuru Toshitaka Shimamura. Toshitaka Shimamura made this.* The combination *kore o tsukuru* in seal form, is very unusual.

No. 725.

Engraved upon an ivory *Netsuke*. SA, meaning *left*, and probably signifying that the artist carved the *netsuke* with his left hand.

No. 726.

Painted in gold upon a small Cabinet of ivory, decorated with lacquer and ornamentation of figures of gold in relief. HOKU-RAKU-SAI JO-SETSU TSUKURU. *Made by Josetsu Hokurakusai.*

No. 727.

Engraved upon an ancient Medicine Box of carved wood. ICHI-ZAN TOSU. *Ichizan carves.*

No. 728.

Painted in gold upon an ivory Dish, splendidly decorated with gold lacquer. SHO-JU-SAI. *Shojusai*, the name of the maker.

No. 729.

Carved upon a wooden *Netsuke*. ROKU-JIU-NI O HAKU——-SHA. The second character of the maker's name is illegible, but the first part of the inscription, *Rokujiu-ni o*, means that he was *an old man, 62 years of age*.

No. 730.

Painted in gold upon a wooden Case, holding an ancient tea-jar of Bizen stoneware. ON-CHA-IRE UYE-YAGI. *Onchaire, Tea-case*. *Uyeyagi*, the name of the maker or of the owner. The prefix ON is used to indicate that the case holds an object dedicated to some honorable or sacred purpose.

No. 731.

Carved upon a wooden Mask used as a *Netsuke*. TEN-KA ICHI, IDE-ME UYE-MITSU. *Uyemitsu Ideme, the first man in the world;* the name of the maker. The lower character is the mark of the maker.

No. 732.

Engraved upon a Flower Pot formed out of a large tusk of ivory, upon which is carved a representation of a battle, probably that of Yashima. IDE-ME SEI-GIOKU; the inscription is not very clear, but the interpretation given is probably correct. *Seigioku Ideme*, the name of the maker.

No. 733.

Carved upon a wooden Tea-jar, decorated with metal ornamentation in relief. KIU-SAKU. *Kiusaku*, the name of the maker.

No. 734.

Engraved upon an ivory *Netsuke.* HO-MIN. *Homin*, the name of the maker; the lower character is his mark.

No. 735.

Engraved upon a Tobacco Box of ivory. ICHI-SHI-DO, MASA-KAZU. *Masakazu Ichishido*, the name of the maker; the lower character is his mark.

No. 736.

Carved upon a Tobacco Box of wood. YU-ZAN TSUKURU. *Made by Yuzan.*

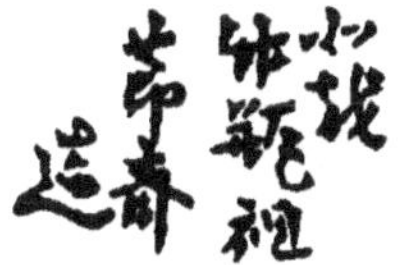

No. 737.

Carved upon a Teapot made from bamboo. HOKU YETSU, *the province of Yechigo, hoku* meaning northern, and *Yetsu* being the abbreviated form of Yechigo; CHIKU-HEI-SO, meaning *the inventor of Bamboo ware;* SETSU-SAI TSUKURU. *Made by Setsusai.*

No. 738.

In relief upon an ivory Box. TANI-NAGA. *Taninaga*, the name of the maker.

No. 739.

No. 740.

Engraved upon an ivory *Netsuke*. MITSU-HISA. *Mitsuhisa*, the maker; the lower characters are his mark.

No. 741.

Engraved upon an ivory *Netsuke*. The larger inscription may probably be read as HIYO-ROKU, but the upper character, in the form of a gourd, is given in place of the word *Hiyo*, which expresses that form; the smaller inscription reads: GIOKU-JU. *Giokuju Hiyoroku*, the name of the maker.

No. 742.

Engraved upon an ivory *Netsuke*. KO-MIN-SAI. *Kominsai*, the name of the maker.

No. 743.

Engraved upon an ivory *Netsuke.* HO-ZAN. *Hozan,* the name of the maker.

No. 744.

Engraved upon an ivory *Netsuke.* TOMO-CHIKA. *Tomo-chika,* the name of the maker.

No. 745.

Engraved upon an ivory *Netsuke.* HO-KEI. *Hokei,* the name of the maker.

No. 746.

Engraved upon an ivory *Netsuke.* MASA NOBU. *Masa-nobu,* the name of the maker.

No. 747.

Engraved upon an ivory *Netsuke.* TAMI-YA. *Tamiya,* the name of the maker.

No. 748.

Engraved upon an ivory *Netsuke.* MASA-HIRO. *Masa-hiro,* the name of the maker.

No. 749.

Engraved upon an ivory *Netsuke*. HISA-NAGA. *Hisanaga*, the name of the maker.

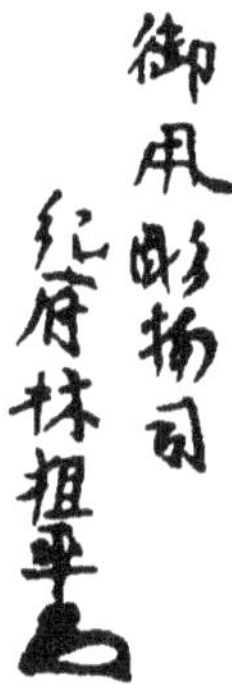

No. 750.

Engraved upon a Group of Rabbits carved in soapstone. GO-YO CHIO-MOTSU-SHI KI-FU, HAYASHI SO-HEI. *Hayashi Sohei, engraver to the prince of Kifu*, the province generally known as Kii.

No. 751.

Painted in black upon a paper Note issued by a daimio in the feudal days. The ornamentation of the note is of a very artistic character. GIN ICHI MOMME. *One silver momme.*

No. 752.

Painted in black upon a paper Note issued by a daimio in the feudal days. GIN ICHI MOMME. *One silver momme.* This inscription is the same as the preceding one, but is written in a different style.

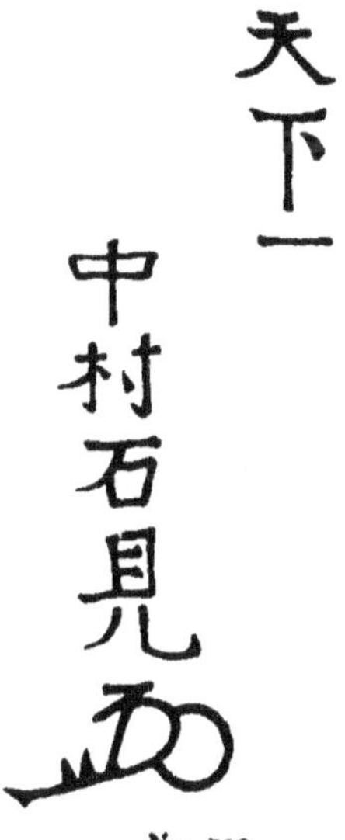

No. 753.

Engraved upon an Inkstone belonging to a lacquer writing case of great beauty. TEN-KA ICHI, NAKA-MURA IWA-MI. *Nakamura Iwami, the first man in the world;* the name of the maker. The lower character is the mark of the maker.

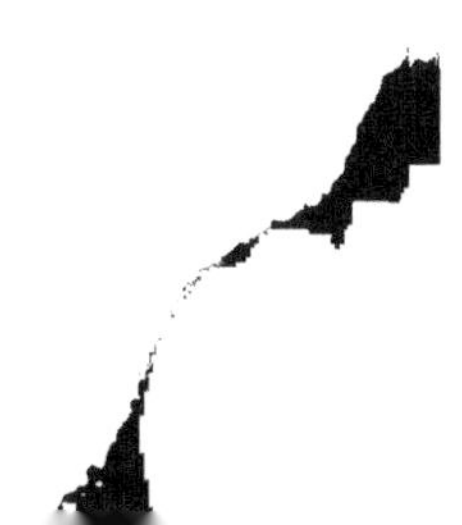

No. 754.

Engraved upon an ivory *Netsuke*. MASA-TSUGU. *Masa-tsugu*, the name of the maker.

No. 755.

Engraved upon an ivory *Netsuke*. KUA-ROKU. *Kuaroku*, the name of the maker.

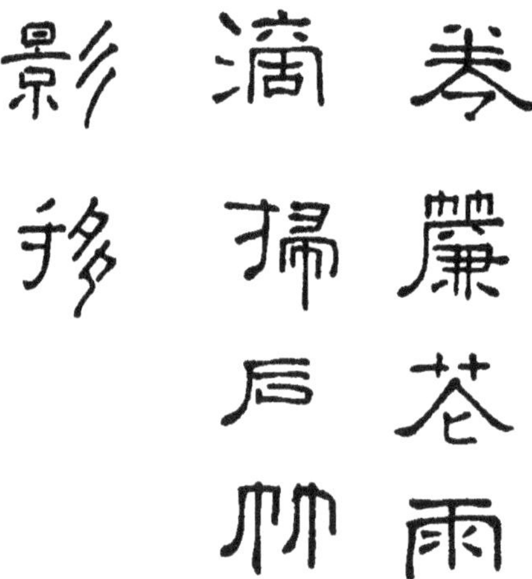

No. 756.

Painted upon a Plate of painted enamel. MAKEBA REN O KA U SHITADARU HARAYEBA ISHI O CHIKU YEI UTSURU. The inscription is read as follows—

Ren o makeba kau shitadaru,
Ishi o harayeba chikuyei utsuru.

It may be translated—

As I raise the curtain the rain drops from the flowers,
As I sweep the stone the shadow of the bamboo is reflected.

No. 757. No. 758. 759.

Upon a Screen enriched with a scene from the Soga Monogatari, executed in ivory and coloured stones carved in relief. Modern work of the most beautiful and skilful execution. No. 757. SHIMA-MURA; TOSHI-TAKA; the seals read, TOSHI-TAKA. No. 758. SHIMA-MURA; TOSHI-MASA; the seal is SEISU, *made by*. No. 759. SHIMA-MURA; TOSHI-AKI; the seals read, TOSHI-AKI. The work was evidently executed by three members of the Shimamura family, named Toshitaka, Toshimasa and Toshiaki.

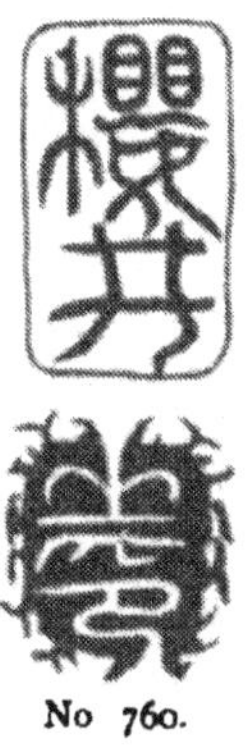

No 760.

Ivory seals upon a Plaque of wood decorated with ornaments of ivory carved in relief. SAKURA-I NO IN. *The seal of Sakurai*, the maker.

No. 761.

Ivory seals upon a Plaque of wood decorated with designs executed in ivory, pearl and coloured stones. TOSHITAKA. *Toshitaka*, the name of the maker.

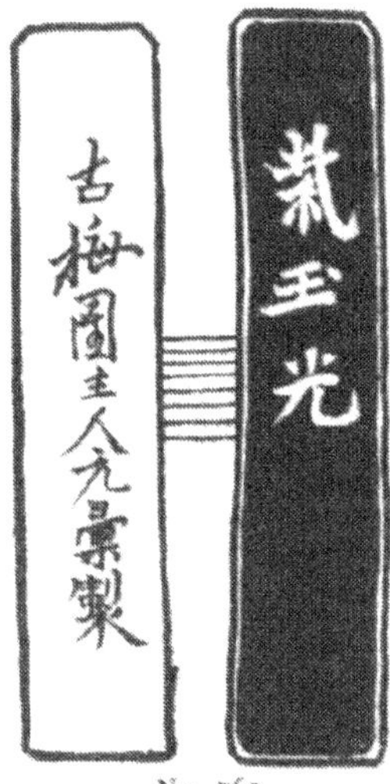

No. 762.

Impressed, and in relief, upon a Stick of Ink. The characters in the right-hand panel are SHIGIOKUKO, the name of the ink. Those to the left read: KOBAIYEN, the name of a celebrated firm in Japan which makes the materials for writing; SHIUJIN MOTONORI SEISU, *made by Motonori, the master* or chief of the firm. The stick of ink from which the above inscriptions are taken was made of the soot from the sacred fire which burns in the temple of Kasuga, in the province of Yamato; this ink is preserved as a sacred object in Japan.

No. 763.

Ivory seal upon a Plaque of wood decorated with designs executed in ivory and coloured stones. RIU-HO. *Riuho*, the name of the maker.

No. 764.

Painted upon a Plaque of plaster decorated with ornamental work in relief. KI-YU, KI-SHIU, UTSUSU CHIO-DO KAN-JIN. *Copied by Kanjin Chiodo during the last Autumn of the Zodiac year of the Cock.* In Japan the Autumn is divided into three periods, first, middle and last, corresponding with the European months, July, August and September. The seal marks are illegible.

No. 765.

Worked upon Embroidered Satin. Ho-KIO NO SHO. *The seal of Hokio.* Hokio is a title conferred upon Artists. The characters in the right-hand half of the seal are HOKIO; the upper ones to the left are NO, meaning *of*, and the lower one is SHO, *The Seal.* The latter word has the same meaning as IN, which is generally used. These characters are written in various ways, as may be seen by the following examples:

RIOYEN NO IN.
The Seal of Rioyen.

MASATAMI NO IN.
The Seal of Masatami.

NO IN.
The Seal of.

RINKO NO IN.
The Seal of Rinko.

SHIJIU NO IN.
The Seal of Shijiu.

In rare instances the character NO is omitted, and that of IN only is given, as in the following mark:

KOU IN.
The Seal (of) Kou.

THE ZODIACAL CYCLE AND YEAR PERIODS.

THE ZODIACAL CYCLE AND YEAR PERIODS.

THE division of time in Japan has been accomplished since the earliest ages by two methods; first, by the Zodiacal Cycle of sixty years, and, secondly, by the Year Periods, which have been fixed from time to time under the authority of the Mikado.

The sixty characters of the Zodiacal Cycle are formed by the combination in regular order of the JIKKWAN, or the elementary signs, with the JIUNI SHI, or twelve calendar or horary signs.

The Jikkwan consists of the words *Kinoye*, *Kinoto*; *Hinoye*, *Hinoto*; *Tsuchinoye*, *Tsuchinoto*; *Kanoye*, *Kanoto*; and *Mizunoye*, *Mizunoto*. These ten characters are used in the Chinese calendar and have been adopted in Japan; they are founded upon the words *Ki*, *Hi*, *Tsuchi*, *Ka* and *Mizu*, which signify, respectively, Tree, Fire, Earth, Metal and Water. They are each used in two forms, it being necessary to have ten characters for the purpose of the calendar, and the duplication of the signs is accomplished by the use of the terminations *no ye* and *no to*, the former signifying, literally, *of the elder brother*, and the latter *of the younger brother*.

The Jiuni Shi group of characters consists of the names in full, or in an abbreviated form, of the twelve animals used to express the calendar signs; they are *Ne*, rat or mouse; *Ushi*, ox; *Tora*, tiger; *U*, hare or rabbit; *Tatsu*, dragon; *Mi*, snake or serpent; *Muma*, horse; *Hitsuji*, sheep or goat; *Saru*, monkey; *Tori*, cock; *Inu*, dog; *I*, wild boar. These characters are used to denote the months of the year, the hours of the day, and the points of the compass, as shown in the table of the signs; they are also used to designate the seasons and the different periods of the day, and occasionally the years; but this latter application of them is incorrect except in combination with the Jikkwan signs, and is only used in Japan by the illiterate.

In forming the Zodiacal names of the years, the first word of each of the two groups is taken, and these together express the name of the first of the sixty years forming the cycle; then the second words in each group are combined in the same manner, and so on in succession until the Jikkwan signs are exhausted, when the process is recommenced, and as there are ten words in one group and twelve in the other, they must necessarily produce sixty different combinations, and at the sixty-first year the name formed by the first words of each group must reappear, and another cycle is commenced.

The second mode of marking time is by the Year Periods, the use of which commenced in 645 A.D.; these periods, which are of varying length, frequently lasting not more than a single year, and seldom extending over ten years, have no special significance, having been arbitrarily fixed by the reigning Emperor according to caprice, or upon the occurrence of some notable event of good or evil import. This system has, however, been changed since the revolution, and it is intended that in future the name of the period shall be changed only upon the completion of each reign; the present period, which commenced in 1868, is named *Meiji*, which signifies a brilliant reign, an appropriate description of that of Emperor Mutsuhito.

Both the Zodiacal system and the Year Periods are in constant use in Japan, and the list of Marks in this Volume affords numerous instances of their use upon works of art. A complete series of the former is given in the following Tables, but it has not been thought necessary to carry the Year Periods to an earlier date than the close of the fourteenth century, as those before that period are of no practical use in connection with this Work. The characters are Chinese, written in the *Kaisho* style.

THE JIKKWAN.

CHARACTER.	JAPANESE NAME.	CHINESE NAME.	CHARACTER.	JAPANESE NAME.	CHINESE NAME.
甲	*Kinoye*	*Ko*	己	*Tsuchinoto*	*Ki*
乙	*Kinoto*	*Otsu*	庚	*Kanoye*	*Ko*
丙	*Hinoye*	*Hei*	辛	*Kanoto*	*Shin*
丁	*Hinoto*	*Tei*	壬	*Mizunoye*	*Jin*
戊	*Tsuchinoye*	*Bo*	癸	*Mizunoto*	*Ki*

THE JIUNI SHI.

CHARACTER.	JAPANESE.	CHINESE.	YEAR OF THE—	THE MONTH, HOUR OF THE DAY, AND POINT OF THE COMPASS.		
子	*Ne*	*Shi*	Rat	November	12 Night	N
丑	*Ushi*	*Chiu*	Ox	December	2 a.m.	NNE
寅	*Tora*	*In*	Tiger	January	4 a.m.	ENE
卯	*U*	*Bo*	Hare	February	6 a.m.	E
辰	*Tatsu*	*Shin*	Dragon	March	8 a.m.	ESE
巳	*Mi*	*Shi*	Snake	April	10 a.m.	SSE
午	*Muma*	*Go*	Horse	May	12 Morn.	S
未	*Hitsuji*	*Bi*	Sheep	June	2 p.m.	SSW
申	*Saru*	*Shin*	Monkey	July	4 p.m.	WSW
酉	*Tori*	*Yu*	Cock	August	6 p.m.	W
戌	*Inu*	*Jiutsu*	Dog	September	8 p.m.	WNW
亥	*I*	*Gai*	Wild Boar	October	10 p.m.	NNW

THE ZODIACAL CYCLE.

YEAR OF THE CYCLE.	CHARACTERS.	JAPANESE NAME.	CHINESE NAME.	THE YEAR OF THE—
1	子甲	*Kinoye-ne*	*Ko shi*	Rat
2	丑乙	*Kinoto-ushi*	*Otsu-chiu*	Ox
3	寅丙	*Hinoye-tora*	*Hei-in*	Tiger
4	卯丁	*Hinoto-u*	*Tei-bo*	Hare
5	辰戊	*Tsuchinoye-tatsu*	*Bo-shin*	Dragon
6	巳己	*Tsuchinoto-mi*	*Ki-shi*	Snake
7	午庚	*Kanoye-muma*	*Ko-go*	Horse
8	未辛	*Kanoto-hitsuji*	*Shin-bi*	Sheep
9	申壬	*Mizunoye-saru*	*Jin-shin*	Monkey
10	酉癸	*Mizunoto-tori*	*Ki-yu*	Cock
11	戌甲	*Kinoye-inu*	*Ko-jiutsu*	Dog
12	亥乙	*Kinoto-i*	*Otsu-gai*	Wild Boar

THE ZODIACAL CYCLE—*continued.*

YEAR OF THE CYCLE.	CHARACTERS.	JAPANESE NAME.	CHINESE NAME.	THE YEAR OF THE—
13	子丙	*Hinoye-ne*	*Hei-shi*	Rat
14	丑丁	*Hinoto-ushi*	*Tei-chiu*	Ox
15	寅戊	*Tsuchinoye-tora*	*Bo-in*	Tiger
16	卯己	*Tsuchinoto-u*	*Ki-bo*	Hare
17	辰庚	*Kanoye-tatsu*	*Ko-shin*	Dragon
18	巳辛	*Kanoto-mi*	*Shin-shi*	Snake
19	午壬	*Mizunoye-muma*	*Jin-go*	Horse
20	未癸	*Mizunoto-hitsuji*	*Ki-bi*	Sheep
21	申甲	*Kinoye-saru*	*Ko-shin*	Monkey
22	酉乙	*Kinoto-tori*	*Otsu-yu*	Cock
23	戌丙	*Hinoye-inu*	*Hei-jiutsu*	Dog
24	亥丁	*Hinoto-i*	*Tei-gai*	Wild Boar

THE ZODIACAL CYCLE—*continued.*

YEAR OF THE CYCLE	CHARACTERS.	JAPANESE NAME.	CHINESE NAME.	THE YEAR OF THE -
25	子戊	*Tsuchinoye-ne*	*Bo-shi*	Rat
26	丑己	*Tsuchinoto-ushi*	*Ki-chiu*	Ox
27	寅庚	*Kanoye-tora*	*Ko-in*	Tiger
28	卯辛	*Kanoto-u*	*Shin-bo*	Hare
29	辰壬	*Mizunoye-tatsu*	*Jin-shin*	Dragon
30	巳癸	*Mizunoto-mi*	*Ki-shi*	Snake
31	午甲	*Kinoye-muma*	*Ko-go*	Horse
32	未乙	*Kinoto-hitsuji*	*Otsu-bi*	Sheep
33	申丙	*Hinoye-saru*	*Hei-shin*	Monkey
34	酉丁	*Hinoto-tori*	*Tei-yu*	Cock
35	戌戊	*Tsuchinoye-inu*	*Bo-jiutsu*	Dog
36	亥己	*Tsuchinoto-i*	*Ki-gai*	Wild Boar

THE ZODIACAL CYCLE—*continued.*

YEAR OF THE CYCLE.	CHARACTERS.	JAPANESE NAME.	CHINESE NAME.	THE YEAR OF THE—
37	子庚	*Kanoye-ne*	*Ko-shi*	Rat
38	丑辛	*Kanoto-ushi*	*Shin-chiu*	Ox
39	寅壬	*Mizunoye-tora*	*Jin-in*	Tiger
40	卯癸	*Mizunoto-u*	*Ki-bo*	Hare
41	辰甲	*Kinoye-tatsu*	*Ko-shin*	Dragon
42	巳乙	*Kinoto-mi*	*Otsu-shi*	Snake
43	午丙	*Hinoye-muma*	*Hei-go*	Horse
44	未丁	*Hinoto-hitsuji*	*Tei-bi*	Sheep
45	申戊	*Tsuchinoye-saru*	*Bo-shin*	Monkey
46	酉己	*Tsuchinoto-tori*	*Ki-yu*	Cock
47	戌庚	*Kanoye-inu*	*Ko-jiutsu*	Dog
48	亥辛	*Kanoto-i*	*Shin-gai*	Wild Boar

THE ZODIACAL CYCLE—*continued.*

YEAR OF THE CYCLE.	CHARACTERS.	JAPANESE NAME.	CHINESE NAME.	THE YEAR OF THE—
49	子壬	*Mizunoye-ne*	*Jin-shi*	Rat
50	丑癸	*Mizunoto-ushi*	*Ki-chiu*	Ox
51	寅甲	*Kinoye-tora*	*Ko-in*	Tiger
52	卯乙	*Kinoto-u*	*Otsu-bo*	Hare
53	辰丙	*Hinoye-tatsu*	*Hei-shin*	Dragon
54	巳丁	*Hinoto-mi*	*Tei-shi*	Snake
55	午戊	*Tsuchinoye-muma*	*Bo-go*	Horse
56	未己	*Tsuchinoto-hitsuji*	*Ki-bi*	Sheep
57	申庚	*Kanoye-saru*	*Ko-shin*	Monkey
58	酉辛	*Kanoto-tori*	*Shin-yu*	Cock
59	戌壬	*Mizunoye-inu*	*Jin-jiutsu*	Dog
60	亥癸	*Mizunoto-i*	*Ki-gai*	Wild Boar

THE YEAR PERIODS.

FROM 1394 A.D. TO THE PRESENT TIME.

CHARACTERS.	NAME OF PERIOD.	COMMENCED A.D.	CHARACTERS.	NAME OF PERIOD.	COMMENCED A.D.
永 應	*Oyei*	1394	正 寛	*Kwansho*	1460
長 正	*Shocho*	1428	正 文	*Bunsho*	1466
享 永	*Yeikio*	1429	仁 應	*Onin*	1467
吉 嘉	*Kakitsu*	1441	明 文	*Bunmei*	1469
安 文	*Bun-an*	1444	享 長	*Chokio*	1487
徳 宝	*Hotoku*	1449	徳 延	*Yentoku*	1489
徳 享	*Kiotoku*	1452	應 明	*Meiwo*	1492
正 康	*Kosho*	1455	亀 文	*Bunki*	1501
禄 長	*Choroku*	1457	正 永	*Yeisho*	1504

THE YEAR PERIODS—*continued.*

FROM 1394 A.D. TO THE PRESENT TIME.

CHARACTERS.	NAME OF PERIOD.	COMMENCED A.D.	CHARACTERS.	NAME OF PERIOD.	COMMENCED A.D.
永 大	*Daiyei*	1521	永 寛	*Kwanyei*	1624
禄 享	*Kioroku*	1528	保 正	*Shoho*	1644
文 天	*Tembun*	1532	安 慶	*Keian*	1648
治 弘	*Koji*	1555	應 承	*Jowo*	1652
禄 永	*Yeiroku*	1558	暦 明	*Meiriki*	1655
亀 元	*Genki*	1570	治 萬	*Manji*	1658
正 天	*Tensho*	1573	文 寛	*Kwambun*	1661
禄 文	*Bunroku*	1592	宝 延	*Yempo*	1673
長 慶	*Kiocho*	1596	和 天	*Tenwa*	1681
和 元	*Genwa*	1615	享 貞	*Jokio*	1684

THE YEAR PERIODS—*continued.*

FROM 1394 A.D. TO THE PRESENT TIME.

CHARACTERS.	NAME OF PERIOD.	COMMENCED A.D.	CHARACTERS.	NAME OF PERIOD.	COMMENCED A.D.
元禄	*Genroku*	1688	安永	*Anyei*	1772
宝永	*Hoyei*	1704	天明	*Temmei*	1781
正徳	*Shotoku*	1711	寛政	*Kwansei*	1789
享保	*Kioho*	1716	享和	*Kiowa*	1801
元文	*Gembun*	1736	文化	*Bunkwa*	1804
寛保	*Kwanpo*	1741	文政	*Bunsei*	1818
延享	*Yenkio*	1744	天保	*Tempo*	1830
寛延	*Kwanyen*	1748	弘化	*Koka*	1844
宝暦	*Horeki*	1751	嘉永	*Kayei*	1848
明和	*Meiwa*	1764	安政	*Ansei*	1854

THE YEAR PERIODS—*continued.*

FROM 1394 A.D. TO THE PRESENT TIME.

CHARACTERS.	NAME OF PERIOD.	COMMENCED A.D.	CHARACTERS.	NAME OF PERIOD.	COMMENCED A.D.
萬延	*Manyen*	1860	元治	*Genji*	1864
文久	*Bunkiu*	1861	慶應	*Keiwo*	1865

MEIJI.

The Year Period which commenced 1868 A.D., and still continues.

INDEX.

INDEX.

ZEN-PEN.
The whole Volume.